NIXON
SPEAKS
OUT

Major Speeches and Statements
by
Richard M. Nixon
in the
Presidential Campaign of 1968

Nixon-Agnew Campaign Committee
450 Park Avenue
New York, N. Y.

Seldom, if ever, has a candidate for any office spoken out as fully on as wide a range of issues as Richard M. Nixon has during the Presidential campaign of 1968.

The Nixon-Agnew Campaign Committee recently published "Nixon on the Issues," a 194-page collection of positions taken by Mr. Nixon on 227 specific issues in the 1968 campaign for the Presidency. These were excerpted from speeches, statements, articles, and the hundreds of interviews, press conferences and question-and-answer sessions he has held since opening his campaign in New Hampshire on February 2.

In this companion volume are collected the full texts of 34 of Mr. Nixon's formal statements and major addresses of 1968, including his series of nationwide radio broadcasts and his speech accepting the Republican nomination for the Presidency. They include both detailed programs for the future and thoughtful analyses of the processes of change and development in American society.

Together, these two volumes represent a publishing event unique in political history—a fuller compilation of a candidate's current views than ever before presented to the public during a campaign.

Nixon-Agnew Campaign Committee
October 25, 1968

TABLE OF CONTENTS

The American System in a Time of Change

To Make Our People One

For a Dynamic Economy

Crusade Against Crime

Unmet Needs and America's Opportunities

Quest for Peace

In the Arena

THE AMERICAN SYSTEM IN A TIME OF CHANGE

THE NATURE OF THE PRESIDENCY

During the course of this campaign, I have discussed many issues with the American people. Tonight, I would like to talk with you about a subject often debated by scholars and the public, but seldom dealt with directly in a Presidential campaign: The nature of the Presidency itself.

What *kind* of leadership should a President give? Is the office too strong, or not strong enough? How can it be made more responsive? Should a President lead public opinion, or follow it? What are the priorities for Presidential attention, and the range of Presidential responsibilities?

Perhaps the best way to begin my own answer is with another question, one I am often asked as I travel around the country: "Why do you seek the office? With all the troubles that we have, why would *anyone* want to be President today?"

The answer is not one of glory, or fame; today the burdens of the office outweigh its privileges. It's not because the Presidency offers a chance to *be* somebody, but because it offers a chance to *do* something.

Today, it offers a greater opportunity to help shape the future than ever before in the nation's history—and if America is to meet its challenges, the next President must seize that opportunity.

We stand at a great turning point—when the nation is groping for a new direction, unsure of its role and its purposes, caught in a tumult of change. And for the first time, we face serious, simultaneous threats to the peace both at home and abroad.

In this watershed year of 1968, therefore, America needs Presidential leadership that can establish a firm focus, and offer a way out of a time of towering uncertainties. Only the President can hold out a vision of the future and rally the people behind it.

The next President must unite America. He must calm its angers, ease its terrible frictions, and bring its people together once again in peace and mutual respect. He has to take *hold* of America before he can move it forward.

1

This requires leadership that believes in law, and has the courage to enforce it; leadership that believes in justice, and is determined to promote it; leadership that believes in progress, and knows how to inspire it.

The days of a passive Presidency belong to a simpler past. Let me be very clear about this: The next President must take an activist view of his office. He must articulate the nation's values, define its goals and marshal its will. Under a Nixon Administration, the Presidency will be deeply involved in the entire sweep of America's public concerns.

The first responsibility of leadership is to gain mastery over events, and to shape the future in the image of our hopes.

The President today cannot stand aside from crisis; he cannot ignore division; he cannot simply paper over disunity. He must lead.

But he must bear in mind the distinction between forceful leadership and stubborn willfulness. And he should not delude himself into thinking that he can do everything himself. America today cannot afford vest-pocket government, no matter who wears the vest.

In considering the kind of leadership the next President should give, let us first consider the special relationship—the special trust—that has developed between President and people.

The President is trusted, not to follow the fluctuations of the public-opinion polls, but to bring his own best judgment to bear on the best *ideas* his administration can muster.

There are occasions on which a President must take unpopular measures.

But his responsibility does not stop there. The President has a duty to decide, but the people have a right to know why. The President has a responsibility to tell them—to lay out all the facts, and to explain not only why he chose as he did but also what it means for the future. Only through an open, candid dialogue with the people can a President maintain his trust and his leadership.

It's time we once again had an open administration—open to ideas *from* the people, and open in its communication *with* the people—an administration of open doors, open eyes and open minds.

2

When we debate American commitments abroad, for example, if we expect a decent hearing from those who now take to the streets in protest, we must recognize that neither the Department of State nor of Defense has a monopoly on all wisdom. We should bring dissenters into policy discussions, not freeze them out; we should invite constructive criticism, not only because the critics have a right to be heard, but also because they often have something worth hearing.

And this brings me to another, related point: The President cannot isolate himself from the great intellectual ferments of his time. On the contrary, he must consciously and deliberately place himself at their center. The lamps of enlightenment are lit by the spark of controversy; their flame can be snuffed out by the blanket of consensus.

This is one reason why I don't want a government of yes-men. It's why I do want a government drawn from the broadest possible base—an administration made up of Republicans, Democrats and Independents, and drawn from politics, from career government service, from universities, from business, from the professions—one including not only executives and administrators, but scholars and thinkers.

While the President is a leader of thought, he is also a user of thought, and he must be a catalyst of thought. The thinking that he draws upon must be the best in America—and not only in government. What's happening today in America and the world is happening not only in politics and diplomacy, but in science, education, the arts—and in all areas a President needs a constant exposure to ideas that stretch the mind.

Only if we have an Administration broadly enough based philosophically to ensure a true ferment of ideas, and to invite an interplay of the best minds in America, can we be sure of getting the best and most penetrating ideas.

We cannot content ourselves with complacency, with an attitude that because something worked once before, it must be good enough for us now. The world is changing, America is changing, and so must our ideas and our policies change—and our pursuit of the new must be an unremitting pursuit of excellence.

When we think of leadership, we commonly think of persuasion. But the coin of leadership has another side.

In order to lead, a President today must listen. And in this time of searching and uncertainty, government must learn to listen in new ways.

A President has to hear not only the clamorous voices of the organized, but also the quiet voices, the *inner voices*—the voices that speak through the silences, and that speak from the heart and the conscience.

These are the voices that carry the real meaning and the real message of America.

He's got to articulate these voices so that they can be heard, rather than being lost in the wail and bellow of what too often passes today for public disclosure. He must be, in the words of Woodrow Wilson, "the spokesman for the real sentiment and purpose of the country."

The President is the one official who represents every American—rich and poor, privileged and underprivileged. He represents those whose misfortunes stand in dramatic focus, and also the great, quiet forgotten majority —the non-shouters and the non-demonstrators, the millions who ask principally to go their own way in decency and dignity, and to have their own rights accorded the same respect they accord the rights of others. Only if he listens to the quiet voices can he be true to this trust.

This I pledge, that in a Nixon Administration, America's citizens will not have to break the law to be heard, they will not have to shout or resort to violence. We can restore peace only if we make government attentive to the quiet as well as the strident, and this I intend to do.

But what of the burdens of the Presidency? Have they, as some maintain, grown beyond the capacity of any one man?

The Presidency has been called an impossible office.

If I thought it were, I would not be seeking it. But its functions have become cluttered, the President's time drained away in trivia, the channels of authority confused.

When questions of human survival may turn on the judgments of one man, he must have time to concentrate on those great decisions that only he can make.

One means of achieving this is by expanding the role of the Vice President—which I will do.

I also plan a re-organized and strengthened Cabinet, and a stronger White House staff than any yet put together.

The people are served not only by a President, but by an Administration, and not only by an Administration, but by a government.

The President's chief function is to lead, not to administer; it is not to oversee every detail, but to put the right people in charge, to provide them with basic guidance and direction, and to let them do the job. As Theodore Roosevelt once put it, "the best executive is the one who has enough sense to pick good men to do what he wants done, and self-restraint enough to keep from meddling with them while they do it."

This requires surrounding the President with men of stature, including young men, and giving them responsibilities commensurate with that stature. It requires a Cabinet made up of the ablest men in America, leaders in their own right and not merely by virtue of appointment—men who will command the public's respect and the President's attention by the power of their intellect and the force of their ideas.

Such men are not attracted to an Administration in which all credit is gathered to the White House and blame parceled out to scapegoats, or in which high officials are asked to dance like puppets on a Presidential string. I believe in a system in which the appropriate Cabinet officer gets credit for what goes right, and the President takes the blame for what goes wrong.

Officials of a new administration will not have to check their consciences at the door, or leave their powers of independent judgment at home.

Another change I believe necessary stems directly from my basic concept of government. For years now, the trend has been to sweep more and more authority toward Washington. Too many of the decisions that would better have been made in Seattle or St. Louis have wound up on the President's desk.

5

I plan a streamlined Federal system, with a return to the states, cities and communities of decision-making powers rightfully theirs.

The purpose of this is not only to make government more effective and more responsive, but also to concentrate Federal attention on those functions that can only be handled on the Federal level.

The Presidency is a place where priorities are set, and goals determined.

We need a new attention to priorities, and a new realism about goals.

We are living today in a time of great promise—but also of too many promises. We have had too much wishful imagining that all the ills of man could be set right overnight, merely by making a national "commitment."

A President must tell the people what cannot be done immediately, as well as what can. Hope is fragile, and too easily shattered by the disappointment that follows inevitably on promises unkept and unkeepable. America needs charts of the possible, not excursions into the impossible.

Our cause today is not a nation, but a planet—for never have the fates of all the peoples of the earth been so bound up together.

The tasks confronting the next President abroad are among the most complex and difficult ever faced. And, as Professor Clinton Rossiter has observed, "Leadership in foreign affairs flows today from the President— or it does not flow at all."

The whole structure of power in the world has been undergoing far-reaching changes. While these pose what may be our period of greatest danger, they open what also may be our greatest opportunity. This is a time when miscalculation could prove fatal; a time when the destructive power amassed by the world's great nations threatens the planet. But it is also a time when leaders both East and West are developing a new, sobering awareness of the terrible potential of that power and the need to restrain it.

The judgments of history can bestow no honor greater than the title of peacemaker. It is this honor—this destiny—that beckons America, the chance to lead the world at last out of turmoil and onto that plateau of peace man has dreamed of since the dawn of time. This is our summons to greatness. If we answer the call, generations yet unborn will say of this generation of Americans that we truly mastered our moment, that we at last made the world safe for mankind.

The President cannot stand alone. Today, more than ever in modern times, he must reach out and draw upon the strength of the people.

Theodore Roosevelt called the Presidency "a bully pulpit;" Franklin Roosevelt called it pre-eminently "a place of moral leadership." And surely one of a President's greatest resources is the moral authority of his office. It's time we restored that authority—and time we used it once again, to its fullest potential—to rally the people, to define those moral imperatives which are the cement of a civilized society, to point the ways in which the *energies* of the people can be enlisted to serve the *ideals* of the people.

What has to be done, has to be done by President and people together, or it won't be done at all.

In asking you to join this great effort, I am asking not that you give something *to* your country, but that you do something *with* your country; I am asking not for your gifts, but for your hands. Together, we can hardly fail, for there is no force on earth to match the will and the spirit of the people of America, if that will and that spirit are mobilized in the service of a common aim.

Let me add a personal note. I made a point of conducting my campaign for the nomination in a way that would make it possible to unite the party after the convention. That was successful. I intend now to conduct my election campaign in a way that will make it possible to unite the nation after November. It is not my intention to preside over the disintegration of America or the dissolution of America's force for good in the world. Rather, I want the Presidency to be a force for pulling our people back together once again, and for making our nation whole by making our people one. We have had enough of discord and division, and what we need now is a time of healing, of renewal and of realistic hope.

No one who has been close to the Presidency would approach its powers lightly, or indifferently, or without a profound sense of the awesome responsibility these powers carry.

Nor should the American people approach this time of challenge without a sense of the majesty of the moment.

Greatness comes from stepping up to events, not from sitting on the sidelines while history is made by others.

History will be made in these years just ahead—history that can change the world for generations to come. So let us seize the moment, and accept the challenge—not as a burden, and not in fear—but in the full confidence that no people has ever had such resources to meet its challenge. Ours is the chance to see the American dream fulfilled at last in the destiny of man. This is the role that history offers; this is the hope that summons us; this is our generation's call to greatness as a nation. This, today, is America's opportunity.

NBC and CBS Radio Networks
September 19, 1968

TOWARD AN EXPANDED DEMOCRACY

In recent years, and tragically in recent weeks, America has been rocked by disorders, shocked by crime, stunned by assassinations, and left in puzzled fury by a wave of unruly demonstrations and mass obstructionism not only in the streets of our cities, but in the halls of our great universities.

Faced with epidemic disorder, one part of the answer is both to strengthen and to use the forces of law. But this by itself is not enough. If we are to restore domestic peace, we sooner or later must bring those who threaten it back within the system.

At the same time, we need a searching new look at our political and social "system" itself.

The Alienated

Much of today's violence and disorder is the product of those commonly called the "alienated"—those people who either have never had faith in America's institutions, or who have lost it. They can be found in student mobs beseiging a university building, or looting in a ghetto riot, or peddling the literature of hate. They challenge our society because they reject what they think are its values; they threaten it, because all too often they also reject its restraints and its procedures for peaceful and orderly change.

Among these alienated there are strident voices, harsh voices, crying out for anarchy for its own sake. These are the extremists who reject all authority except their own, and whose heroes are the Che Guevaras of the world—men for whom the act of revolution is an end in itself, and the particular cause a mere excuse for violent means.

But if we look closely, we see that these extremists are a small minority. When they are isolated from their followers, they can readily be dealt with by the forces of law.

Most of the alienated are not so extreme. But they *are* people with a long catalogue of dissatisfactions with things as they are. It's worth examining this catalogue. When we do, some curious facts emerge.

Let's look at some of the things they're angry about:

9

- A paternalism that robs the individual of his sense of self.
- A widening gulf between the individual and his government, as effective power moves further and further away.
- A political dialogue littered with broken promises, with false phrases and inflated hopes.
- A racial dialogue still studded with the old stereotypes—on both sides—that reinforce old fears and play on old distrusts, in which old arguments about past guilt block new perceptions of right and wrong.
- A deep sense of social injustice—of a fundamental conflict between the "power structure" and "human rights."
- A welfare system that breaks families apart rather than holding them together, and that robs the person of pride and privacy as the price of filling his stomach.
- A disillusionment with wars that seem avoidable, in places that seem remote.
- An anxiety about the future, and about the place of the individual—who more and more seems alone and powerless against an overwhelming society.

Through all these complaints, there runs a common thread: that society in the mass is losing touch with the individual in the flesh; that the sense of community—of a place of belonging where leaders listen and respond—has crumbled; that the power to control decisions immediately affecting one's life is vanishing; that that unique, precious, indescribable thing—the *individual* human mind, heart and spirit—is being injured, or neglected, or slighted.

What's significant is that in this, the alienated are not alone.

The Quiet Revolution

In part, their complaints echo the complaints of millions of other Americans, people who are neither young nor poor, and who are proudly in the mainstream of American life and determined to stay there.

During the past five months, I've campaigned in twenty-two states, and talked with thousands of people from every walk of life. I've had a chance to sense the mood of America, in the way that only a candidate who goes to the people senses it.

10

And I've found something.

If we listen, we'll discover that the white man in the Boston suburb shares many of the same frustrations as the black man in the Chicago ghetto. Not all, of course. But he, too, wants to be heard. He too, wants a voice in the decisions that shape his life. He, too, wants dignity—the dignity of being a man, not a number, not a category or a census statistic.

Those protesting college students who carry signs reading: "Do not fold, bend, staple or mutilate. This is a human being," speak not only for the student revolt, but for the frustrations of Americans everywhere.

Beyond the disorders, there's another rebellion going on today. This other is a quiet revolution. It's a rebellion by the great, quiet majority—those who pay their taxes, go to their jobs, perform their civic duties, send their children to school or college. I'm sure it includes many of you listening tonight.

In part, this quiet revolution is a protest against the violence and the excesses that have marked a time of tumultuous change, and also against the heavier-and-heavier demands of an age of impatience.

It's a rebellion against taxes, and against the ever-higher piling of Federal tax on state tax on local tax.

It's a demand for moderation—moderation in the tone of public discourse, in the style of public protest, in the posturing and promises of public officials.

But it's also something more.

The people who make up this great quiet majority want a voice in the shaping of their own future. They're not against change; what they want is to participate in the process of change, to help mold the future to their own designs rather than be swept along by impersonal forces.

They too want a voice.

In fact, if there is one thing common to all groups, all races, all ages, in America today, it is this: a deep, gut feeling that they want to be a part of things, to have a say in things, to have a *voice*—and to have that voice heard.

The First Step

Today's conflicts are part of a pattern of social upheaval and generational upheaval, at a time when the old ordering of forces is being challenged by new.

The task of our generation is to resolve these conflicts and bring peace among these forces.

Finding that we do have shared grievances is the first step toward breaking down those barriers that have set group against group, generation against generation. It's the first step toward finding answers.

When we look closely, we see that much of what is lacking in our society today is precisely what America was established to provide.

Ours was conceived, in the eloquent simplicity of Lincoln's words, as a government of the people, by the people and for the people.

As we look back over this middle third of the century, we find that we have been getting more and more government *for* the people, but less and less government of the people and by the people.

And in this lies the root of much of today's frustration.

Loss of Community

Our whole development as a nation has been a great experiment, a continuing process of trial and error.

We have a system today that's an outgrowth of the experiments of the 30's—when the nation, faced with crisis, turned in fear and desperation to Washington. To make its experiments work, Washington took more and more power into its own hands. At the same time, we were becoming a truly continental nation. Air travel was beginning to link the coasts. Radio and the movies were beginning to give us a national culture. East and West, North and South, all were discovering one another. Then came television, which more than ever broke down the sense of local community. All across the nation, people were not only hearing the same words but seeing the same pictures, in their own living-rooms, night after night.

There was World War II, which brought the nation together in a shared, sustained intensity of experience not equalled before or since—and which again, and necessarily, centralized power in the Federal government. After

12

World War II we went through a new kind of experience, a wrenching readjustment not only to an uneasy peace, but to a new and unaccustomed role of world leadership and world responsibility.

The nation's horizons were thrust wide. Suddenly, what happened in Rangoon or Rio de Janeiro mattered to America, and what happened in Washington mattered in Rangoon and Rio.

At the same time, of course, this was a period of sweeping social change, of technological revolution, a time when the forces that shaped our lives kept getting bigger and more remote.

It seems obvious, now, that this would have been a time in which the place of the individual, his sense of security, of uniqueness, of belonging, would be gravely threatened.

Roots of Disorder

No great movement, no trend, takes place in a vacuum. The spread of violence and disorder is obviously no accident; obviously, it has roots in the patterns of current history.

These roots are many and complex. But I am suggesting tonight that one of the central roots is this: the steady erosion of the sense of person, of a place within the system, that we have allowed to accompany the development of our mass society.

As everything around him has gotten bigger, the individual has gotten smaller by comparison. He's been lost in the mass of things, his voice drowned out in the chorus.

The machinery of government seems increasingly remote, increasingly incapable of meeting his needs when action is needed. The community itself begins to appear less relevant, and its standards and restraints become less effective.

He feels that the *system* has left *him*.

One reason people are shouting so loudly today is that it's so far from where they are to where the power is. If we fail to bring power closer—if we persist in treating complex local needs from remote centers—we'll be repeat-

13

ing tomorrow mistakes that already have added dangerously to the frictions of today.

Revolution of Ideas

I have pointed out tonight that, in differing degree, the alienated and the rest of us share many of the same frustrations, and I have traced these to the patterns of our recent history.

Can we do anything about it?

We can.

Among many of our leading thinkers, there's been another quiet revolution going on—a revolution of ideas about the way the nation should be organized to deal with its problems.

After a third of a century of concentrating power, an old idea is winning a new acceptance: the idea that what we need is a dispersal of power. What we need is not one leader, but many leaders; not one center of power, but many centers of power.

Richard Goodwin stated this proposition cogently: "Whatever our particular position, the one overriding goal of political life must be to help restore and strengthen that faith of the individual in himself which is the source of national direction and generosity of deed."

This is a concept in which I deeply believe.

It also is the clearest-cut issue of this year's Presidential campaign.

The man who is most likely to be nominated by the Democratic party—Vice President Humphrey—is a man I respect. He is a man of honor and a man of his convictions. And he honestly believes in the old ways.

I believe in a new way.

Power has been flowing to Washington for a third of a century, and now it's time to start it flowing back—to the states, to the communities, and most important, to the people.

Every program I offer in this campaign will be tested against this standard: Does it increase the power of the people, or diminish it? Does it enhance the self-respect, the pride, of the individual human being, or reduce it?

14

Time to Modernize

We now are at a great turning point. We have to decide which way to go: whether to take the old road that leads to a government getting bigger and bigger, and more and more impersonal—the road that leads to more rebellions, more frustrations—or whether we take a new road.

Every idea has its time. And the time is now for the idea of an expanded democracy, of moving government closer to the people, of breaking massive problems into manageable pieces. This way the people can participate, they can be involved, their voices can be heard and heeded.

It's time to think anew and act anew.

Our government today is a propeller-age structure in a space-age world. In giving a new pride of place to the individual, the need is not to dismantle government, but to modernize it.

A Searching Reappraisal

One of the first tasks of the next President should be to set in motion a searching, fundamental re-appraisal of our whole structure of government—not only of the Federal departments and agencies, but also of state and local government, and its relation to the Federal structure.

The two Hoover Commissions, which studied the organization of government for Presidents Truman and Eisenhower, performed a major public service. But thirteen years have passed since the second Hoover Commission made its report, and during those years our population has grown by some 35 million; three new Cabinet departments have been created; and the whole pattern of relationships among governments and people on all levels has been profoundly changed.

There are new relationships between city and suburb; new patterns of direct Federal involvement in the cities and in education; new ventures in regional co-operation; and new layers upon layers of authority for the individual citizen to fight his way through.

The Commission on Government Re-Organization I am now proposing would be a commission with a difference. It would have a far broader mandate than those given the Hoover Commissions.

15

It would thoroughly study ways of increasing the efficiency of government organization. But its focus would be equally on the *responsiveness* of government.

Toward this end, it would be charged with searching out every feasible means of decentralizing government, of getting it closer to the people, of transferring functions to state and local governments, of creating new instrumentalities where appropriate to involve the people at the community level directly in the decisions that affect their own lives.

It would seek new ways to transfer functions from government to private enterprise, and also to the great, vital voluntary sector—to enlist the energies of those millions of Americans who stand ready and eager to serve and to help, in the best American tradition.

Its broadly-based membership would include the best management talent, the best government talent, and also the best academic talent from many disciplines. And one of its charges would be to start from a new premise: to search out what the people *want* from government today, and then to proceed to the question of how those wants can best be satisfied.

Vice President's Role

I have said that if I were President, I would give the Vice President major additional duties in helping administer the domestic functions of government. One of the first of these duties would be to involve himself directly and personally in this entire effort to move government closer to the people, and to make it more responsive. And in making the decision on the Vice Presidential nominee, this is one of the major factors I will consider.

This new, decentralized approach will require a strengthening and modernizing of state and local governments, so they can adequately discharge their new responsibilities. It will require a time of readjustment, perhaps even of difficult transition. It will require trial and error. But trial and error is itself a part of the new concept, for the concept is rooted in a basic belief that no one man, and no one group of men, has all the answers.

This new distribution of authority will mean different things to different people.

To the black man, it will mean not only the opening of doors to the larger community that have previously been barred, but also greater control, greater independence, within his own community.

For the student, it will mean a greater share in the decisions that affect *his* own community—not necessarily in matters of educational curriculum, or basic university administration, but in the personal things—the rules of living —that mean so much.

For all, it will mean a chance to be heard. It will mean responsive government. It will mean a continuing process of give-and-take. It will mean burying the old concept that you can't fight City Hall. It will mean the power of doing represented by thousands of voluntary associations with millions of members.

Re-Establishing Community

It's in this way that we can re-establish the sense of community, and thus the framework within which *all* the elements of our society at last can function.

I don't think we can buy off the alienated with more money.

I don't think we can suppress them with more police.

But I do think that as we make government more responsive, as we re-kindle trust and re-establish a sense of community, we can bring many back within the system. By improving the means of orderly change, we can reduce the temptation to disorderly change.

But we shouldn't take this new path just to bring peace to our cities, or just to bring calm to our campuses, or just to bring contentment to the suburbs. We should do it because it's right—because people do matter, and people do have rights, and because the securing of those rights is the first business of government.

What we need is nothing less than a revolutionary new approach. Government hasn't kept up with the times. The times have been rapidly changing, but government has been only growing. As it's structured today, government simply can't keep abreast of the mushrooming complexity of the country.

17

Power has to be spread out; otherwise it can't be responsive. We have to make our government structures into a set of precision instruments, tooled for particular functions.

That's the government side of the coin.

Enlisting the Energies

The other side is that we need a massive effort to ensure that private energies *are* enlisted, that local governments *are* modernized, that the voluntary sector *does* step up to the ball.

This can't be let go by default.

For let me be very clear: in turning away from ever bigger government we are not turning our backs on ever bigger problems. Our aim is not to ignore the problems, but better to solve them. It's not to neglect the poor, but better to serve their needs. It's not to sit idly by while our air and water are polluted, but to establish the most direct and effective means of control. It's not to give up in despair at snarled transportation, but to enlist the energies of those most directly affected in straightening out the snarl.

As we turn away from the old paternalism of the 40's and toward the expanded democracy of the 70's, we'll discover a new dignity, a new unity, a new stability in America. We'll discover anew that this land *is* our land, all of us together, that its destiny is our destiny. We *are* one nation, together and inseparable, and if that proposition has been tested in these past years, tested in the fires of our cities, tested in war and in the bitter debates the war engendered, tested in demonstrations and civil disobedience and in the wondering conflict of the generations, the nation has shown it can pass that test. Despite our troubles, there's a gathering today of the forces that are going to cement our society back together again—determined that decency and justice *will* prevail, and determined that reason shall rule.

Emerson wrote that "governments have their origin in the moral identity of men." Woodrow Wilson told us: "I believe in democracy because it releases the energy of every human being."

To make its expanded democracy work, America will need the willing hands of millions of individual people—proclaiming by their deeds that moral

18

identity which is the rock our freedom rests on. America will need their involvement. It will need their ideas and their energies.

That is why, in this campaign, in this watershed year, I am asking not just for your votes in 1968, but for your continued help in the next Administration. That is why I ask not just your support, but also your enlistment in this great adventure that stretches before us.

CBS Radio Network
Thursday, June 27, 1968

A NEW ALIGNMENT FOR AMERICAN UNITY

Great movements and changes in the political scene are seldom recognized while they are happening.

They are perceived long afterward. Historians, looking back in American history, can spot the great shifts:

There was the time, 140 years ago, just after the Era of Good Feeling, when Andrew Jackson re-introduced the two-party system in America.

There was the time, 100 years ago, after the collapse of the Whig Party, of a new coalition that became the Republican Party.

And there was the time, 35 years ago, when Franklin Roosevelt assembled a Democratic coalition of organized labor, minority groups and the "solid" South.

That last assemblage of power blocs dominated the middle third of the Twentieth Century in America. But as we enter the last third of this century, it is time we recognize a profound change that has taken place in American politics.

Parallel Ideas

Without most of us realizing it, a new alignment has been formed.

Most Americans have not been aware that this new alignment has been gathering together. Yet it has happened, and it is an exciting, healthy development.

More than a century ago, Alexis de Tocqueville put his finger on the mysterious formation of a new opinion:

> Time, events, or the unaided individual action of the mind will sometimes undermine or destroy an opinion, without any outward sign of the change. It has not been openly assailed, no conspiracy has been formed to make war on it, but its followers one by one noisely secede; day by day a few of them abandon it, until at last it is only professed by a minority . . .

> They are themselves unaware for a long period that a great revolution has actually been effected . . .

20

The majority have ceased to believe what they believed before, but they still affect to believe, and this empty phantom of public opinion is strong enough to chill innovators and to keep them silent and at a respectful distance.

This new alignment is already a new majority; it will affect the future of all Americans for generations to come whether they are part of it or not.

The new majority is not a grouping of power blocs, but an alliance of ideas.

Men and women of all backgrounds, of all ages, of all parties, are coming to the same conclusions. Many of these men and women belong to the same blocs that formed the old coalitions. But now, thinking independently, they have all reached a new conclusion about the direction of our nation. Their very diversity of background provides a basis for a new unity for America.

The Republican Voice

Listen to the conclusion as expressed by one group, the most visible one, voiced by many Republicans for many years:

"This nation has become great not by what government has done for people but by what people have done for themselves. The more centralized and domineering a government gets, the less personal freedom there is for the individual.

"The role of government is to do for people what they cannot do for themselves: to open up new opportunities, to mobilize private energies to meet public needs, to protect and defend every citizen, to create a climate that enables every person to fulfill himself to the utmost — in his own way, and by his own choice."

That's the Republican voice, the voice of both liberals and conservatives within the party, and its good sense is becoming more appealing to millions of Democrats and Independents. That traditionally Republican thinking is the well-spring of the new alignment.

21

Voice of the New Liberal

But there is another voice saying much the same thing in a different form. It is the voice of the New Liberal.

That voice of the New Liberal calls for a workable form of "participatory democracy." It demands a political order close to the people who are governed, in which the people play a vital part. That voice demands more personal freedom and less government domination.

Thoughtful critics like Daniel Moynihan and Richard Goodwin — both liberals — are giving the word another dimension. A century ago, to be a "liberal" meant to be against the domination of governmental authority, to put personal liberty ahead of the dictates of the State. Only recently has the term "liberal" come to mean the dependence on federal action to meet people's needs.

The future meaning of liberal is likely to return to the reliance on personal freedom. But it will have a difference: it will see that a key role of government is to provide incentives for the free enterprise system to accept more social responsibility.

In that context, liberals and conservatives will find themselves coming closer together, rather than splitting apart.

Just as there is a difference between the New Deal Liberal and the New Liberal, there is a big difference between the New Liberal and the New Left.

The New Liberal recognizes that progress and order go hand in hand. He points to the channels of protest open to those who dissent, especially through the electoral process. In this way, the American system can be a force for change without changing the American system itself.

The extremists of the New Left strongly — even violently — disagree. They say that the respect for dissent, the protection of their civil rights to protest peaceably, are only safety valves for the Establishment.

The very processes that permit gradual change are resented by these extremists. That is because they would find it much easier to break a rigid structure than to break our flexible one.

22

They feel — quite wrongly — that they have to tear down in order to build, shaking society to its foundations, leading us to anarchy. The New Left has a passion, while the New Liberal has a program.

And yet I have a feeling that many of the young people who call themselves New Leftists now are in fact far more closely attuned to the voice of the New Liberal. When it comes to a choice between getting something off your chest or getting something done, sooner or later most people choose to get something done.

Voice of the New South

There is a third voice — the voice of the new South. Not the old solid South of the Thirties, of automatic voting habits and a declining economy.

The new South is no longer prisoner of the past; no longer bound by old habits or old grievances or the old racist appeals. The new South is building a new pride, focusing on the future, pressing forward with industrial development through resurgent private enterprise, forging a new place for itself in the life of the nation.

Politically, the new South is in ferment. It is breaking the shackles of one-party rule. Its new voices are interpreting the old doctrines of states' rights in new ways — those of making state and local governments responsive to state and local needs.

Voice of the Black Militant

There is a fourth voice — the voice of the black militant. There is a deep and widening division between today's black leadership and the doctrinaire welfarist.

When you listen to these black voices, you hear little about "handouts" or "welfare." Instead, you hear the words "dignity," "ownership," "pride." They do not want to be recipients, they want to be participants.

The message of giveaway, of handout, of permanent welfare is no longer of interest to people who want dignity and self-respect.

The nation, in its present economic crisis, cannot afford an increase in these giant welfare programs today.

What we can and should do immediately, is to respond to their demands for a share of American opportunity, for a legitimate role in private enterprise.

The Silent Center

There is a fifth element to the new alignment — a non-voice, if you will.

That is the silent center, the millions of people in the middle of the American political spectrum who do not demonstrate, who do not picket or protest loudly. Yet, these people are no less committed to seeking out this new direction. They are willing to listen to new ideas, and they are willing to think them through.

We must remember that all the center is not silent, and all who are silent are not center. But a great many "quiet Americans" have become committed to answers to social problems that preserve personal freedom. They have rejected the answers of the Thirties to the problems of today.

As this silent center has become a part of the new alignment, it has transformed it from a minority into a majority. That is why we are witnessing a significant breakthrough toward what America needs: peaceful, orderly progress.

Disharmony in the New Alignment

My point is this: these voices — the Republicans, the New Liberals, the new South, the black militants — are talking the same language.

Let's not oversimplify. The voices are not joined in any harmonious chorus — far from it. The ideas of the new alignment differ in emphasis. But they do not conflict the way the old alliance of power blocs used to conflict.

The differences within the new alignment are differences of emphasis, not of fundamentals; differences in the *speed* of change, not so much in the *direction* of change.

Now, the new alignment's greatest need is to communicate with all its elements, rather than march along in parallel lines that never converge.

24

Strange Bedfellows

You can be sure that the members of the old power blocs will try at first to dismiss this new majority as just an assortment of strange bedfellows.

But despite the differences in appearance, despite the differences in ways and means, despite the lack of communication, despite all the pains of realignment, the *fundamental agreement is there.* Even men who find each other disagreeable at first, can find themselves in agreement.

The Straddlers

I do not claim to be the only one who notices the formation of this new alignment. On the campaign trail today you can see the politicians of the old order adjusting their appeals. It may be awkward, but they speak about "more Federal billions now for the cities" in one breath and then, in the next breadth, talk of "an end to the old welfare system and a return to private enterprise."

These politicians are trying to have it both ways. On the one hand, they are reluctant to abandon the old power alliances that have served them so well in the past. On the other hand, they don't want to miss the new boat as it leaves the dock.

People today, and the political figures who appeal to them, will have to make the hard choice: whether to cling to the old power-bloc alliances of the middle third of this century, or to join the new alignment of ideas that will shape the final third of this century.

Promise of Unity

And therein lies the great excitement of this new alignment. Right now, we see our differences all to clearly; in the future, those of us in the alignment will see our similarity of methods and goals much more clearly.

The mark of a good insight is when everyone says "Of course — that's what I've been thinking all along, only I never put it that way." That is what is at the heart of the new alignment: the crystallization of what is on the minds of the American people today.

Tomorrow, as we focus the new movement more clearly, America will gain a new unity.

We will not seek the false unity of consensus, of the glossing over of fundamental differences, of the enforced sameness of government regimentation.

We will forge a unity of goals, recognized by men who also recognize and value their own diversity. That is the great advantage of an alignment of ideas over the coalition of power blocs.

As we coalesce the elements of this new alignment, some surprising things will begin to happen. As frustration ends, violence will wane; as runaway government is curbed, personal freedom will grow; as demeaning welfare systems are replaced, individual initiative will take the lead; as peace returns to the American city, America will be better able to build peace in the world.

Joining the New Alignment

The new alignment speaks in many accents, and approaches its point from many directions. But the common message is there:

People come first, and government is their servant. The best government is closest to the people, and most involved with people's lives. Government is formed to protect the individual's life, property, and rights, and to help the helpless — not to dominate a person's life or rob him of his self-respect.

The concept is great not because it is new, but because it is right and it is relevant.

Victor Hugo pointed out that there is nothing so powerful as an idea whose time has come. The time has come for this idea. No one leader has drawn together this new alignment; it has been drawn together by the magnet of an idea that is right for our time, that speaks to us now, that has special meaning today.

How do you become part of the new alignment?

You don't have to be a member of any special party, or any union; you are not required to live in any region or any city; you don't have to be rich

26

or poor, young or old. Because we're not dealing with blocs — we're dealing with an idea.

If you believe that people do come first; if you believe that dignity must replace the dole; if you believe that order and progress go hand in hand; if you are idealistic about personal freedom; — then you don't have to worry about where to go to join the new alignment.

You are already a part of it.

Rising to the Crisis

The great re-alignments of our history did not take place in normal, quiet times. They took place when America was in trouble, or when the existing majority could not come to grips with the needs of the nation. And so, without realizing it, a new majority is formed and lasts as long as it meets the need for change. This is what we mean by "the collective wisdom of the people."

This is the unspoken voice of America, in its majesty and its mystery, demanding articulation by men who sense its new meaning.

That is why new faces with more of the old answers miss the point. That is why new leadership is needed now — leadership with a proven record of fighting for the action the new majorty now demands.

No man can predict the ultimate shape of the alignment that is happening in America today. But I know this: It is alive, it is moving forward, it is rooted in reality, and it calls out for you to come aboard. In the years to come, I believe that historians will record this:

> That in the watershed year 1968, America, in a time of crisis, responded as it has responded before — with new ideas, with great traditions, with a new alignment and with the fresh hope that comes from a new unity.

CBS Radio Network
Thursday, May 16, 1968

A COMMITMENT TO ORDER

In the course of this year's Presidential campaign, I will be discussing with the American people many issues — what I see as the nation's needs and its strengths; it problems and its purposes; the dangers we face, and the opportunities that are ours to seize.

Tonight I would like to talk with you about the number one issue of 1968 — the number one issue in the United States — and the number one issue in the world.

This is the problem of order.

By order I mean peace at home, and peace in the world. I mean the containing of violence, whether by armies or by mobs or by individuals. I mean the essential stability, the decent regard for the rights of others, that makes life livable and progress possible.

It was more than a quarter-century ago that President Franklin Roosevelt proclaimed "freedom from fear" as one of the Four Freedoms. And yet today, fear stalks our lives as never before.

There are many kinds of fear today — fear of the loss of individuality, fear of human obsolescence, fear of economic deprivation — but the central fear is the most primitive — the fear of physical violence.

We live today at a time of deep and fundamental questioning, when millions of Americans are asking whether their country can survive, and whether their world will survive. Both abroad and at home, the forces of destruction threaten our lives and our institutions.

Here at home, we have been amply warned that we face the prospect of a war-in-the-making in our own society. We have seen the gathering hate, we have heard the threats to burn and bomb and destroy. In Watts and Harlem and Detroit and Newark, we have had a foretaste of what the organizers of insurrection are planning for the summers ahead. The President's National Advisory Commission on Civil Disorders now cautions that "in the summer of 1967, we have seen in our cities a chain reaction of racial violence. If we are heedless none of us shall escape the consequences."

Abroad, we have lived for a generation with the abrasive tensions of the cold war, with the threat of nuclear weapons, with the explosive instabilities of a rapid dismantling of the old colonial empires. We have fought World War II, Korea, Vietnam, and the peace is still elusive. Still we live in a world in which tyranny and greed and fanaticism march behind the barrels of guns. Are we, then, to be divided forever into warring worlds?

And here at home, are we to become two nations, one black, one white, poised for irrepressible conflict?

On both counts, the answer is no. But we cannot have peace abroad by wishing for it. And we cannot heal the wounds of our nation either by blind repression or by an equally blind permissiveness.

The peace we want in our cities is not the illusory peace of an abdication of authority, and not the sullen peace of the dispirited, but the peace that springs from participation — participation in the processes of growth and change, in the excitement of the present and the promise of the future.

As they survey the prospects of our cities, some cry out in despair that all is lost, that nothing can be done, that The Fire Next Time already is licking at the window-sills. Even President Johnson said not long ago that "we will have a bad summer," and "we will have several bad summers before the deficiencies of centuries are erased."

This is not a time for Pollyannas, but neither is it a time to throw up our hands in helplessness. Violence in a free society is never inevitable — unless we accept its inevitability.

The first responsbility of leadership is to gain mastery over events, to shape the future in the image of our hopes. If the present Administration persists in its weary voice of defeatism, its tired counsels of despair, it will have abdicated this great responsibility.

We should not for a moment underestimate the threat to our safety and our stability. But neither should we underestimate the means we have of countering that threat. Above all, we should make clear to those who threaten that these means will be employed — and thus that they cannot hope to carry out their threats and get away with it.

For a generation now, America has had the chief responsibility for keeping the peace in the world. In meeting this responsibility, we have been learning the uses of power — and specifically the uses of power in preserving the peace. We have learned from our successes, and I would hope that we have learned from our failures. Those lessons are needed today at home as never before.

The first lesson is that the best time to display both power and the will to use it is before trouble starts — to make transparently clear to a potential aggressor that the price of aggression is too high, and the chances of success too slight.

A second lesson is that force alone is not enough. Force may deter a great power. But force is no answer to despair. It is no answer to those who think they have nothing to lose, whether among the hungry nations of the have-not world, or among those in our own cities nursing the grievances of centuries.

Only if we can light hope in the ghetto can we have peace in the ghetto — but that hope has to be real, and achievable, and it has to rest, not on the expectation of being *given* something, but on the chance to *do* something. It has to be the kind of hope that builds responsibility, not dependency.

In the case of our threatened cities, I am not making any flat predictions. But I will say this: 1968 *can* see a cooler summer, rather than a hotter one. I say it can for three reasons:

First, because we have been warned. The violence being threatened for this summer is more in the nature of a war than a riot. A riot, by definition is a spontaneous outburst. A war is subject to advance planning. But if those threatening war can plan, those being threatened can also plan.

The second reason I say it could be a cooler summer is this: among responsible Negro leaders, there is a growing spirit of resistance to the extremists. After all, the great, quiet majority of America's Negroes *do* live by the law, and do share the ideals of the society we all belong to. Yet it was *their* neighborhoods that were destroyed, their homes ravaged, their lives made hostage to terror. And now their voices are being heard, providing a climate once again more receptive to the common-sense Negro leadership that recognizes that the only lasting way to progress is the peaceful way.

30

The third reason I say that it could be a cooler summer is that this is a Presidential election year — a fact which provides a peaceful focus, a political focus, for the great challenge of combining peace with progress, and through peaceful progress bringing about a new spirit of racial reconciliation.

But we can expect a cooler summer only if we do two things, and do them both with compelling urgency.

On the one hand, we must take the warnings to heart, and prepare to meet force with force if necessary — making it abundantly clear that these preparations are made, and that retaliation against the perpetrators and the planners of violence will be swift and sure.

But on the other hand, we must move with both compassion and conviction to bring the American dream to the ghetto.

I spoke a moment ago about lessons we learned abroad that could be applied here at home. There also are lessons from our experience at home that are relevant abroad. One of these is, quite starkly and quite simply, that what happened in Watts and Detroit could happen in the world, unless we move with a sense of urgency to create among the lagging nations and peoples of the world a sense of belonging, of participation, of hope, that has been lacking in the slums of our own cities.

The world is becoming a great city — a city in which communication is instantaneous, and travel nearly so; a city in which civilizations centuries apart in development are suddenly side by side. It is becoming a city in which the extremes of national wealth and national poverty cannot forever co-exist in explosive proximity, without inviting upheaval — and the difference between the violence we have experienced in our cities and the violence this would invite is the difference between Molotov cocktails and the ultimate weapons of annihilation.

Another and more immediate lesson is that we dare not let the forces of violence get out of control.

All history has been a struggle between man's thrust toward violence and his yearning for peace. One measure of the advance of civilization is the degree to which peace prevails over violence.

Today, the apostles of violence are testing their doctrines — in Vietnam, in Thailand and Laos, along the border between North and South Korea, in Africa, in Latin America, where roving bands of Castro's guerrillas operate. The old violence parades today in a new uniform. Both at home and abroad, it has wrapped itself in propaganda.

At home, it may masquerade as "civil disobedience," or "freedom," and it sometimes marches under the banner of legitimate dissent.

Abroad, violence calls itself a "war of national liberation," and tries to justify terror and aggression with slogans of social revolution. But the new war is still the old imperialism.

The sloganeering of the new violence confuses many people. That's what it intends to do. But when the slogans are stripped away, it still is violence plain and simple, cruel and evil as always, destructive of freedom, destructive of progress, destructive of peace.

The war in Vietnam is a brutal war, and a terrible war, as all wars are brutal and terrible. It has cost us heavily in lives, in dollars, in hostility abroad and division at home — in part because of the Administration's failure convincingly to strip away its masquerade. But the men dying there are dying for a cause fundamental to man's hope: the cause of checking aggression, of checking violence, and of moving us one step closer along the difficult road to a lasting peace.

I have long been a vigorous critic of the conduct of that war. Our *military* power has been frittered away in a misguided policy of gradualism; if we had used our power quickly, we could have ended it with far less than we are now using.

The Administration's failure to inform the American people of the full costs of the war — its failure to take the people fully into its confidence on the war — has sown distrust and suspicion about the war, both here and abroad.

But even more fundamentally, the Administration has failed to understand the nature of this new kind of war. This is different from other wars, and far more complex. It is a war for people, not for territory, and it cannot be won by military means alone.

32

Because of its failure of understanding, the Administration has failed to press those non-military measures — diplomatic, economic, psychological, political — that could have vastly increased the effectiveness of the military effort. It has failed to use diplomacy effectively with the Soviet Union, to enlist the Soviets on the side of peace. It has failed to do enough to enlist the South Vietnamese fully in their struggle — enough to train their military, and enough to give their people the hope, the stake in the future, the spirit of independence, that are needed if they are to have something to fight *for,* as well as against.

Only when our political, economic and diplomatic efforts are given a priority equal to our military effort will this war be brought to a successful conclusion.

Only this way can we get the negotiated end of the war that we want — not a military victory in the conventional sense, not unconditional surrender by the other side, but a durable peace in which the right of self-determination of the South Vietnamese people is respected by all nations, including North Vietnam.

I think that with different policies the war could have been ended before this. I think that with new policies it could be ended sooner — though not as quickly or as cheaply as if those policies had been adopted when they should have been.

It is essential that we end this war, and end it quickly. But it is essential that we end it in such a way that we win the peace. And just as the cause we are fighting for is larger than Vietnam, the peace we must be concerned with is larger than Vietnam. The peace we must be concerned with is peace in the Pacific for the balance of this century. But Vietnam alone will not secure that peace. It requires a preventive diplomacy, designed to concert the rapidly growing strengths of the Asian nations themselves.

We are a nation of 200 million people, powerful and rich. But there are more than 2 billion people in the free world. In Korea, the United States furnished most of the arms, most of the money — and most of the men. In Vietnam, the United States is furnishing most of the arms, most of the money — and most of the men.

As we look to the future, we must establish conditions in which, when others are threatened, we help if needed — but we help them fight the war for themselves, rather than fighting the war for them. This means that the other nations in the path of potential aggression must prepare to take their own measures, both individually and collectively, to contain the aggressor. They must not be allowed to suppose that they can continue indefinitely to count on the United States for go-it alone protection.

This is not a retreat from responsibility, and not a new isolationism. It recognizes three fundamental facts:

First, that the job of keeping the peace is too large for the United States alone;

Second, that among nations as among individuals, self-reliance is the foundation of pride and the cornerstone of progress;

And, third, that by establishing new collective security systems, the total effective strength of the free world will be increased, and thus the communist powers' temptation to launch new wars will be reduced.

We as a nation must still do our share, but others must do their share, too. In the long run, peace can be maintained only if the responsibility for maintaining it is shared.

What then are the prospects, both at home and abroad?

Are we doomed to live with an ever more terrible violence? Are the bitter agonies of these wars of the past and the present — the war in Vietnam, and the war in our cities — to be magnified? Or is it possible that finally, after three foreign wars in a generation, and after the battles that have set our cities aflame and seared the soul of the nation, we can move on now to a peace of understanding abroad and a peace of reconciliation at home?

I say it is possible. It is not only possible, but imperative. But we live in a world of hard facts and harsh realities, and these make firmness and fortitude necessary.

Eventually, we can and must look forward to the day when the Communist powers will abandon the pursuit of their ambitions by military means.

We can and must do all in our power to enlist them, too, on the side of peace and not on the side of war. I am convinced that in the term of the next President substantial progress on this front will be possible. But it will only be possible if we persuade them, first, that aggression does not pay — that just as they finally learned in Korea that they could not expand by the old-style war, they must be shown in Vietnam that they cannot achieve their goals by the new-style war.

The war in Vietnam is not a war to end war. But it is a war to make a larger peace possible. Only if this war is ended in a way that promotes that larger peace, will the cost be justified.

If we are to achieve a peace of reconciliation here at home, there is one thing we must make crystal clear.

We increasingly hear angry cries that ours is an unjust society, that the whole "power structure," the whole social and economic and political structure, is evil and ought to be destroyed. Whether the cry comes from extremists in the Black Power Movement, or from the far fringe of the New Left, the message is still one of intolerance and hate, and it still is wrong.

These mounting threats of violence come when there has never been less cause for violence, and never less excuse for rebellion. Never have we been so close to the achievement of a just and abundant society, in which the age-old wants of man are met and the age-old grievances of the disinherited set right.

There are injustices. There are inequities. But there also is a massive popular will to correct those inequities and right those injustices.

Equally important, we have the means to correct them in peaceful and orderly fashion. America was born in revolution. But the architects of the new nation saw clearly that if the society was to be secure, the means of peaceful change had to be provided. They built into our structure what the colonies had rebelled for lack of: a system by which the people of America could be masters of their own destinies, in which all could be heard, and the power of persuasion substituted for the power of arms as a means of bringing about progress and change.

This points up a major deficiency in emphasis in the recent report of the President's riot commission — its tendency to lay the blame for the riots on everyone except the rioters.

Among the causes of the riots the commission noted that "frustrated hopes are the residue of the unfulfilled expectations aroused by the great judicial and legislative victories of the civil rights movement and the dramatic struggle for equal rights in the South."

It might also have included the inflated rhetoric of the War on Poverty, which added to the dangerous expectation that the evils of centuries could be overcome overnight.

One thing worse than not keeping a promise is making a promise that cannot be kept.

The commission rightly sounded a note of urgency, and it rightly pictured the task ahead in the cities' slums as massive.

But it would be unrealistic to raise hopes that the vast programs the commission proposed might all be done at once.

And it would also be a disservice to suggest to the dwellers in those slums that they need only wait for Federal housing, Federal jobs, a Federally guaranteed income.

Jobs, housing — all the things of the better life — will come, ultimately, when two things happen: when private enterprise gets into the ghetto, and when the people in the ghetto get into private enterprise — as workers, as managers, as owners.

We can and must make far greater progress than we have, but we can only do so by a far greater enlistment of private enterprise in rebuilding the cities, in providing the jobs, in constructing the housing.

During the course of this campaign I will be recommending programs to move us toward this goal.

More than almost any of the great issues facing America today the tortured problem of race requires a careful balance and a clear perspective. Much that is desirable, much that is urgent, takes time to achieve.

America still is going through an agony of transition.

It takes time for old myths to give way to new awareness.

It takes time to erase the old stereotypes.

But the point is that we are moving forward, and moving rapidly, toward what the riot commission refers to as a "single society" — one nation, one people, one common ideal, in which each person is measured as an individual, and in which legal rights are fleshed out with actual opportunities.

We must do more. But if progress is to be made, the first essential now is order.

The riots shook the nation to a new awareness of how deep were Negro resentments, how explosive the grievances long suppressed. But that lesson has been learned. And those who now cry "burn" tempt a new conflagration that could engulf not only the cities, but all the racial progress made in these troubled years.

Excesses on one side bring excesses on the other; we could too readily be drawn into a spiral of violence and vengeance. We can ill afford the destruction of our cities; we could even less afford the ravaging of our society.

We cannot be complacent about our country's faults, but neither should we be apologetic about its strengths.

What began in rebellion nearly 200 years ago has become a peaceful revolution and a permanent revolution — a revolution that has transformed the world, and that has stood for these two centuries as a beacon for man's aspirations and a symbol of his liberties.

This permanent revolution is not yet finished. Lincoln freed the slaves. Our uncompleted task is to free the Negro. Franklin Roosevelt promulgated the old, negative freedoms *from*. Our uncompleted task is to make real the new, positive freedoms *to*.

The architects of our country provided the means for peaceful change. Our uncompleted task is to damp the fires of violent change, to cement our mastery of the pace of change, and to make the most of our opportunity for constructive change.

Change is the essence of progress. But there can be no progress without order, no freedom without order, no justice without order.

And so our first commitment as a nation, in this time of crisis and questioning, must be a commitment to order.

This is the commitment that makes all else possible. This is the commitment that is needed if our unfinished agenda is to be finished, and the American Resolution — the permanent peaceful revolution — is to fulfill its promise to mankind.

NBC Radio Network
Thursday, March 7, 1968

LEARNING TO SHARE RESPONSIBILITY

Never before in the history of Presidential campaigns have four weeks been more unpredictable, or in a political sense more exciting, than those we have just experienced. All the signs indicate that this year's campaign will be one of the historic political battles of our time. But the question lingers: will this battle move America forward or backward?

At its worst, this campaign could be seriously destructive of the great goals we seek. At its best, it can make a great contribution not only to better understanding of the issues, but also to the charting of a new direction for the nation as we enter this final third of the twentieth century.

This promises to be a year of great debates — both within the two parties, and between the parties.

These debates will be a test of our political system — a test of the nation's ability to deal rationally with the harsh problems of a distant war; a test of our capacity to move from violence to reconciliation in our cities; a test of the mood and spirit of the nation, and of our capacity as a people to rise above the tensions and distractions of a deeply troubled time.

The questions facing us this year are difficult — far more difficult than those that ordinarily constitute the "issues" in a political campaign, precisely because they are so much more fundamental. Both abroad and at home, we are confronted by far-reaching questions of the balance of power, the distribution of power, the exercise of power and the limits of power. Both abroad and at home, we face the wrenching readjustments of a time of rapid transition.

Never has the United States been in more trouble in more places than it is today — in Europe, in Latin America, in the Middle East, in Southeast Asia, and in the cauldrons of our cities here at home.

Never have we more needed an intelligent, rational and dispassionate discussion of the great issues. And yet seldom has debate been more raucous and more irresponsible.

Senator Kennedy accuses his fellow Democrat, President Johnson, of "calling upon the darker impulses of the American spirit." The President and his supporters too often respond in kind by savage attacks on the motives of his critics.

The Great Society is becoming a bitter society — bitter in its mood, bitter in its frustration, bitter in the sense of foreboding that poisons the atmosphere of discussion.

We need a new unity — but not a unity which discourages dissent. We need a unity within which a diversity of view and expression is welcomed. True unity can only be hammered out on the anvil of free debate, and the sparks from that debate are what today must light the fires of hope. We need dissent — but we need a creative dissent, one that contributes to the dialogue and to the fund of fresh ideas from which practical approaches can be drawn.

What we need is not less debate or more debate, but to improve the quality of our debate. For the decisions facing us cut to the heart of our structure as a society and our purpose as a nation.

The future of peace and freedom in the world depends on the manner in which the United States meets its responsibilities — and also on the way in which those responsibilities are defined and shared.

One of America's strengths has always been its abiding streak of idealism. But unless we temper this idealism with realism, it can prove our undoing. We must be idealists about the goals we seek, but realists about the means of reaching those goals. We must be realists about what is necessary, and also about the limits of the possible — about the extent to which our resources can be stretched, and about what our power can accomplish.

We have come to a time when America must reappraise — in a most searching, measured and fundamental way — its role and its responsibilities in the world, and the resources which we and which other nations can bring to the meeting of those responsibilities.

We need to fashion a new diplomacy which can readjust the balances within the free world, as well as those between the free and the communist worlds.

Economically, diplomatically, militarily, the time has come to insist that others must assume the responsibilities which are rightly theirs. We must do our full share, both in maintaining order and in helping the have-not nations onto their feet. But the free world can no more base its security and prosperity on a system of permanent welfarism abroad than the security and prosperity of our own cities can be based on permanent welfarism here at home.

Since World War II, the United States has moved into a new and unfamiliar position — often an uncomfortable position — of power and of responsibility. We have inherited by default the role of the world's chief keeper of peace and guardian of freedom. This is a role we did not ask; it is one history thrust upon us. But our not asking it makes it no less ours.

However, conditions have changed since we first assumed that role. The other nations of the West have grown in strength. Japan has moved into the first rank of industrial powers. All around the rim of China the nations of non-Communist Asia are building a new prosperity and developing a new cohesiveness, which together suggest that they should be able to play far more assertive roles in their own defense.

The Soviet drive for strategic supremacy — which the Soviets already have very nearly achieved, while the United States has passively watched — is deeply troubling and seriously threatening. No longer is it possible for the thinly stretched power of the United States to play the decisive role that it has in many crises in the past. Even where it can be deployed, it is not backed today by the nuclear superiority which in the past has made it credible.

The United States has been able to keep the peace since World War II, as far as another world war is concerned, because we have had an overwhelming balance of power in our favor.

But we have let that balance slip, and with it we have seen an erosion of our ability to keep the peace in the world.

This has profound implications not only for the United States, but for the rest of the free world.

For one thing, it means that what has always been an elusive goal must now be made a reality: the other nations of the world must begin, and quickly, to pick up a greater share of the burden of the common defense.

To insist that others share more fully in the responsibilities of defining and maintaining the conditions of peace is not a retreat into a new isolation. Rather, it recognizes that today there are new realities of power. It recognizes, to put it very bluntly, that even if the United States had the will, it no longer has the capacity to do all that needs to be done. If the other nations of the free world want to remain free, then they must rise in their own defense. They can no longer afford the luxury of relying on American power.

We must, then, do three things. We must move quickly and persuasively to enlist the other nations of the free world more fully in the tasks which must be done. During this critical time of transition, we must continue to bear the burdens which are inescapably ours until a new system of stability can be constructed. At the same time, we must restore at least a part of the strategic advantage that we once held — not because we want power, but because in the world as it is we need power if we are to be secure.

Vietnam has been a deeply troubling lesson in the limits of U.S. power. But it is not enough simply to lament those limits, or to criticize the commitment, or to wish that history had dealt differently with that tormented part of the world.

The crucial point is that we must confront the reality of the world as it is, even as we press toward the goal of what we want it to become.

The war itself is the latest and the grimmest battlefield in a larger, continuing struggle. This struggle is in part between the United States and the Soviet Union, and between the United States and Communist China, but more fundamentally between those nations that want stability and those that want instability; between those that want order, and those that want disorder; between those that want peace, and those that seek domination.

As we approach the day of nuclear parity between the United States and the Soviet Union, we approach the moment of truth in the relations between East and West. What strategists called the "Cuban power environment" no longer exists. In 1962, at the time of the Cuban missile crisis, the balance of strategic power made it possible for President Kennedy to deliver a fully credible threat of nuclear retaliation. The balance was then sufficiently in our favor so that the Soviet ability to destroy the United States with an inferior missile force was doubtful, while the capacity of the U.S. bombers and missiles to destroy the Soviet Union was certain. In these circumstances, the President was able to face down the Soviet leaders, and to force them to withdraw their offensive missiles from Cuba. But the United States no longer has such a decisive power advantage.

Nor do we command either the allegiance or the respect that were ours in the world at large only a few short years ago. No longer do our words receive the hearing they once enjoyed. Those who once *followed* the United States now *observe* the United States.

The world has lost much of its respect for our power. When we possessed an overwhelming strategic superiority, as well as mobile forces that could be dispatched to world trouble-spots both quickly and safely, without leaving other frontiers unguarded, then we had to be listened to.

Our ideals no longer communicate the fire, the passion and the promise that they did only a few short years ago. The passion we have been demonstrating lately is the passion that tears a society apart rather than the passion that builds unity and hope.

The world has lost its confidence in our dollar. It has lost its faith in our purposes, its respect for our judgment, its trust in our word.

If we delay our reappraisal of the U.S. role; if we delay moves to establish a new structure of security adequate to the age; if we delay these until the war in Vietnam has ended and the dust settled, then we will have delayed too long. Vietnam must be the last agony of the old order, because there is question whether the old order could sustain another.

Both abroad and at home, the dominant trend of the middle third of the 20th century was toward the concentration of responsibility. What we need now is a dispersal of responsibility.

Abroad, a world that in the early thirties had many centers of power developed in the years after World War II into one dominated by the two superpowers and divided into two great blocs.

The fact that recent years have seen a growing polycentrism in the communist world and a fracturing of the Western alliance signals a major crack in the essential bi-polarity of this division. But it has not altered the fundamental fact of a continuing confrontation between communist ambition and Western resistance.

However, the growing strength of the nations of Western Europe, of Japan, and of other nations now emerging into a new prosperity does indicate the capacity of the non-communist world to move toward a dispersal of responsibility that accords with the new distribution of power.

Here at home this last third of a century has been a time of rapid accumulation of federal power. I do not maintain that big government is necessarily bad government, or that federal power necessarily limits personal freedom. But the problems facing our country today simply cannot be handled by the federal government alone. The complexity of our national life today requires a dispersal of power here at home that accords with the diversity of our society and the variety of its needs.

Devising the most effective ways of achieving this is one of the central tasks of our time.

I am not suggesting that we should be trying to undo what has been done, that we should turn back the clock or renounce the great progress that has been achieved.

I am suggesting, rather, that we have reached a point at which we need a new direction. This is a cause in which liberals and conservatives increasingly are finding common ground. The old New Deal was born in response to despair and desperation. We now need a new vision that embraces the hopes of an age of opportunity.

America has been learning the lessons of reality the hard way, but also the best way — by trial and error, by pursuing hopes and confronting disappointments. We are learning better what government can do, and what it cannot.

We already have learned a great deal about our society — its strengths and its shortcomings. The explosion of bitterness in the Negro ghetto has driven home a dramatic lesson that there are many whom this society has tragically failed. But if it has shown this, it also has shown that the old approaches — the government charities that feed the stomach and starve the soul — have also failed.

44

The American opportunity is neither a black nor a white opportunity —
but if we are to make our nation whole again by making our people one,
we must begin with the recognition of a need for a greater black opportunity.
The only way to set right the power balance in our cities is to put a greater
measure of power in the ghetto. By this I speak not of "Black Power" as
some of the extremists would interpret it — not the power of hate and
division, not the power of cynical racism, but the power the people should
have over their own destinies, the power to affect their own communities,
the power that comes from participation in the political and economic
processes of a society.

This is a goal. The nation still is struggling and stumbling toward the
best, the most effective and the most equitable means of reaching this goal.

On the goal, I am convinced there can be no compromise. On the means
there must be cooperation, accommodation, a searching out of the possible,
a testing of what works and what does not.

I have cited these examples to illustrate the point I want to make
tonight: that the questions facing America in 1968 *are* fundamental ones,
and they *do* require the best and the most dispassionate thinking we can
mobilize.

The tortured problems of Vietnam cannot be solved by an emotional
jingoism, or by impassioned laments for the agonies of war that ignore the
hard requirements of peace.

Neither can they be solved by a stubborn intransigence that seeks to
justify the mistakes of the past by carrying them to futile extremes, when
new approaches are needed.

Whether in defining our role abroad, or in remaking our society at home,
we must recognize that we live in a complex and difficult world, in which
the realities of power can be cruel and in which the answers are seldom
simple.

The issues before us this year center on the most fundamental questions
of all: about the conditions that may determine whether peace and freedom
survive, and indeed whether civilization as we know it survives. They
require a new enlistment of the people of America in the shaping of their

own destiny — whether on college campuses, or in industry, or in the slums of our festering cities. We need a new freedom from dogma, freedom from the old ideologies and the old isms.

We need to restore to our political dialogue the sense that it *matters* — that the processes of democracy still *are* effective, even for dealing with the complexities of the modern day. I share the view of those who say that Senator McCarthy's campaign has contributed significantly to this goal: that his enlistment of the enthusiasm, the energy and the faith of many who had given up on the political process is a step toward the restoration of that process itself to the place it deserves, and must have if our system of government is to work.

But we need to do more than focus dissent. We also need to enlist energy and enthusiasm in the fashioning of realistic programs that can achieve the promise of this final third of the century. We need the same energy in *positive* causes that negative causes enlist. We need helping hands, not marching feet.

The tragedy of the Johnson Administration is not a tragedy of mean intensions or of ignoble motives, but simply a tragedy of failure. Never has an Administration so misjudged a people, so underestimated their promise, or so missed the challenge and the opportunity of its time.

I believe that the role of the Republican party in 1968 is larger than party — that it centers on a cause bigger than differences among Republicans, and bigger than the differences between Republicans and Democrats. The role of the Republican party in 1968 is to assemble a new coalition — a coalition of those dissatisfied with things-as-they-are, with politics-as-usual and slogans-as-usual and drift-as-usual.

During twenty years in public life, studying the problems of our nation and of the world as a public official and as a private citizen, I believe I have found *some* of the answers. Because I *have* seen the range and complexity of our problems, I would not presume to suggest that I have all of the answers. But I do have certain convictions about the values that are important, and about the kind of means that are most effective.

And I think I know the questions.

In the months ahead, I will be talking with all of our Republican Governors, with the Republican Senators and members of Congress, with the mayors of our cities, and with other leaders of thought in all fields without regard to party. I will be asking their ideas, and seeking out their answers. The problems of America today are not Democratic problems or Republican problems. They require the marshaling of the best brains America can produce, and the broadest range of experiences that can be brought to bear. If the debates of 1968 can serve this end, then they will have served their purpose — and the American system will have passed its test.

And now, a final word: We can never master our problems unless we measure our opportunities.

For too long, we have listened to the tired voices of defeatism, the bitter voices of negativism.

But this *is* a moment of opportunity for America. We all can sense that opportunity when we put aside what's wrong with America, and look at what's right with America. We can feel it in the pride that has never been stilled — pride in our ideals, pride in our strength, pride in the fact that for all its faults, ours *is* the society that has come closer to realizing man's age-old dreams of liberty and abundance than any other, any time, any place.

The dimensions of this opportunity are what give force to our drive to surmount the problems of an age of challenge. For if we can put these problems behind us, the horizons of the possible stretch almost without end.

The world's future depends on the leadership America gives. And that leadership depends ultimately on the spirit of America's people. Unless we have faith in the basic strengths of our system, in the basic idealism of our people, in the basic workability of our institutions, we can hardly expect to inspire that confidence abroad that our effort to establish a new system of order in the world requires.

But I believe we have that faith, and that capacity, and that by giving new life to our ideals at home we can and will provide an example for the world.

NBC Radio Network
Thursday, March 28, 1968

47

THE AMERICAN SPIRIT

Williamsburg is a revered place in America.

Here was the capital of Colonial Virginia; here was a revolutionary war headquarters of George Washington and here, during the Civil War, was the scene of a bloody battle between Blue and Grey forces.

In modern times, Williamsburg has been restored to its historic setting; today, men of the twentieth century can walk through a village of the eighteenth century, absorbing the mood that surrounded the men who built this nation.

It is fitting, then, to pause in the election campaign of 1968 at a place steeped in our heritage; this is a proper moment to examine our past for some keys to our future. Perhaps we can draw some strength and gain some insight from what has gone before.

We we recall the days of our Revolution, we think of the phrase "the spirit of '76." That is not just a slogan; there was a real "spirit of '76." That spirit was the driving force within most Americans of that revolutionary era.

I believe that a nation, like a person, has a spirit.

I believe that a national spirit comes to the fore in times of national crisis.

I believe that each time a national spirit makes itself felt, it speaks to its own time with a different message directed to the problems of that time.

That is why a searching look at the American spirit is needed today. The American spirit, as I envision it, is not the visitation of some ghost of the past; rather it is the affirmation of a deep national yearning that all of us feel today.

Whenever America falls short, that spirit appears—not to comfort us, but to make demands on us. Not to salve our conscience, but to spur our conscience.

Our history shows that as a people we have responded to these new demands each time they were made.

48

Almost two centuries ago, at the time of our Revolution, the American spirit demanded political liberty. And so a nation was born.

A century and a half ago, the American spirit demanded a choice in national leadership, calling for a framework that encouraged the cut and thrust of controversy. And the two-party system was born.

A century ago, at the time of our Civil War, the American spirit demanded an end to slavery and an end to sectionalism. And so the nation was born again, this time into a deeper unity.

At the turn of this century, the American spirit demanded a fair share for all in the fruits of our economic system; trust-busting was born and the labor movement gained momentum.

A generation ago, with tyranny on the march, the American spirit stirred again; a new internationalism was born, and America shouldered her world responsibilities.

With hindsight, we can now see how the American spirit reappeared time after time in our history; looking back, it is easy to detect its differing demands and the great changes it achieved.

But the Americans living through those times did not have the benefit of hindsight. The men who gathered at places like Williamsburg two centuries ago were not then a distinguished group of statesmen known as Founding Fathers—they were a band of practical idealists risking the gallows by talking of revolution.

The great eras of changes are clear enough for us in retrospect. But to the men living through those times, America was upset and uncertain; strong cross-currents of opinion roiled the waters and hatreds flared.

That is the kind of era we are going through right now. The textbooks of the next century—if textbooks are still in use—may sum up the new demands of the American spirit in a sentence or two. But now it is up to us to work it out for ourselves.

Here in 1968, what is missing from American life that has called up this spirit of change? What void in each one of us needs to be filled?

Of course, we think first of the obvious answers. We need peace in the world; we need the good life for all; we need justice for all, in the framework of law. But let's go a step beyond.

We are told of a man who was seen digging around the walls of his house; when he was asked why, he gave this strange and intriguing answer: "I am letting the dark out of my cellar." That is what we must do now; as we dig for the demands of change, we must let the dark out of our cellars.

I believe that an underlying reason for the feeling of emptiness in so many hearts today stems from the loss of personal freedom.

I believe that the American spirit is reappearing now to demand the return of that personal freedom.

As in our past, these demands are thundered in stormy times. Some of us are all too noisy; some of us are all too silent; but each of us knows that this is the time to stand up for his own individual identity.

We won our fight for political freedom two centuries ago; we won a battle for human freedom a century ago; today, we are in a fight for our personal freedom.

Personal freedom, to me, is at the root of human dignity.

Personal freedom is room to turn around in life. It is the right to grow in your own way, to learn what is not yet being taught; it is both the right to privacy and the right to participate.

Personal freedom is not a license to disrupt, but it is a liberty to dissent; not a duty to destroy, but an obligation to challenge.

Personal freedom will not ensure that every man will get all he desires; it will ensure that every man will get all he deserves.

Those Americans who once had personal freedom and lost it, now want it back; those who never had it at all, want it now.

In striving for a worthy goal—security—we have lost a worthy asset— individuality, the hallmark of personal freedom. In trying to provide for the material needs of all, we have stolen from the personal freedom of each.

Where did we lose our way? Where did we begin to trade away our personal freedom?

Some would say we lost our way when we began our ever-expanding welfare programs. Others would say we lost our way when we took on the responsibility of helping to defend the free world.

I don't agree. These were steps that changed the course of history; these were steps in the right direction.

We were right to want to help the poor, the sick, the unemployed, the elderly. We were right to want to help advance the cause of democracy around the world.

But in making these advances, we lost something. We became so busy doing so much for the "people" that we forgot about the person. We became so obsessed with the collective needs that we overlooked the individual need.

At first we didn't feel the loss. Our American system had so much momentum; there was so much to be done and so much to do it with. We could not detect the slow erosion of our personal freedom, the gradual diminishing of human dignity.

But now, a generation later, we feel it. And we miss what we lost. We miss it in the feeling so many Americans have of being hemmed in; of being a cog in a huge machine; of being no longer in control of our own lives; of not having our own important say in the direction of our communities and our nation.

Well, what are we going to do about it? We cannot turn back the clock; we must not undo all the good we have done, as we try now to regain the freedom we have lost.

Nor can we throw up our hands and say that one man does not count anymore—that we've traded personal freedom away for the security of a big, paternal government.

We do have another choice. We must find a way to make government work for all of us without dominating any one of us. We have to establish new respect for the qualities of initiative, personal sacrifice, and readiness to seize opportunity, that made the individual American the wonder of the world.

And we have to reawaken this respect the hard way: without tearing down the structure we have built to help those who cannot help themselves.

That is why a political promise of "more of the same" is wrong, and why a promise of "less of the same" is just as wrong. We need neither more nor less of the "same"—we need an approach that is entirely different.

Welfare is too important to be left to the Welfare Staters. We are going to change our welfare system to make it fit the American system, to provide each person with a means of escape from welfare into dignity. This is not an impossible dream. America needs it: with leadership that understands the American spirit, America is going to get it.

And that's not all. Each of us wants to get back that sense of participation in government, that hand in our own destinies.

We are going to reverse the flow of power to the Federal Government in Washington, and channel more power back to the states and localities. Tax sharing; bloc grants; decentralization; local option; community participation; this is the direction I believe America is about to choose.

What's more, the pendulum is going to swing back to an emphasis on individual opportunity. But something new will be added: genuinely equal opportunity, starting from childhood. The industrious person will get ahead and the lazy man will fall behind, no matter what their background or heritage or skin color.

How can I be so certain about all this?

Because I believe that is what the American spirit now demands. Because the American people are not "the masses"—they are 200 million individual persons who are discovering what they have lost, and are determined to get it back.

Our present leaders are out of touch with this new mood and cannot comprehend this new need. They see the future as bearing down on us. They are fearful of the future, fearful of the change it will bring, and they brace themselves for the shock that they know will come.

In the eyes of the fearful, tomorrow is a threat that must be faced; in the eyes of the hopeful, tomorrow is a vision that must be realized.

An American poet put it this way: "dive for dreams, or a slogan may topple you." We must turn away from the old slogans that trigger responses that are no longer responsive; we must dive for the dreams we can make come true.

The way to the future is not along the path of least resistance. We will only earn back our personal freedom along a path of great resistance.

The American spirit is presenting its demands today, as it did in different terms to generations before us. Once again, those demands require sacrifice and ingenuity:

The American spirit demands an explosion of education into the mind of every child in every corner of this land;

It demands a career—not just a job, but a career—open to every man and woman who has the capacity to get ahead;

It demands an end to the slamming of doors, with the answering echo of gunfire that we have heard in the past;

It demands a plunge into community service by each of us, rather than delegating compassion to government;

The American spirit of today demands that the helpless be cared for, and the hopeless be cared about;

It demands that there be greater rewards for initiative and hard work and self-reliance;

It demands that privacy be respected, that the individual be respected, that the law be respected.

Most of all, the American spirit today demands the self-determination of the human being. This means a shift from Federal rule to home rule, a shift from faceless manipulation to personal participation.

There is a mystery to America that its detractors have never been able to grasp.

53

Just when our idealism appears to be swamped in a sea of material wealth; just when our native morality seems to be flooded by a wave of crime and disorder; just when our international power and prestige appear frustrated by the ineptness of our leadership—something remarkable happens.

The American spirit wells up and we snap out of it. We let the dark out of our cellar. We choose new leaders with new ideas and we tell them we're ready to make any sacrifice required to set our nation right.

We don't ask new leadership to put us back to sleep. We don't ask new leadership to fix everything without bothering us. Instead, we demand to know what we need to do—what each individual one of us must do.

At watershed moments like these, the unconquerable American spirit comes alive. We stand at a pivot point; the nation is poised to turn and move in the direction the spirit of America demands.

That is why I have been saying that the choice in this election year is perhaps the most important in our lives. If we fail to seize this moment, if we let slip this chance to recapture our personal freedom—the moment may never come again in our lifetime.

Therefore, let us not lightly dismiss the agony of the American spirit today as only "growing pains."

Let us recognize it as hunger pangs, for now is a time that our body politic hungers for new directions, new answers to new needs.

At moments like these throughout our history, it has been America's genius and good fortune to satisfy this appetite for orderly change. This generation of Americans shall not be the first in 200 years to deny the demands of the American spirit.

Rather, I believe this generation will choose to rise to the challenge: we shall promote the general welfare, yes—but we shall preserve our personal freedom as well.

We shall hold fast to the quality that made America great, as we reach out for new qualities that will make America greater.

54

Woodrow Wilson described the challenge of such a moment. The year was 1913. The nation was badly torn; a third party movement had split the majority vote. There was war in the Balkans that threatened to spread to the rest of the world.

In his first Inaugural Address, this is what Wilson told his countrymen: "Men's hearts wait upon us; men's lives hang in the balance; men's hopes call upon us to say what we will do. Who shall live up to the great trust? Who dares fail to try?"

In this campaign, my fellow Americans, we can feel the American spirit stirring.

It calls upon us to make a mighty effort to rekindle our hope, our courage and our passion for personal freedom. We dare not fail to try.

The American spirit today demands an awareness of the need for change.

It requires the exploration of new horizons of justice.

It insists on the rediscovery of the worth of the individual.

It will accept nothing less than a reach for greatness.

The next President of the United States could possibly serve until 1976, the 200th anniversary of the birth of our nation.

That next President will lead this nation in its reach for greatness only if he summons a new "spirit of '76"—a spirit conceived in old glories, born to speak to its own time, destined to shape a glorious future.

Williamsburg, Virginia
October 2, 1968

TO MAKE OUR PEOPLE ONE

BRIDGES TO HUMAN DIGNITY, THE CONCEPT

Every age has its special set of problems, and every problem has its special catch-phrases. Today, we commonly speak of "the urban crisis." And yet the problems wrenching America today are only secondarily problems of the cities. Primarily, they are problems of the human mind and spirit.

Over and over again, we ask ourselves whether our cities can survive, whether they can remain livable, whether the races can coexist within them, whether poverty and squalor must inevitably consume the inner city. In asking these questions, we are asking, in effect: how long can Americans ignore the race condition?

How long can we endure the discord, the prejudice, the dependency, the difficulty of bringing white and black together in peace?

The challenge confronting America today is as broad as the world and as complex as humanity itself.

It is a question of whether the pain, the injustices, the angers that stem from a century of fear and misunderstanding, now can at last be put behind us.

It is a question of whether we believe in the essential dignity of man, and if so, whether we are prepared to act on that belief.

For years now, the focus of talk, of debate, of action, has been on "civil rights" — and the result has been a decade of revolution in which the *legal* structure needed to guarantee equal rights has been laid in place.

Voting rights, schools, jobs, housing, public accommodations — in all these areas, new laws have been passed, old laws struck down. Segregation, Jim Crow, "all deliberate speed," freedom rides — these terms which aroused such passion a few years ago, have lost much of their relevance as basic goals have been won. The old vocabulary of the civil rights movement has become the rhetoric of the rearview mirror.

And yet these victories have not brought peace or satisfaction or the fullness of freedom. Neither have the old approaches of the 30's — the government charities that feed the stomach and starve the soul.

59

No "More of the Same"

For too long, white America has sought to buy off the Negro — and to buy off its own sense of guilt — with ever more programs of welfare, of public housing, of payments *to* the poor, but not *for* anything except for keeping out of sight: payments that perpetuated poverty, and that kept the endless, dismal cycle of dependency spinning from generation to generation.

Our task — our challenge — is to *break* this cycle of dependency, and the time to begin is now. The way to do it is not with more of the same, but by helping bring to the ghetto the light of hope and pride and self-respect.

We have reached a point at which more of the same will only result in more of the same frustration, more of the same explosive violence, more of the same despair.

I have said recently that the fiscal crisis now confronting America is so great and so urgent that only by *cutting* the Federal budget can we avert an economic disaster in which the poor themselves would be caught calamitously in the undertow.

The reality of the national economic condition is such that to talk of massively increasing the budget in order to pour additional billions into the cities *this* year is a cruel delusion.

But this does *not* mean that because we cannot do more of the same, we must do nothing new. Only those who are locked into the solutions of the past, who measure progress by billions spent rather than by results achieved, will let themselves be stopped by a budgetary wall.

Activating Our Resources

In the long run, I think history will judge it fortunate that the United States was forced by economic crisis to turn to people, rather than government: forced to explore new and imaginative means of activating the real resources of America. For the plain fact of the matter is that all the money in the world wouldn't solve the problems of our cities today — whether those are thought of as problems of race, or of housing, or of education, or even as problems of poverty.

60

We won't get at the real problems unless and until we rescue the people in the ghetto from despair and dependency.

There's no pride at the receiving end of the dole, and unless and until there is pride in the ghetto — personal pride and racial pride — we're not going to get anywhere in tackling the real problems of a real world.

Let me be very clear. As we look down this final third of the twentieth century, a period in which the population of our cities will double, the costs of both physical and human regeneration will increase greatly. No fiscal sleight-of-hand can restore and renew the cities without our having to pay the bill. And governments at all levels will have to join with private enterprise in meeting that cost.

But this is long-term.

Right now we face a short-term fiscal crisis, a crisis that William McChesney Martin, the Chairman of the Federal Reserve Board, calls the worst in a generation. Unless we save the dollar, we may have nothing left to save our cities with.

At such a time, it is gross irresponsibility to promise billions of new Federal dollars for the cities or even for the poor. One thing worse than not keeping a promise is making a promise that cannot be kept.

If the ghettos are to be renewed, their people must be moved by hope. But hope is a fragile thing, easily destroyed and even more easily weakened — and nowhere is it more fragile than among those whose hopes over the years have been repeatedly raised only to be cruelly dashed.

What we do *not* need now is another round of unachievable promises of unavailable Federal funds.

The Bridges Needed Now

What we *do* need is imaginative enlistment of private funds, private energies, and private talents, in order to develop the opportunities that lie untapped in our own underdeveloped urban heartland.

It costs little or no *government* money to set in motion many of the programs that would in fact do the most, in a practical sense, to start building a firm structure of Negro economic opportunity.

We need new bridges between the developed and underdeveloped segments of our own society — human bridges, economic bridges, bridges of understanding and of help.

We need incentives to private industry to make acceptable the added risks of ghetto development and of training the unemployed for jobs. Helping provide these incentives *is* the proper role of government; actually doing the job is not — because industry can do it better.

This is one kind of a bridge.

Another bridge is the bridge of black success — a bridge that can only be built by those Negroes who themselves have overcome, and who by their help or their example can *show* that the way to the American Dream is not barred by a sign that reads, "Whites Only."

A third bridge is the development of black capitalism. By providing technical assistance and loan guarantees, by opening new capital sources, we can help Negroes to start new businesses in the ghetto and to expand existing ones.

Educational bridges can be built, now, at little cost — bridges of tutorial help, of business training, of remedial assistance, using volunteers who in case after case have shown themselves both willing and effective.

Bridges of understanding can be built by revising the welfare rules, so that instead of providing incentives for families to break apart, they provide incentives for families to stay together; so they respect the privacy of the individual; so they provide incentives rather than penalties for supplementing welfare checks with part-time earnings.

From Welfare to Dignity

We must make welfare payments a temporary expendient, not a permanent way of life; something to be escaped from, not to. Our aim should be to restore dignity of life, not to destroy dignty — and the way welfare programs are too often administered today, their effect is to destroy it. They create a permanent caste of the dependent, a colony within a nation.

62

In another nationwide radio address next Thursday I will spell out a number of specific programs for building these bridges, and also others. The point about all of them is that they *can* be done *now*; they don't require billions of dollars that the government doesn't have, and they don't require waiting until billions more become available. They are not the whole answer. But they are part of the answer — and a vital part, without which no amount of money can do the job.

These are the kinds of approaches that get directly at the matter of dignity and pride and self-respect; these are the kinds of approaches that can break the shackles of dependency, just as the laws of the past decade have finally broken the shackles of bondage.

Human Rights, Property Rights

Much in this area can be done through private initiative — for example, by groups such as John Gardner's forward-looking Urban Coalition. What they require is *commitment*, by private citizens as well as by public officials.

It's long been common practice among many to draw a distinction between "human rights" and "property rights," suggesting that the two are separate and unequal — with "property rights" second to "human rights."

But in order to *have* human rights, people need property rights — and never has this been more true than in the case of the Negro today. In order to enjoy the human rights that ought to be his, he has to acquire the property rights on which to build. What do I mean by property? Many things — but essentially, the economic power that comes from ownership, and the security and independence that come from economic power. Rights are never secure unless protected, and the best protections for a person's basic rights are those he can erect himself.

Black extremists are guaranteed headlines when they shout "burn" or "get a gun." But much of the black militant talk these days is actually in terms far closer to the doctrines of free enterprise than to those of the welfarist 30's — terms of "pride," "ownership," "private enterprise," "capital," "self-assurance," "self-respect" — the same qualities, the same characteristics, the same ideals, the same methods, that for two centuries have been at the heart of American success, and that America has been

63

exporting to the world. What most of the militants are asking is not separation, but to be included in — not as supplicants, but as owners, as entrepreneurs — to have a share of the wealth and a piece of the action.

And this is precisely what the central target of the new approach ought to be. It ought to be oriented toward more black ownership, for from this can flow the rest — black pride, black jobs, black opportunity and yes, black power, in the best, the constructive sense of that often misapplied term.

Black Enterprise

Philosophies, wars, power structures, all have turned historically on the basic questions of ownership — who owns the means of production, who owns land — for the simple reason that with *ownership* goes power, prestige, security, the right to decide and to choose.

We should *listen* to the militants — carefully, hearing not only the threats but also the programs and the promises. They have identified what it is that makes America go, and quite rightly and quite understandably they want a share of it for the black man.

For a long time, we too have been talking about preservation of the private enterprise system, about enlisting private enterprise in the solution of our great social problems, about profits as the great motive power of our fantastically productive economy. What many of the black militants now are saying, in effect, is this: "We believe you, and now we want a chance to apply those same principles in our own communities."

Our reply should not be to reject this request, but to seize upon it — and to respond to it.

The ghettos of our cities will be remade — lastingly remade — when the people in them have the will, the power, the resources, and the skills to remake them. They won't be remade by government billions; the sad history of urban renewal, for example, has shown how often this results in an actual decrease in the number of housing units available for the poor, with one slum torn down and another created — because the basic *conditions* of slum life haven't been changed. These conditions are what we have to get at — the human and social conditions, the conditions of the spirit — and these

64

in turn rest in large part on our laying in place the *economic* structure that can support a rebirth of pride and individualism and independence.

Free Enterprise in the Ghetto

For the individual, a job is the essential first step — whether toward independence, toward family responsibility, or toward advancement — but even jobs have to be provided *within a framework* that establishes dignity and the pride of the black man as well as the white.

It's no longer enough that white-owned enterprises employ greater numbers of Negroes, whether as laborers or as middle-management personnel. This is needed, yes — but it has to be accompanied by an expansion of black ownership, of black capitalism. We need more black employers, more black businesses.

Integration must come — but in order for it to come on a sound and equal basis, the black community has to be built from within even as the old barriers between black and white are dismantled from without.

We have to get private enterprise into the ghetto. But at the same time we have to get the people of the ghetto into private enterprise — as workers, as managers, as owners.

The Demand for Dignity

At a time when so many things seem to be going against us in the relations between the races, let us remember the greatest thing going *for* us: the emerging pride of the black American. That pride, that demand for dignity, is the driving force that we all can build upon. The black man's pride is the white man's hope — and we must all, black and white, respond to that pride and that hope.

These past few years have been a long night of the American spirit. It's time we let in the sun.

It's time to move past the old civil rights, and to bridge the gap between freedom and dignity, between promise and fulfillment.

It's time to give a new dimension to our American concept of equal justice under law — time to give an answer of the spirit to America's crisis of the spirit — and it's a time to face our challenges not in despair, but with zest — not with a heavy heart, not bowing sullenly to duty, but as an *opportunity* for America to redeem and enrich its heritage.

Ours is a chance today to change America, and, by our example, to help America change the world.

CBS Radio Network
Thursday, April 25, 1968

BRIDGES TO HUMAN DIGNITY, THE PROGRAMS

In a radio address last week, I stated this conviction: that the economic crisis confronting America today is so acute that it rules out a massive transfusion now of additional Federal funds into the nation's cities. Rather than spending more, the Federal budget must be cut by some $8 billion if the fiscal crisis is to be averted and the dollar itself preserved.

But I also stated that a lack of available Federal funds ought not to stifle our ingenuity. I spoke of bridges that can and should be built between the developed and the under-developed parts of our society — between rich and poor, white and black — human bridges, economic bridges, bridges of understanding and of help.

Tonight I would like to describe some of those bridges.

These programs represent a beginning; they illustrate the new direction that our efforts to reconcile the races and to rescue the poor ought to be taking.

They will not by themselves eliminate poverty now or even in the next decade. They will not guarantee complete racial harmony. But they will point the way toward our becoming at last one nation and one people. For they aim at breaking the dismal cycles of despair and dependency, which have created a welfare class catered to by a welfare bureaucracy. And the point about them is that they are all things which *can* be done *now* — which do not require the massive spending which can be neither realistically promised nor responsibly delivered.

The old approach was custodial: to *care* for the poor with Federal doles, Federal housing, Federal make-work jobs. The new approach is remedial: to involve the poor in the rebuilding of their own communities, and in the fostering of self-reliance and self-respect.

The first need is to replace dependence with independence.

This means laying the economic stepping-stones of meaningful and productive jobs securely in place. Beyond this, it also means encouraging black pride through the vigorous development of black management and of black capital ownership, and thus helping remove the ceiling from black aspiration.

The possible answers to our nation's problems are infinite in number — the product of the ingenuity of the American people multiplied by their commitment of the cause of justice. But here are some of the things — specific, practical things — that can be done *now* to get private enterprise into the ghetto, and the people of the ghetto into private enterprise.

Core City Credits — Rural Development

Tax incentives — whether direct credits, accelerated depreciation or a combination of the two — should be provided to those businesses that locate branch offices or new plants in poverty areas, whether in the core cities or in rural America.

Free enterprise goes where the profits are. Tax incentives can place these profits where the people are, and where the need is.

I include rural America in this incentive program for two reasons.

The first is need. We don't see rural America exploding on television, but these harsh realities cannot be overlooked: more than half the Americans living below the poverty line live in rural America. Unemployment on the farm is twice what it is in the city. More than half the nation's inadequate housing is in rural areas.

The second reason is, quite simply, that many of the cities' problems are rooted in rural decay. As workers are forced off the farms, they crowd into the cities — often as unprepared for city life as they are for city jobs. To the extent that new jobs can be opened in rural America, to that extent will the pressure be lessened on the cities.

New Capital

If our urban ghettos are to be rebuilt from within, one of the first requirements is the development of black-owned and black-run businesses. The need is more than economic. Black ownership — of homes, of land, and especially of productive enterprise — is both symbol and evidence of opportunity, and this is central to the spirit of independence on which orderly progress rests.

Establishing new businesses requires both capital and know-how.

Too often, the normal sources of capital are unavailable for ghetto enterprises. The risks are considered too high.

As the President's Riot Commission has recommended, the Small Business Administration's loan program should be substantially expanded in these areas.

Beyond this, additional loan guarantee programs can be combined with active efforts to enlist traditional lending institutions in ghetto development.

Reinsurance programs cost little to establish, and these can reduce the risk of investment in poverty areas.

Dr. Andrew Brimmer, a Governor of the Federal Reserve Board, has urged a greater use of correspondent relationships between large, white-controlled lending institutions and smaller, black-controlled ones, which again would increase the capital available for ghetto business loans.

Churches, unions, and corporations doing substantial business in poverty areas, might choose to keep some of their cash deposits in banks that serve those communities.

Federal and state banking authorities might join with private banking institutions to provide technical and capital assistance for the establishment of more new, black-controlled banks.

Senator Javits has proposed creation of a Domestic Development Bank, roughly comparable in concept to the World Bank. This would make loans and guarantees for businesses that either are located in poverty areas or draw most of their employees from poverty areas, with preference given to those enterprises that are locally-owned or that allow residents of the area to participate in ownership.

New Enterprises

A New Enterprise program should be established to serve the Negro in the central city, helping black employees to become employers.

Under such a program, successful businessmen and business school teachers could provide training in the techniques of business management. If such a program were organized, surely enough could be found who would volunteer their time — and, as an extra inducement, I would suggest an individual tax deduction equivalent to the rate of pay of an instructor in a business school for the time individually put in, and corporate tax deductions for those companies that loan their executives.

Human Investment

Next, I urge immediate enactment by Congress of the Republican-sponsored Human Investment Act, providing tax incentives to corporations which hire and train the unskilled and upgrade the skills of those at the bottom of the employment ladder.

A few years ago, American industry was given a seven per cent tax credit for the modernization of equipment. The credits were widely used. Productivity increased, and the entire economy benefited. A similar tax credit for increasing the productivity of people is overdue, and along with it should go a vigorous effort — led by the President — to persuade industry to utilize it to the fullest. Workers, business and the nation would benefit.

Critics have questioned such tax-credit proposals on the ground that each dollar of tax credit increases the budget deficit by as much as a dollar of new spending.

But in this case, it wouldn't work that way. In the first place, those put on payrolls will be taken off welfare rolls or unemployment — compensation rolls; and in the second place, as industry is moved into the job-training field, government can be moved out of it.

The Job Corps, for example, has proved a costly failure. It costs some $10,000 a year to train a Job Corpsman for a job that often turns out not to exist. Under the Human Investment Act, industry itself — which creates the jobs — would be training men at far less cost for jobs that did exist.

Computer Job Bank

Part of the unemployment problem is simply a matter of getting the man and the job together.

Last month, while the Department of Labor reported that three million

American men and women were looking for jobs, classified pages all across the nation were thick with "Help Wanted" ads.

This is an area in which modern technology can serve human needs. If computers can match boys and girls for college dates, they can match job-seeking men with man-seeking jobs.

Thus I have recommended the creation — immediately — of a National Computer Job Bank.

Under this plan, computers would be located in areas of high unemployment, both urban and rural. These would be programmed with data on available jobs and job training programs — locally, statewide and nationwide. A jobless man could tell the computer operator his employment background, his skills, his job needs — and in minutes he could learn where to find the work or the training he seeks.

These economic programs all are simple in concept and modest in cost. They lack the drama of a $2 billion or a $20 billion pricetag. But they are aimed at enlisting the real engines of American progress — individual initiative, private capital, voluntary services; the dynamic four-fifths of our economy *not* accounted for by government.

Now let us turn to education.

When it comes time for budget-cutting, this is one area that must *not* be shortchanged. Doing so would shortchange the future of our children, and the future of the nation.

The Federal government has an immensely important role to play in advancing education, as do the states and the local communities.

But there also is a great deal the *people* can do.

Student-Teacher Corps

Young Americans have shown their idealism and their dedication in the Peace Corps and in VISTA. To these now should be added a National Student Teacher Corps of high school and college students; carefully selected, paid volunteers who would work at the tutoring of core-city

71

children. What they might lack in formal teaching skills, they could make up in the personal bonds of friendship and respect.

A comparable program already is at work in New York City where Homework Helpers — supervised high school seniors — are tutoring fourth-to-sixth grade students. Both helper and pupil have benefited. The Riot Commission has commended the program — and it represents the kind of helping hand needed across the nation.

Extended Training

Compensatory education is the first step toward bringing quality education to slum schools. Without it, the children of poverty will never catch up with the children of abundance.

I recommend inauguration of Extended Training Programs in core-city schools, in which classes in basic language and communication skills would be made avaliable after regular school hours and during the summer months. For those willing to take advantage of them, these programs would provide an essential and often missing foundation for further learning.

Teacher-Veterans

One of the key needs in the ghetto is for more black teachers and administrators, highly trained, highly motivated. As Floyd McKissick put it a few months ago, "We need a black authority figure . . . with whom our children might be able to identify and to whose position they might aspire."

Among the nation's greatest underutilized assets are the returning Negro veterans of Vietnam. These include thousands of officers and non-commissioned officers, trained and proven in leadership. Many of these would be superbly qualified for training as teachers.

The universities and schools for teacher training should intensify their recruitment among these veterans. For its part, the Department of Defense should set up a special information program to make Vietnam veterans, black and white alike, aware of the opportunities and rewards of teaching.

The black soldier has written a proud record in Vietnam — and that pride is needed in the ghetto schools.

Home Ownership

People who own their own homes don't burn their neighborhoods; rather, in pride and self-interest, they turn to fixing up their communities and making them livable for themselves and their neighbors.

Exciting new trails are being blazed toward more widespread home ownership.

Senator Percy's National Home Ownership Foundation plan, for example, would provide a private sector device for channeling mortgage capital into the slums and for enabling the poor to own their own homes — and it would do so at only a minute fraction of the cost of packing them into public housing.

Flanner House, a private self-help organization in Indianapolis, has shown dramatically that "sweat equity" can be made to work as a means of getting the poor into their own homes; some 400 families there have built their own homes from scratch. The example should be widely copied.

The FHA is largely limited today to "safe" mortgages. It should be turned in the direction of taking greater mortgage risks, so that it can function effectively in slum areas where now it does little.

I have tried tonight to set forth a few example of low-cost steps that could be taken now to attack the problems of slum housing, rather than spending hundreds of millions to clear more slum acres, to displace more families, and to build more public housing.

The basic principle here is the same as in the job programs I outlined: imaginative enlistment of the private and the independent sectors, encouragement of private ownership, development of the pride that can only come from independence.

Significantly, some of the nation's outstanding Negro leaders have shown the way. Men like Dr. Leon Sullivan in Philadelphia and Dr. Thomas Matthew in New York have established private programs which have opened doors of opportunity to thousands of Negroes who might never have benefited from a government program.

The old way — the government way — will no longer do. The old way is still the conditioned reflex of those whose policy approaches are rooted in the 30's — the old way of massive spending piled on massive spending, and of looking to Washington to solve the problem of Watts.

The old ways have failed, because the Crisis of the Old Order is not the crisis of today. In the ruins of downtown Washington, of Detroit and Watts and Newark, lie the ruins of a philosophy of government that has outlived its origins and no longer speaks to its time.

It's time now for a new way, which yet is the oldest way of all — the way that begins with people, marshaling their own energies, moved by their own will, pursuing their own dreams.

The people are responding — individuals, voluntary organizations, businesses, universities.

People are *asking* what they can do. Businesses are *looking* for ways to enlist.

Our legislative goal should be the maximum mobilization of this will and these resources, with government's primary role not to do the job by itself, but to assist in getting it done.

Through this creative interaction of public and private, of government and people, the poor can finally receive what law alone cannot provide — the hope, the help, the fellowship of human dignity, which stem from that greatness of heart that lies at the heart of America's greatness.

NBC Radio Network
Thursday, May 2, 1968

THE VOLUNTARY WAY

These years of turmoil have shocked Americans into a recognition of how enormous are the social tasks ahead of us, and how urgent.

Faced with an urban crisis, the first instinct of many has been to demand vast new government programs and vast new expenditures—whether a "Marshall Plan for the cities," or a doubling of public housing funds or a government-guaranteed income for everyone.

Yet even at best, these government programs would only scratch the surface of need. They would drain the Federal treasury to soothe the public conscience, but they would fail—because they would leave untapped the greatest reservoir of neglected resources in America today: the energies and the spirit of the American people themselves.

Enlisting People

Government has an important role. But it's only part of the mix. We need to enlist the energies of that dynamic four-fifths of our economy represented by private enterprise, and we also need to enlist those millions of Americans who stand ready to serve and to help, if only they knew what to do and how.

It's small wonder that more and more people, and not only the young, are in a mood of open revolt against the machinery and the men of government—against an increasingly impersonal bureaucracy, a top-heavy Washington, a statistical model of services that dehumanize man and perpetuate a cycle of dependency.

Program after program aimed at "establishing domestic tranquility and securing the general welfare" has had almost the opposite effect—less tranquility and more violence, more public "welfare" and less personal well-being.

As government has strained to do more, our people have felt constrained to do less. The more the Federal government has tried to solve *all* of our problems, the more it has seemed to fail.

Public programs are attacked by the very people for whom they were created; and our young people, our most precious resource, are disillusioned and disaffected by the results.

The problem lies not with the American people, but with a government that has lost touch with the people.

Six months ago I delivered a series of two nationwide radio addresses titled "Bridges to Human Dignity." In these, I outlined a new approach to break the cycle of dependency. I detailed an extensive list of programs to bring the races together in peace, and to bring hope to the hopeless. I focused primarily on things that could be done now by government, and by private enterprise—and especially on new ways in which government incentives could be used to mobilize private enterprise more effectively in meeting our public needs.

Third Set of Bridges

Tonight, I want to talk about the third set of bridges we need—the bridges of voluntary action by people who care.

In many ways, these are the most important of all. For the tasks we face are, above all, human tasks. Unless the personal element is restored, we cannot succeed. But if our human resources are enlisted on the scale required, we can hardly fail.

Those resources are available—willing and waiting.

Voluntary Organizations

There are more than a million independent, voluntary organizations in America today. There are 320,000 churches, with more than a hundred million members. There are two thousand United Funds and Community Chests, 3,500 voluntary hospitals, six thousand private foundations, more than 100,000 voluntary welfare agencies. Thirty-six million Americans belong to fraternal and service organizations.

The potential is greater still. The Gallup polling organization has estimated than *61 million* adult Americans would be willing to contribute *245 million man-hours every week* to voluntary activities.

76

Think of what that could accomplish!

It's more than twice as many man-hours as all the civilian employees of the U.S. government could put in, even if they worked full-time on nothing else.

That's the measure of the American willingness; that's one dimension of the American spirit.

It's also a measure of our neglected opportunity.

This voluntary tradition is deeply rooted in American history, and in the American character. More than a century ago Alexis de Tocqueville described it as our most "distinguishing characteristic." Today, it's needed as seldom before—needed in the cities, needed in the depressed rural areas, needed where government has failed.

"Citizen Initiative"

Beginnings are being made. All across America, there's a springing up of "citizen initiative" in public planning and problem-solving. We see it in the insistence by local school boards on greater control over the quality of education; in the establishment of neighborhood development corporations; in the creation of private student aid funds and the organization of ghetto industries.

Exciting new trails are being blazed—and in city after city, determined people are showing the reach of private ingenuity.

Just the other day, for example, I met in Detroit with a group of people assembled by Governor Romney. They were men, women; black, white, of all ages and backgrounds, but they had one thing in common: they have been putting the voluntary principle into practice with phenomenal success.

These were people who cared; who acted—and their achievements are an example for all America.

One of them had set up a program for the hard-core unemployed, not only to train them for jobs, but also to give them the basic understanding of how to get and hold a job that so many lack. Another had a program that had led thousands of school drop-outs to go back to school and finish

77

their education. Another had pioneered a program of home ownership for the poor. Another had established a community-owned business development corporation that provided loans and technical assistance for new businesses in the ghetto. Others had found jobs for thousands of unemployed, or found ways to turn a neighborhood without pride into a community with pride, or provided basic education that allowed workers at the bottom of the ladder to move up. And there were more.

Motivation, Pride, Dignity

The point is that in jobs, housing, education, and more fundamentally in those intangible but vital factors of motivation and pride and dignity, these people had actual, functioning programs that had changed the lives of tens of thousands of people—and they had done it through voluntary effort.

What they have done can be multiplied, and it must be.

In the course of that meeting in Detroit, a question that strikes at the heart of America's need was trenchantly put—in three simple words—by a remarkable young Negro schoolteacher, Mrs. Carole Williams. She was describing what had lead her, a year ago, to establish a Volunteer Placement Corps for graduates of Detroit's ghetto high schools.

A survey had revealed a shocking statistic: that in the first few months after graduation, only 10 per cent of those graduates were being placed in jobs, colleges or job training programs. As Mrs. Williams pondered that failure and its cost, she was led to wonder what could be done about it and who could do it—and then, she said, she put the question to herself this way: "Is it I?"

Was *she* the one who could help?

In putting the question, she found the answer. Yes, And she acted— at first alone. Already the placement corps that she founded only a year ago has nearly 500 volunteers who scout job and college scholarship opportunities, and who counsel and advise high school seniors both before and after graduation. Of the 2,000 June graduates reached by her program, 85 per cent have been placed, and more than 500 of them are in college.

"Is it I?"

If every American would take those words into his heart, the nation would be transformed. For they reach what government cannot: the qualities of heart, of caring, that are the difference between impersonal bureaucracy and personal concern. It's these qualities that make efforts like Mrs. Williams' succeed where government programs fail. It's these that bridge the human gulf, that touch the spirit, and spark that sense of personal worth so essential if the cycle of despair is to be broken.

One-to-One Relationship

Time and again, those who have run successful private anti-poverty programs make this point: that the key to success lies in the one-to-one relationship, in the person-to-person bond—in the knowledge that some one person cares enough to help. This, government cannot create; only a person can.

These voluntary efforts won't have the place they deserve until we have leaders in Washington who are genuinely committed to the voluntary way. Those who consider government programs the first resort will look down on voluntary efforts as a last resort. The result will be what we have today: lack of information, lack of co-ordination, active competition by government agencies for attention and for staff. The result will be a bureaucratic attitude that either ignores voluntary efforts or tries to subordinate them to Federal programs.

Simply by providing information, the government can give an enormous stimulus to volunteer activity.

For almost every community problem that exists in America, solutions have been found somewhere. Slums have been successfully rehabilitated, unemployables have been employed, cities and rural areas have been beautified, pollution has been curbed, student activism has been channeled into productive action.

But all too often, the only people who know about it are those who live where it's been done. People willing and eager to help don't know where to turn or what to do.

National Information Clearing-house

As one of the first tasks of the new Administration, therefore, I intend to set up a national clearing-house for information on voluntary activities—on what's been tried, what the difficulties have been and what the solutions are. By setting up a comprehensive, computerized data bank, the government can make it possible for groups or individuals anywhere in the country to discover at once what the experience of other communities has been, whom to contact for more information, where particular skills can be utilized and where needed skills are available.

But I intend to go beyond making information available. I will expect Federal departments concerned with social problems all to be actively dedicated to the stimulation of new voluntary efforts—and I will expect the Secretaries of those departments to make this a personal responsibility.

It's time for the Federal establishment to winnow out its own programs, and determine those for which primary reliance can be placed on voluntary efforts. Then it must encourage voluntary organizations to move in and take over.

But it should lead, not push; it should encourage, not coerce.

The whole strength of the voluntary sector lies in its voluntary nature. To trifle or tamper with this voluntary nature is to risk destroying it.

The usual task of government is to exercise authority: to tax, to regulate, to give orders or instructions. Yet these are things it cannot do where private initiatives are concerned.

Too often in the past, Federal assistance has led to Federal planning; the result has been to subordinate volunteer efforts to government efforts, and to erode initiative. We cannot afford to let volunteers become mere foot-soldiers in a battle directed from Washington.

As the nation's first citizen, the President should be the chief patron of citizen efforts.

Marshalling Moral Authority

I intend to marshal the moral authority of that office to the fullest, to set priorities, to point out where the needs are, to encourage and reward citizens efforts to meet those needs.

The President has immense power to confer recognition on a worthy cause. For example, Franklin Roosevelt did so for the March of Dimes; the next President can do so for those activities designed to help the disadvantaged, to make our cities livable and to bring the light of hope to those who have no hope.

In a Nixon Administration, there will be a new measure of reliance on voluntary efforts, and a new level of official public recognition of their immense contribution to the betterment of life in America.

There will be new awards for public service, and a new place for the leaders of voluntary activity in the councils of government. It's time Washington listened more to those who have been on the firing-line in the battle for better communities. It's time they told Washington their needs, and Washington adjusted its policies to fit those needs, rather than the other way around.

For this is the American way.

Leadership That Believes In People

To accomplish this, we need leadership that believes in people; leadership that will concentrate government efforts on what *it* can do best, and that will summon the people to do what *they* can do best. In asking the people to lend their hands and give of their hearts, the next President will be asking America to be itself again.

This is one of the great questions the election of 1968 is about: whether we continue to rely more on government and less on people, or whether we turn our ingenuity toward finding new ways to enlist the people in shaping a future that is genuinely their own.

The present Administration has been so transfixed by Federal power that it has ignored the power of people.

The next President must move consciously and deliberately to inspire those voluntary efforts that bring freedom alive. Only if we restore the spirit of voluntarism to its historic place can we heal the deeper troubles we suffer from. In people helping people, we can find the spiritual cement to put our country together again, and to make our nation whole by making its people one.

ABC Radio Network
Sunday, October 6, 1968

A BETTER DAY FOR THE AMERICAN INDIAN

The sad plight of the American Indian is a stain on the honor of the American people.

Historically, these native Americans who shared the first Thanksgiving and guided restless explorers across the American continent have been deprived of their ancestral lands and reduced by unfair Federal policies and demeaning paternalism to the status of powerless wards of a confused Great White Father.

Today, many of the 600,000 American Indians living on reservations suffer limitations, disabilities, and indignities that few disadvantaged groups in America suffer in equal measure.

Their infant mortality rate vastly exceeds the average for the nation as a whole.

Their education level is inexcusably low in spite of increased Federal spending on Indian education, and their motivation is sapped by an educational structure which forces them to reject their own culture as the price of educational advancement.

Their unemployment rate is 10 times the national average.

Their average family income is far below the national average and, in some areas, below $500 per year.

Ninety-five per cent of their housing is totally inadequate and improvements are stymied by bureaucratic restrictions on efficient production.

Off the reservations, many Indians, some of them unwisely relocated by the Federal government, have not been successfully assimilated and find themselves confined to hopeless city reservations of despair because of lack of education and skills.

The causes of these tragic problems cannot be confined to the 19th century era of expansion or excused as the growing pains of the nation.

The Indian people have been continuous victims of unwise and vacillating Federal policies and serious, if unintentional, mistakes. Their plight is a bitter example of what's wrong with the bankrupt old approach to the problems of minorities. They have been treated as a colony within a nation—to be taken care of. They should—and they must—be made part of the mainstream of American life.

To their great credit, the Indian people are not occupying themselves with the errors of the past. Many of them—seizing thin threads of opportunity—have made great contributions to our society. Now they are striving for a brighter future.

To help them reach the goals that they themselves have set and will set, my Administration will be pledged to the following policies:

The special relationship between the Federal government and the Indian people and the special responsibilities of the Federal government to the Indian people will be acknowledged.

Termination of tribal recognition will not be a policy objective, and in no case will it be imposed without Indian consent.

We must recognize that American society can allow many different cultures to flourish in harmony, and we must provide an opportunity for those Indians wishing to do so to lead a useful and prosperous life in an Indian environment.

The right of self-determination of the Indian people will be respected, and their participation in planning their own destiny will be encouraged.

I will oppose any effort to transfer jurisdiction over Indian Reservations without Indian consent, will fully support the National Council on Indian Opportunity and ensure that the Indian people are fully consulted before programs under which they must live are planned.

I will appoint a qualified Indian member to the Indian Claims Commission, will see to it that local programs and Federal budgets are operated with minimum bureaucratic restraint and in full consultation with the Indian people who should achieve increasing authority and responsibility over programs affecting them.

Independent school boards, funded at government expense, must be urged for each government-run school. Tribes should be urged to take over reservation law and other programs. Road construction and repair activities should be under Indian management. School service contracts for running school busses or for operating a school lunch program, should be funded as they are now but should be an activity of the Indian people themselves rather than of the Federal government.

The economic development of Indian reservations will be encouraged and the training of the Indian people for meaningful employment on and off the reservation will have high priority.

To date, the basic error of attempting to train the Indian work force only for off-reservation jobs has been the major cause of the lack of normal progress on the reservation.

My Administration will promote the economic development of the reservation by offering economic incentives to private industry to locate there and provide opportunities for Indian employment and training.

Large companies which have already located on reservations have been highly impressed with the reliability and productivity of Indian workers. Such companies can provide a stable economic base for a reservation and can and should be encouraged to permit the Indian people to share in the fruits of their enterprise.

The special development problems of smaller reservations will also be recognized, and the administrators of government loan programs will be encouraged to take businessmen's risks in sponsoring Indian enterprises.

Moreover, the recreation and tourist potential of Indian reservations can be improved as a source of continuing independent income which would in turn fuel further Indian-sponsored development.

Job training for Indian people must be accelerated on and off the reservation. I have promised my full backing to the Vocational Education Act and will see to it that the Indian people enjoy the full benefits of its provisions.

The administration of Federal programs affecting Indians will be carefully studied to provide maximum efficiency consistent with program continuity.

A first priority of my Administration will be a thorough study of the executive branch by an independent commission patterned on the Hoover Commission. The coordination of the various programs affecting the Indian people will be an important matter on the agenda of that commission.

I will particularly direct that attention be given both to the ultimately desirable administration of Indian affairs and to methods by which a smooth transition from the existing structure can be effected. I will instruct the commission to eliminate needless bureaucratic levels which insulate decision-making from the Indian people.

Improvement of health services to the Indian people will be a high priority effort of my Administration.

The Eisenhower Administration revitalized health programs for the Indian people and sharply reduced the death rate from tuberculosis and the infant mortality rate. Now new progressive steps are direly necessary.

Looking to the future, my Administration will stress programs of preventive medicine, additional modernization of health facilities, and assure greater progress in the delivery of health services to the Indian people.

The Indian people have long responded to deprivation and hardship by seeking to utilize the processes of orderly change. Through their own ability and determination, not a few of them have achieved notable success. We must seek to demonstrate to them all that our society is responsive to their patient pleas and help them to live among us in prosperity, dignity, and honor.

Omaha, Nebraska
September 27, 1968

FOR A DYNAMIC ECONOMY

A NEW DIRECTION
FOR AMERICA'S ECONOMY

In this year of violence and turmoil, the capacity of the American people to govern themselves is being questioned as never before.

Terrible and tragic events have thrown a dark cloud of self-doubt across our society. At home and abroad, voices are heard castigating America as "sick." Many are ready—even eager—to write the epitaph of the world's oldest republic and to write off mankind's greatest experiment in democratic self-government.

I reject the false argument that all Americans are somehow responsible for the evils that have befallen us and the grave dangers we face. We are a nation made up, not of a faceless mass, but of 200 million individuals. In recent months, in a thousand different conversations, people across the country have opened their hearts and minds to me. These Americans have not given up on themselves. These Americans are vital, hopeful, and idealistic—they still dare to believe in the triumph of dreams in a time of nightmares.

If there is a single quality that sets Americans apart, I believe it is their openness to change. They do not merely cope with change; they embrace it. They are committed to it. They gladly accept the wrenching pain of change in order to seize its exciting promise. Our republic has survived, our great experiment has flourished, because Americans have always regarded their revolution on behalf of human freedom, dignity, and fulfillment as unfinished, perpetually in the process of *becoming*.

Politics of Responsibility

I shall not attempt to minimize the impact of the profound shocks we have experienced in this fateful year. Nor do I believe that we should surrender ourselves to what Vice President Humphrey has called his "politics of joy." This is no time for taking refuge in comforting self-delusions. America is in more trouble, in more places, than ever before in its history.

Now is the time, I firmly believe, for facing the truth, for seeing it clearly, and for speaking it plainly. Now is the time for the kind of democratic self-government too long neglected. Now is the time for the politics of maturity and responsibility.

Under our system, the people do not await commands from on high. As free men, they know where they want to go and what they hope to achieve. They look to the leaders they elect for guidance, for purposeful direction of the nation's vast energies and immense resources. In the role of manager of the nation's economy, any Administration affects the American people intimately for good or ill. As trustee of the economy and guardian of the dollar, the Johnson-Humphrey Administration, in my judgment, has failed the people abysmally.

Climate of Uncertainty

This role is much broader than the formulation of sound economic policies. We look to our government, first of all, for the creation of a climate in which our common ideals and objectives are secure, so that each of us can be free to pursue his individual goals. Such a climate does not exist in America today. The Johnson-Humphrey Administration has failed in its first and most basic reponsibility—the preservation of order in the society. When Americans look toward tomorrow apprehensively, uncertain of what it may bring, they have not lost confidence in themselves. They have lost confidence in those to whom the safekeeping of the future was given.

The rise of a climate of fear and uncertainty, of crime and anarchy, can be traced partly to the emergence of a vacuum of leadership at the center of our federal government. Under our system, there must be a continual dialogue between the people and their leaders, a healthy exchange which insures government truly representative of the popular will. Today, there is no such dialogue. Today, there is a sad estrangement between the people and their government. Where there should be purposeful men listening and leading, guiding the forces of change, there are only weary and confused men, grasping for expedients, talking to themselves, and appointing commissions to study problems for which the supposed leaders have no solution and no plan of action.

The American people are not sick—they are massively frustrated. They speak and no one heeds them. The leaders speak and no one takes their words at face value. What appears to some to be a collapse of the system is in fact a breakdown of the democratic dialogue, a mutual withdrawal of trust between the people and their leaders who have failed them.

In its mismanagement of the economy, we see a particularly revealing failure of the Johnson-Humphrey Administration. It illustrates the erosion of trust, the retreat from responsibility, the growth of a paralysis at the top of the government.

False Prosperity

It may appear that talk of idealism and dreams is unrelated to the cold realities of economics. Quite to the contrary, America's economy is the means by which dreams, individual and national, are realized. The dollar in our pocket is the token of our labor and our aspirations. If its value is protected, the rewards of our labor are secure. If the dollar loses its value, to that extent we labor in vain, and if an uncontrolled loss of value occurs, we are denied the means to achieve the dreams we have deferred until tomorrow.

Until fairly recently, the Johnson-Humphrey Administration could hardly find superlatives glowing enough to praise its management of the economy. Month by month, we were told of the longest economic expansion in the nation's history. Then suddenly, these torrents of self-praise were turned off and the flood-gates of gloomy warnings were opened wide. We have been told, by President Johnson himself, that the nation faces "the worst financial crisis of the post-war era."

What kind of prosperity is it, Americans must ask, which suddenly carries us to the brink of disaster?

It is a false prosperity, founded on a timeless device of deception—inflation.

Runaway Inflation

In the last five years, the Johnson-Humphrey Administration has undone the work of the previous decade. Since the last Presidential election, the general price level—that is, the price level of our total output of goods and services—has risen over 10 percent.

Not only has the price level been rising, the rise has also been accelerating. Inflation occurred at the rate of just under 2 percent in 1964; at more than 2 percent the following year; at more than 3 percent the next year. Last year, the rate was 3.5 percent. So far this year, the rate is above 4 percent. Next year, if the most stringent measures are not taken, the rate of inflation could climb above 5 percent.

What does this mean in practical terms?

It means almost everything costs more—the food we eat, the clothes we wear, the apartments and homes we live in. It means that the cost of services, especially hospital and medical services, are skyrocketing. At every turn in our daily lives, we encounter the hidden tax of inflation, requiring that we pay more for the same or for less. Even the price of bread is up a cent—and in some supermarkets, the "pound" loaf now weighs only 15 ounces.

Inflation means that those who have put money aside in the bank, and who believe they are earning interest at the rate of 4 percent, are in fact earning nothing. Inflation has robbed them of the reward of their thrift and sacrifice.

In terms of dollars, Americans are earning more than they ever did. In terms of what those dollars will actually buy, many Americans are worse off than they were two or three years ago. When higher social security and income taxes are deducted, when the invisible tax of inflation is deducted, the average weekly pay-check of the non-farm worker is actually less than it was in 1965—and he is steadily losing ground.

The "Money Illusion"

American breadwinners and their wives realize that they are victims of the "money illusion." Those workers who can bargain for higher wages are trying hard to keep ahead of the wage-price spiral. Collective bargaining in 1964 brought wage settlements averaging 3.2 percent; the following year, 3.8 percent; the next year, 4.8 percent. Last year, new wage contracts jumped

5.7 percent. This year, the increase is above 6 percent. But unchecked price inflation all but destroys these seeming wage gains. Each rise in wages now brings a rise in prices. We are caught up in a deadly cycle of futility.

In the beginning of a period of inflation, only its temporary good effects are seen in rising wages and employment. But as the artificial stimulant wears off, as the dosage is increased and increased again, the good effects disappear and the bad effects—the lasting and deeply harmful effects —come into view.

We no longer hear about the Johnson-Humphrey Administration's War on Poverty. But on the neglected front of inflation, the government has inadvertently blocked the advance of the poor—just one of many unforeseen but tragic side-effects of irresponsible fiscal policies.

To those who have little or no bargaining power, to those who are trying to live on fixed incomes, steadily worsening inflation means steady reduction in an already low standard of living. The poor—whose plight evokes such sympathy in Washington—are made even poorer.

The Balance of Promises

Fiscal irresponsibility also produces unforeseen but seriously harmful consequences overseas. Certainly, it was not the intention of the Johnson-Humphrey Administration to weaken American prestige and influence abroad. Certainly it was not the Administration's intention to diminish America's credibility when its policies in Vietnam were under worldwide attack. America, as the leader of free nations whose allegiance cannot be coerced, can keep its allies only by keeping its word. But the Administration's word has been undermined by its deeds—and even more, by what it has left undone.

In recent years, Americans have become familiar with a complicated and seemingly remote problem—the balance of payments crisis. We can understand it better if we think of it as simply a balance of *promises* crisis. America, as the financial bulwark of the free world, promised foreign nations holding dollars that those dollars were as good as gold. Year in and year out, however, more dollars poured out from these shores than our overseas trade and investments could earn. And year in and year out, the Administration promised an early end to this deficit.

Last spring, the confidence of foreigners collapsed and the slow retreat from the dollar became a panic-stricken, headlong flight. For a few days in March, Americans traveling abroad suffered an unexpected and unthinkable humiliation when hotels and merchants refused their dollars and traveler's checks. How could anyone doubt the mighty dollar! But skeptical foreigners did, and so did their governments. Our reserves of gold, which had been trickling away, suddenly gushed out. These reserves now stand at the lowest point since the Great Depression, a sadly revealing measure of the decline of American prestige.

By a combination of expedients and renewed promises of swift reform, the decline of the dollar has been temporarily slowed. But the Administration has bought only time; it has not regained the confidence its policies forfeited. Only a truly convincing shift to new policies of prudence and restraint can accomplish this all-important objective.

This brings me to the central question concerning the threat of inflation. Can the Administration which created the peril be relied upon to meet it squarely? I believe the answer is no.

The Economics of Popularity

The Johnson-Humphrey Administration, since it admitted the danger, has tried to blame everyone and everything but itself. There is no mystery about what causes inflation. It springs from the desire of politicians to bestow upon the people more favors than the people are prepared immediately to pay for. In every year since 1961, the federal government has spent more money than it has taken in. Through the end of the current fiscal year, which has just begun, these cumulative deficits will total a staggering nearly $70 billion.

When federal expenditures are enormously more than federal revenues, the politicians pursuing popularity through inflation turn to the Federal Reserve system and create money literally out of thin air. To finance the Treasury, the Federal Reserve system has expanded the money supply at

94

a breathtaking rate. During 1967, the money supply grew at 7 percent, the fastest rate of growth in the entire period since World War II.

Stop-as-you-go

William McChesney Martin, chairman of the Federal Reserve Board, is a dedicated public servant who has occupied his position longer than any other man. He sincerely believes in the prudent management of America's finances. But he has been left holding the bag. The Johnson-Humphrey Administration, by refusing to put the nation's fiscal affairs in order, forced Chairman Martin to assume, with the limited powers available to him, the whole responsibility for curbing inflation. The result has been a stop-and-go policy of monetary restraint and ease, in which every attempt to slow down the expansion of the money supply has been defeated by the urgent necessity to finance the Treasury's huge deficits.

In the summer of 1966, the Federal Reserve's efforts to tighten up caused near-panic in the markets and resulted in a brutal credit squeeze. The housing industry was thrown into a recession from which it has not yet fully recovered. As money was alternately tightened and eased, and as federal deficit spending continued, the expectation of further inflation became fixed in the minds of lenders. Interest rates have now soared to their highest levels since the Civil War. Prospective homebuyers face mortgage rates of more than 7 percent. Interest rates are likely to remain high for some time to come, with all the bad effects for the economy that this implies.

Vietnam Alibi

The Johnson-Humphrey Administration left Chairman Martin to battle inflation alone as long as it could. When it could no longer ignore the plain consequences of its own policies, the Administration found a convenient excuse for inflation—the Vietnam War. It claimed that all the trouble began in mid-1965 when the American commitment to the war was greatly expanded.

This is simply not true. Inflation was evident in the rising prices of raw materials as early as the fall of 1963. By the summer of 1964, the average level of all wholesale prices was climbing fast. Clearly, inflation had taken hold and become widespread many months before Vietnam began having significant financial or economic consequences.

Between mid-1965 and mid-1968, federal expenditures grew by $60 billion. Less than half of this increase, some $25 billion, could be attributed to the war. The rest was in civilian programs.

When President Johnson faced the moment of truth on the battlefield in Vietnam, he committed the troops and resources necessary to stave off imminent defeat. However, he flinched on the home front. There was no moment of truth in America because the President did not take the people into his confidence. He escalated the war by stealth; he encouraged the belief that Americans could go on enjoying guns-and-butter and the deficit-financed favors of the Great Society without giving the war in Southeast Asia a second thought.

Self-deception

By deceiving himself, the President deceived the American people. By failing to mobilize the American economy for war, he guaranteed serious economic disorder. History may record that the President's refusal to establish clear priorities was the pivotal error of his Administration, a decision *not* to choose that forced all subsequent choices to be bad ones as events slipped out of control.

As the war expanded, the Administration's deception of itself and the American people grew. Early in 1966, as the Administration prepared its budget for fiscal 1967, the defense portion was based on the assumption that the war in Vietnam would end by the middle of the summer of 1967. It was further assumed that the 185,000 American troops in Vietnam would rise to only 250,000. At the same time, however, General Westmoreland was asking for a force of 400,000 troops. And it was evident even to outsiders, that the strategy approved by the Pentagon and being pursued on the battlefield would require at least that many troops.

General Westmoreland eventually was given the troops he requested, and the cost of fighting the war, which the Administration had set at $10 billion, soared to $20 billion in fiscal 1967. (It has since risen to nearly

96

$30 billion). Throughout 1966, information on the actual costs of the war—as opposed to the unreal costs set forth in the budget—was held very closely in the Pentagon and the White House. Not only Congress, but even the Treasury, was kept in the dark. If the true costs had been made known, of course, the President might very well have been forced to seek a tax increase or to accept reduced spending on his Great Society programs. The President gambled on an early end to the war—and the entire country paid for that foolish wager and will still be paying for it long after Lyndon Johnson leaves the White House.

The Political Budget

The crucial defense budget for the fiscal year 1967 was inspired, not by economic realities, but by political motives. When the President at last asked for higher taxes, in January, 1967, that request—made belatedly and without any great show of urgency—bore the unmistakable stamp of political motivation. The President then asked for a tax increase of only 6 percent, to be effective at mid-year. But he did not couple this request with a promise of reduced federal expenditures. On the contrary, deficit spending would continue as usual.

What's more, within a few weeks of making the tax request, which would have the effect of restraining the economy, the Administration actually stepped up its efforts to stimulate demand. Funds for housing and highways, which had only recently been frozen, were released. The President requested that Congress reinstate the investment tax credit for machinery and equipment—thus asking for a substantial tax cut for business firms only a few weeks after asking for a tax increase. Instead of facing up to the threat of inflation, the Administration behaved as though the economy were headed into a recession.

Such obvious contradiction and political calculation cost the Administration the trust of members of the Congress and the informed public. When, in August, 1967, the President warned of the onset of ruinous inflation and urgently requested, not a 6 percent tax increase, but a 10 percent increase, he was simply not believed. And he widened the already yawning "credibility gap" by refusing to cut back on federal spending.

Trend Still Inflationary

I have traced this dreary record at length and in some detail because it helps to explain an unparalleled situation. For more than a year and a half, in the face of overwhelming evidence of its necessity, it was impossible for the President and the Congress to agree on a policy of fiscal restraint. The American people were willing to tax themselves to pay for the war in Vietnam, and to forego civilian programs that are not essential. The Congress was willing to act responsibly. But the President had to be virtually dragged to the performance of his duty—namely, to cut the deficit spending which is the cause of our present inflation.

Now the 10 percent surcharge on personal and business incomes has finally been enacted into law. As the price of the tax bill's passage in Congress, the President has reluctantly agreed to cut $6 billion from this year's $186 billion budget.

Let us consider the practical effects of this program. Individuals and businesses will pay higher taxes—that much is certain.

The expenditures of the federal government, however, will *not* be reduced next year; they will increase. All the President has promised is to reduce the *rate* of increase in federal spending and thereby reduce the federal deficit. Assuming these promises are fulfilled, there will still be a substantial budget deficit this fiscal year—perhaps as much as $10 billion.

The chief *intended* effect of the tax increase and spending slowdown is to reassure concerned observers at home and overseas that the Administration at last means to halt inflation. Here, the Administration is saying, is tangible evidence of our resolve to reform.

Will it be persuasive? I seriously doubt it. The long record of irresponsibility has encouraged deep skepticism. What is most worrisome is *not* a particular year's deficit but the persistent *trend* of inflationary policies in Washington. A one-shot exercise in restraint may be regarded as merely a pause in a trend which has yet to be reversed.

The Spending Momentum

Beyond the very sizable federal budget deficit next year lies uncertainty. Programs launched during the heady days of the Great Society at a fraction of their eventual cost are expanding rapidly. The costs of the war are un-clear. In no sense has the expansion of federal spending been brought under effective control. No one can say with confidence that the budget deficits which lie at the heart of our troubles will not stretch on indefinitely.

Not long ago, Chairman Martin declared: "I happen to believe that the dollar is stronger than gold. I happen to believe it rests on the resources and productivity of the United States. It's government that you have to rely on. Basically, you can't rely on a metal for solvency. Whether we like it or not—there are people in the world who doubt we have the capacity to handle our problems."

These doubts will not be dispelled by a one-shot show of responsibility. Confidence abroad will be restored when the American people bestow *their* confidence on a new Administration, free of the necessity of justifying the past and unburdened by promises that have not been kept.

The American economic system has enormous latent strength and re-siliency. But I do not believe it can survive four more years of abuse by irresponsible federal managers without suffering grave and permanent damage.

Balancing the Economy

There are times when the Federal Government can and should use credit wisely to invest in the future. What we need is not a mechanically balanced budget, but an intelligently balanced economy. We have not yet taken the first step toward such balance—toward regaining control over federal deficit spending and the ever-increasing federal debt. The debt is still expanding and still spreading distortions throughout the economy.

Never in the history of the world has a nation been so abundantly blessed with the economic means to achieve its goals—provided these are clearly defined and skillfully pursued.

The first task is to halt the inflationary trend in our fiscal and monetary policies, to check the drift that defeats our purposes and steadily narrows our range of choices.

If this is done, the dollar will swiftly recover much of its strength, and the essential work of modernizing the world monetary system can go forward on the basis of long-term confidence and not short-term expediency.

Re-directing Foreign Economic Policy

I believe we must re-examine the whole sweep of America's foreign economic policies. We should not try to shore up the past; we should build for the future. All too often, the Johnson-Humphrey Administration has taken its vision of the future from the rear-view mirror. It has tried to preserve existing arrangements and relationships simply because they do exist and without asking whether they fit dramatically changing realities. Ironically, the early postward goal of creating a true international economic community has receded as a result of these policies, and we are in danger of slipping backward into narrowly nationalistic rivalry and competition. An Administration dedicated to the old politics of irresponsibility, of promise-and-spend regardless of the consequences, has hastened the crisis of the international economic order which grew out of the Second World War.

Our allies and trading partners no longer need our protection as much as they need our example. The guiding principle of America's foreign economic policies should be the expansion of the community of free and mutually responsible nations. Instead of limiting the movement of capital and goods, as the present Administration has, a fresh and practical commitment should be made to openness, to the lowering of all barriers—political, economic, and ideological. To the extent that weakness forces our withdrawal from such a commitment, we lose precious influence over the flow of events and the shape of the future international environment.

Economic Order in the Cities

If Americans have recently become less outward-looking, it is largely because they have been forced to turn inward and face the upheaval centered in our riot-torn cities. America does not lack the resources to deal effectively with the urban crisis. However, the Johnson-Humphrey Administration's mismanagement of the economy has greatly reduced the nation's freedom in the face of this challenge.

100

The need for modernization of urban America—of the nation that seven out of ten Americans now inhabit—is desperately urgent. Too many of our cities are failing—in physical, economic, and above all, *human* terms. Too much of the wealth created in our failing cities is pumped out of them and into the remote bureaucracies of Washington. The fraction that does return comes in the form of rigid programs which do not meet the real needs of the cities. For example, federal funds are available on a lavish scale to build often disruptive urban highways, but not to improve languishing mass transit or decaying housing or deteriorating social services.

The cities are reduced to the status of paupers by obsolete institutional arrangements. The cities do not need larger federal handouts; they need a larger and more equitable share of the wealth they produce. But before new economic resources are committed to the cities, they must receive an infusion of the nation's best intellectual resources, drawn not only from the government and the academic community, but also from the relatively untapped business and financial community. In the last century, men of action built the cities. In the next stage of America's urban growth, men of thought and action must use new ideas to rebuild the cities.

The old politics of irresponsibility and the old economics of promise-and-spend have denied America much of its flexibility in dealing with onrushing change. We can and must break out of the economic straitjacket fashioned by the present Administration. We can and must regain the freedom that comes from sound and sustainable economic growth. Under intelligent management, the economy can grow in a way which makes possible not only tax cuts but also non-inflationary expansion of federal spending out of our increasing national wealth.

The Trillion-dollar GNP

If our economy enjoys sound expansion, I can foresee a gross national product of a trillion dollars by 1972—and I mean a trillion dollars of stable purchasing power. In the same period, I can foresee 82 million civilian jobs—6 million more jobs in the term of the next President—for the American people, whose wages and well-being would increase in real and not illusory terms.

101

I believe the American people are more than willing to live, not on inflated promises, but on the real wealth they produce.

I believe they are far more mature than their distrustful present leaders assume.

I believe a tide of discontent is running deep and strong within the people, a powerful current which will sweep away falsehood and duplicity, and carry our country again to the firm and high ground of principle.

When America was young, hard work and sacrifice were the only way the people knew to put their dreams and ideals into practice. Now that America is mature, at once seasoned and beset, there is still only one way—the way of responsibility.

New York, New York
July 6, 1968

THE THREAT TO THE AMERICAN ECONOMY

Only a hundred days remain before the American people pass the judgment of this generation on the Johnson years. Based on this Administration's role as guardian of the American dollar and trustee of the American economy, that verdict will be guilty of inexcusable neglect.

During the Eisenhower Administration, the United States achieved several economic milestones. Wartime inflation was brought to an end. A stable wage-price relationship was established. A solid foundation was laid on which future prosperity could be built. Yet, in less than 5 years, the Johnson Administration has squandered the inheritance of a decade's solvency.

In 1964 prices for food and clothing and medicine and housing were already moving up at a rate of just under 2 percent. Today, they are rising at more than 4 percent, the most severe inflation since the Truman Administration.

In 1964 America was enjoying a period of relative labor peace. Today, the number of man hours lost annually through strikes has doubled and continues to rise.

In 1964, the Presidential wage guideposts stood at 3.2 percent nationally. In 1968 those wage guideposts have been breached, abandoned and forgotten. Any worker settling for a "Presidential" pay raise in 1968 would be settling for a cut in purchasing power.

In 1964, mortgage interest rates stood at 5.8 percent. By 1966 they had risen to 6.3 percent, setting off a depression in the housing industry. Today, they are over 7 percent, the highest since the Administration of Ulysses S. Grant.

In 1964 American gold reserves amounted to nearly $15 billion. In the last four years, foreign countries have removed $5 billion from America's gold reserves. These reserves have fallen to the lowest level since the Depression.

Why are prices rising faster than they have in a generation? Why is the American dollar viewed with greater suspicion in the central banks of Europe than it has been for a century? Why is the American taxpayer groaning under the heaviest tax burden in history? Why has the purchasing

103

power of the American worker not risen a dime in two years? The answer is one and the same—because for 5 years this Administration has refused to keep federal spending within federal means.

We need more economy in government and less government in the economy.

The total deficit run up in the budgets of the Johnson years will amount to more than $55 billion. This massive deficit has wracked and dislocated the economy; this massive deficit has plunged the free world monetary system into a profound crisis of credibility.

The war in Vietnam is not so much the cause of our economic problems as it is the ready excuse of the Administration. Much less than half the massive new outlays in federal funds in the past 5 years are traceable to the war in Asia. A government that had guided the economy with the prudence and restraint dictated by the expanding war in Asia could have foreseen and avoided every major pitfall in the last 5 years.

The economy cannot afford 4 more years of abuse from irresponsible Federal managers without suffering grave and perhaps permanent damage. The damage done thus far can and must be repaired by a new administration committed to the economics of responsibility. There is nothing the matter with the engine of free enterprise that cannot be corrected by placing a prudent and sober engineer at the throttle.

Needed in Washington today is new leadership with both an understanding of modern economic conditions and an appreciation of traditional economic principles. The new Administration will recognize that deliberate inflation is deliberate injustice—a form of government aggression against the thrifty, the retired and the poor.

In the last five years the Administration has caused the erosion of more than 10 percent of the value of every dollar Americans earn and save. By encouraging this inflation, this Administration has broken faith with our friends abroad and our own people at home. It has stood silently by while they were robbed of 10 percent of their savings and income—and it has profited politically from their losses.

We need a government in Washington that will recognize that economics is more than a question of politics; it is also a question of justice. We need a government that does not weigh a 4 percent increase in the price level in terms of whether it wins or loses friends or votes—but in terms of whether it is right or wrong.

The rising winds of inflation pose no grave threat to the economic bastions of big business and industry and organized labor. But those winds do imperil the economic security and future of those individuals who can find no shelter from the storm in the safe harbors of the real estate market or the stock exchange.

The old politics of spend-and-elect have not only worked an injustice on the American people; they have denied Americans much of its flexibility in dealing with onrushing change. We can and must break out of the vicious circle fashioned by the present Administration. We can and must regain the freedom that comes from sound economic growth sustained by the dynamism of free enterprise.

If our economy enjoys sound expansion I can foresee a gross national product of a trillion dollars by 1972—and I mean a trillion dollars of stable purchasing power. In the same period I can foresee more than 82 million civilian jobs—more than 6 million new jobs in the term of the next President —for the American people, whose wages and well-being would increase in real and not illusory terms.

I believe the American people are more than willing to live, not on inflated promises, but on the real wealth they produce. I believe they are far more mature than their distrustful present leaders assume. I believe a tide of discontent is running deep and strong within the people, a powerful current which will sweep away falsehood and duplicity, and carry our country again to the firm and high ground of principle.

When America was young, hard work and sacrifices were the only way the people knew to put their dreams and ideals into practice. Now that America is mature, at once seasoned and beset, there is still only one way— the way of responsibility.

Submitted to Republican National Convention
Committee on Resolutions
July 31, 1968

TO MAKE A DOLLAR WORTH A DOLLAR

Our country today is a nation of wealth, of power, and of paradox. We find our people affluent and afflicted—free and yet frustrated. Government is larger and more powerful than ever—and less effective. The people are more affluent than ever—and seem less fulfilled. We daily exceed the wildest dreams of our ancestors in productivity, wealth, and power. Yet we feel an undermining current of despair—as if the dreams were better than their achievement, or as if in the course of fulfilling our material dreams, we failed the American dream.

There is a lack that makes our leaders seem victims rather than masters of change. In an effort to increase our power over events, we have replaced our ancestral faith in free men and individual initiative with a new faith in government. But we have discovered an extraordinary paradox of bureaucracy: it renders powerless not only its subjects, but also its leaders. Thus, in making government bigger we find we are making both its master and beneficiaries smaller. In enlarging Washington we diminish America.

I believe that the frustration in the land is related to the over-centralization.

Tonight I want to discuss a major cause both of centralization and of frustration in the Great Society, namely, inflation of the currency and the cost of living. John Maynard Keynes once quoted Lenin as saying, "The best way to destroy the capitalist system is to debauch the currency." Keynes explained that:

> "By a continuing process of inflation, government can confiscate, secretly and unobserved, an important part of the wealth of their citizens . . ."

This is the danger we will face if current policies are pursued much longer. The continuing process of dollar debauchery is today robbing our citizens of their wealth and aggrandizing the power of Washington.

Inflation penalizes thrift and encourages speculation. Because it is a national and pervasive force—dramatically affecting individuals but beyond their power to influence—inflation is a source of frustration for all who lack great economic power.

106

What is inflation? Technically, it is an excess of money over goods in the economy. As a result the value of money goes down, your dollar buys less. In fact today the dollar has 17 cents less buying power than it had at the end of the Eisenhower Administration. Over the last three years alone inflation has totalled more than ten percent and in recent months has been proceeding at an annual pace of almost six percent.

The frustration caused by inflation is obvious. Any worker whose income is increasing annually by less than six percent finds his paycheck actually buys less each year. Because of rising taxes, in fact, he must average well over six percent in raises to improve his position. Since the average wage increase is now little more than six percent throughout the economy, the average American is losing money.

A great many Americans, however, are not "average". Depending on relatively low or fixed incomes, they find their situation has been getting worse. The chief impact of inflation falls on those with the least power to get more money. Inflation insidiously robs the old of their pensions, the small businessman of his savings, the laborer of his wages. Retirement funds saved 25 years ago are now worth only half as much in terms of buying power; the working man earns *less* today in real purchasing power than he did about three years ago. Inflation has, in fact, more than nullified any benefits of the celebrated Great Society programs.

It is not only the impoverished who are victimized. Inflation also hits with special force other key groups in the society: the farmer and the urban wage earner and homeowner.

Since farm marketing receipts have shown almost no improvement in recent years while farm costs soar, farmers find themselves in an ever tightening bind. The farmer has to buy his equipment on the inflated retail market but the prices of his goods in many cases have been going down. This pinch has helped to drive almost 5 million people off the farms since 1960.

With a great many of the people on the farms going to the cities, it is not encouraging that city dwellers suffer an equally frustrating and in some ways even more demoralizing predicament. People go to the cities largely to take advantage of economic and cultural opportunities there. Yet they find their higher wages eaten away by higher living costs. They invest their savings in a new home, and find it subjected to steadily increasing property taxes while its value is jeopardized by the general deterioration of the urban environment. Crime and delinquency, pollution and congestion, all converge on urban dwellers while their Federal taxes go up to pay for welfare and other programs that in some cases make the problems worse. They find their city repeatedly paralyzed by strikes among workers attempting to escape the blight of inflation and rising taxes. In the cities as on the farms it is a palsied prosperity that the present administration has produced.

The foreign impact of the Administration's inflation is no less severe. It has reduced our export growth by pricing American goods out of international markets. It has made foreign goods more competitive here, thus bringing a major surge of imports. The result has been a dramatic decline in the U.S. trade surplus and a chronic deficit in our balance of payments.

This decline in the U.S. trade and financial position has prompted foreigners to accumulate large dollar reserves, but doubting the stability of our currency, they have been turning dollars in for gold in ever increasing amounts. To stop the flow we were forced to stop freely selling our gold. Today our gold reserves are lower than at any time since the depression. Last year the U.S. had to turn to the International Monetary Fund for help in shoring up the dollar.

This crisis is not simply an American embarrassment, though it certainly *was* embarrassing for the Americans in Europe that day last March when European bankers would not accept dollars in exchange for local currency. The crisis of confidence in the dollar—which is in fact a crisis of confidence in our willingness to stop inflation—represents a dire threat to the world economic system and to our most important foreign policy goals. The dollar is more than the currency of American economic strength. It is also a fundamental medium of exchange for the entire free world. Continued erosion of faith in the dollar could destroy the expansion of world trade that has spurred the marvelous growth of the world's free economies.

The threat is clear. At the moment of our highest prosperity we also face the gravest dangers. If we continue on our present course, we could possibly cause a world economic depression.

Vietnam, of course, is part of the problem; our military frustrations in Asia agonize and perplex the entire society and strain the economy. But we should remember that inflation was accelerating in 1964 long before the massive expansion of our combat effort. The war is not an excuse for fiscal irresponsibility.

Another contributor to the frustration felt by many citizens is simply progress. Some modern technology requires institutions so large that little room seems left for the individual. But this problem is a mandate for a new commitment to humane technology; it is no excuse for despair. The major problem is the tendency of those in the present Administration to promise far more than they can deliver through government or pay for through taxes. In recent years Americans have often believed the promises and exchanged their own wealth and freedom for bureaucratic solutions to their problems. But the problems have remained, and the Administration has demanded still more Federal money and power.

Rather than relinquish programs that it regards as crucial to political success, the Administration has responded to public tax resistance by financing new programs through budgetary deficits. In fact the U.S. has not had a balanced budget since the last full fiscal year of the Eisenhower Administration. The total deficit since then and through the current fiscal year will have reached nearly $70 billion.

This is the cause of inflation and a major cause of our current frustration. The greatest irony is that inflation hurts the very people—the poor and aged —whom Great Society programs are designed to help. In fact inflation has hurt the impoverished far more than the War on Poverty has helped them. Inflation is a major help to only one agency in the society: the Bureau of Internal Revenue. For by moving Americans into higher tax brackets without enlarging their real income, inflation raises the percent of income going to taxes without officially increasing tax rates. Moreover, the present Administration has raised the Federal government's share of the average worker's paycheck not only by the recent ten percent surcharge, but also by another estimated 11 percent through the hidden tax of inflation.

The question today is whether we can afford four more years of these policies. My opponent once labeled himself a big spender, and he has made it absolutely clear that if elected, he plans a massive stepup in Federal spending programs. But he has not told us how he will pay for them.

This is a prescription for further inflation. I believe it is also a prescription for economic disaster.

For at a certain point in the inflation game—however much my opponent may wish it were not so—the intentions of government must give way to the laws of economics. As sure as a binge leads to a hangover, an inflationary boom, if pursued too long, leads to a deflationary bust and massive unemployment. Unless current policies are changed as a matter of highest urgency, we are all in for a dreadful headache in 1970 and beyond.

The excessive inflation which impends if present policies continue would cause major economic distortions that could be redressed in only two ways, equally catastrophic. The psychedelic economics of the present Administration can lead to the police economics of wage and price controls, or to a major recession with widespread unemployment, as the economy's way to bring itself back into balance. My opponent already has indicated his probable choice: wage and price controls. On August 5th, Secretary of Labor Willard Wirtz said that time may be running out for private wage and price decision-making. Vice President Humphrey recently issued a task force report that unless voluntary restraint was exercised by labor and management "a statutory approach will become unavoidable."

In the international arena the present Administration has already displayed a propensity for controls. Rather than make a serious attempt to put our finances in order when the crisis developed in our balance of payments, the Administration attempted first to restrict travel abroad and then in fact imposed controls on U.S. overseas investment and bank lending. This isolationist approach will ultimately hurt the American economy and foreign policy by reducing international trade and economic growth in the free world.

It is quite clear that in order to avoid a recession of the economy, my opponent is quite prepared to have a recession of our liberty. It never seems to occur to him that it would be preferable to avoid this dilemma altogether through adoption of responsible fiscal policy. Let no one imagine that police economics merely contracts the freedom of a few corporations; in order to control wages and prices, it would be necessary to embark on a road from which it is very hard to escape without major damage to the freedom of all.

I do not believe the American people should be forced to choose between unemployment and un-American controls. There is a further choice: the American way of responsible fiscal policy that allows the American people to be both affluent and free.

If I am elected I pledge that I will adopt this approach redressing the present imbalances without increasing unemployment or controls.

This does not mean a mechanical balancing of the budget every year. It means the intelligent balancing of the economy over the business cycle. It absolutely prohibits the use of Washington's fiscal powers to increase the Administration's political control—and it absolutely prohibits the use of inflation as a deceitful way to raise taxes without facing the people. I pledge that a Nixon Administration will not ask you to exchange your liberties for a spurious currency of promises. I promise only freedom and opportunity for all.

Walt Whitman once called our history an open road. Everything seemed possible for America on the frontier. Now in a sense we have come to the end of the open road. And at the end of the open road we do not find the promised land, we find the Great Society, and its bureaucracies have become the great roadblock.

It is time now to reopen the American way—return to the open road, where free men master change rather than passively await it. It is time to renew our dedication to the fundamental principles of the American economic miracle. We must maintain policies of fiscal order and responsibility. Only then can we assure freedom and peace.

CBS Radio Network
Wednesday, October 23, 1968

MODERN AMERICAN AGRICULTURE:
AN OPPORTUNITY FOR SERVICE IN THE 1970'S

In the Congress and as a member of the Eisenhower Administration, I learned long ago of the immense importance of modern American agriculture to the health and strength of our country. Nowhere else in the world do so few farmers and ranchers produce so much, so efficiently, and so reasonably for so many.

In only the past 20 years applied technology has vastly increased production, and in the process American consumers have benefited tremendously. Last year they spent only 17.7 percent of their disposable income for the world's highest quality food—by far the lowest percentage paid anywhere in the world.

Our agriculture also means jobs and markets. Today three out of every ten jobs in our country are directly related to agriculture. Last year farmers spent nearly $35 billion on agricultural production and over $12 billion for the things . . . cars, food, clothing, appliances . . . that other Americans buy.

Moreover, the productivity and industry of our farmers and ranchers are major sources of local, state and federal revenues, and our exports of agricultural products are a vital component of our trade balance and balance of payments. Some 23 of every 100 harvested acres are now devoted to producing crops for overseas outlets. Our annual export acreage is equal to all the cropland of this great agricultural State of Iowa and the combined cropland of Nebraska, Kansas and North Dakota as well.

So the impact of agriculture in many areas is of great importance to our people—and yet, there is a widely held misconception of what farmers think and feel. Agriculturalists, of course they are—but they are first of all good, patriotic Americans, and we must never forget it.

Farmer discontent over the war, taxation, interest rates, and inflation—their alarm over civil disorders and crime—are as intense as the same concerns of citizens in other enterprises. It reflects on the good citizenship of America's people in agriculture to regard them as a group apart, concerned not about their nation but only their livelihood. The broad issues that today trouble all our people may well influence farmer judgments more this year than anything said or done about agriculture alone.

Plainly, however, our farmers and ranchers have been the stepchildren of the Great Society.

Their amazing productivity has been exploited to offset fiscal excesses in other areas and the farmer has been caught in a vicious economic squeeze.

During the past decade his taxes have gone up 78 percent, his labor costs 46 percent, his machinery costs 30 percent, his debt interest 59 percent. Everything he has to buy has gone up; everything he has to sell has gone down. The parity ratio has shriveled to a mere 74 percent—the lowest since the darkest days of the depression.

There is little to be served by reciting the whole Humphrey-Freeman catalogue of failure. A member of Secretary Freeman's own official family, so disillusioned that he resigned in protest, described the problem more persuasively than I could hope to do. Mr. Frank LeRoux of the U.S. Department of Agriculture's Foreign Agricultural Service from February 1961 to September 1966 said it in these words:

"This has been the worst 5 years for the American farmer of any administrative period, regardless of party in power, in modern American agricultural history. The lowest share of gross national product, lowest return on gross sales, lowest return on total capital investment, lowest return on capital investment per farm, lowest share of the consumer dollar, lowest share of the food dollar, lowest level of parity of income, lowest return for farmers versus government salaries, lowest return for farming versus all other major businesses, and the lowest performance on campaign promises."

That was 1961 through 1965. It's worse today!

Realized net farm income in 1967 dropped nearly $2 billion under the year before, and the latest estimates for 1968 indicate no substantial improvement.

As noted earlier, the farm parity ratio which measures farm costs against farm prices has dropped over six points in the past seven years and stands now at a dismal 74. It averaged 84.5 in the eight Eisenhower Republican years.

There has been a 31 percent increase in the cost of production, farm debt is up 90 percent, and 903,000 farms have disappeared from the countryside just since 1960.

Some ten instances of intentional depression of farm prices have been documented by the Republican Task Force on Agriculture in the House of Representatives, so I need not repeat them here. Suffice it to say that the present Administration's record is a sad and sorry one . . . and rural America knows it!

A salute to the great works of agriculture for America and rejection of the Humphrey-Freeman failures are not enough. America verges upon the decade of the 70's, and we must make this a period of unmatched progress for agriculture.

I propose that our nation commit itself to a national agricultural policy that will maintain an efficient, flourishing agricultural economy keyed to opportunity and abundance, with family farm enterprise as its cornerstone. As we develop this policy, I will base my decisions on these approaches:

First, there must be an honest and explicit recognition of the importance of a sound agriculture to our national well-being, together with an understanding, fair and reasonable approach to the many difficult problems of the farm community.

It is far more important than the details of individual programs for farmers to be certain of the basic honesty—the believability—of an Administration and of its real attitudes and posture toward the people and the economics of agriculture. With a leadership in Washington that is responsible and candid—a leadership eagerly responsive to the needs of rural people—the details of programs will fall into the right pattern. I promise an Administration sincerely interested in the farmer, not just in his vote.

Second, farmers are entitled to a commitment that their special problems will be treated quickly and sympathetically. This too I pledge.

To this end I intend to bring to bear the vast intellectual and practical competence of farmers, other rural people, farm organizations, the dedicated careerists in the U.S. Department of Agriculture, the agirculture extension leaders, and college research and technical people. And I also pledge there will always be an open door for agriculture at the White House.

Third, we must substitute good common sense for pretty partisanship in and with agriculture.

An attempt, for example, suddenly to revolutionize agriculture in pursuit of a new economic or political ideology would be calamitous. It is one thing to move with prudence and deliberation toward improved programs that will shore up the foundations of agriculture and assure its long-term vigor, strength, and prosperity. It is something else—in my view, irresponsible—to junk everything in an impatience to reach the millennium overnight. What I am saying is, we mean to improve, not destroy; we will not plow under farmers while trying to help them.

It is this approach that led me some weeks ago to favor temporary continuance of the 1965 Farm Act, which now awaits Congressional action. This law is a patchwork of older legislation and unsuitable for the long-term, but an adequate time is required for farmers to plan their crops and to let a new Administration carefully prepare improvements to take effect when the extended law expires.

Fourth, it is high time we had a Secretary of Agriculture who will spend his time not telling off the farmers of America, but instead will talk *for* them. I pledge an end to the disastrous on-the-job training at the top of the Department of Agriculture.

Instead of having a politico-lawyer Secretary of Agriculture, next January we will have a Secretary undeniably expert and practically experienced in agriculture—one, by the way, who will not politically manipulate and slip, slide, and duck, or will disparage and oppose what farmers need. Rather, he will forcefully and knowledgeably advocate the cause of agriculture in the highest councils of government, and in this he will have my support. He will not need to be pressed to solicit the views of rural people; he will be one who *wants* their views, who has the background to understand these views, and then will honestly reflect them in his dealings with the power centers of Washington.

Within this framework of honest recognition of the importance of agriculture, common sense in approaching its problems, qualified leadership of the Department of Agriculture and a ban on petty partisanship, let us proceed to specific policy directions that I believe will better prepare agriculture for service in the 70's.

These policy directions include:

- Dedicated efforts to improve market prices and strengthen our market economy so farmers and ranchers will be able to prosper in relation to the prices they must pay for other products—and let's have this flatly understood: 74 percent of parity is intolerable in my book; farmers are *entitled* to better, they want not merely to receive better but also an opportunity to *earn* better, and I pledge that in my Administration they will *have* better;

- Encouragement of farmers to improve their bargaining positions through their co-operatives;

- Responsible management of our nation's economic policies to brake inflation and ease interest rates;

- Increased emphasis on agricultural exports while reversing the half-billion dollar drop in farm exports suffered last year, together with protection against foreign dumping and unfair competition;

- Management of the Commodity Credit Corporation's inventory of grains and other farm commodities to improve farm prices, not depress them;

- Improvement of programs for the distribution of milk and other food to schools and needy people;

- Continuation and improvement of the Eisenhower Food for Peace program, emphasizing commercial market development and the export of greater agricultural technology to a hungry, underfed world;

- Assistance to farm cooperatives, including adequate funding of the rural electric and telephone programs;

- More and better research on industrial uses of farm commodities, the development of new markets and new products, and the development of new and better methods for cost-cutting in production and marketing;

- Particular attention to the need for revitalizing Countryside U.S.A., stressing farm prosperity and the creation of favorable economic conditions in our small towns and cities;

- Concentration of more vocational traning, industrial development and human resources in the rural areas from which heavy migration to our crowded cities has come;

- Improvement of credit programs within the Farm Credit System and the U.S. Department of Agriculture to meet the capital requirements of modern agriculture, especially for young farm families trying to get a decent start;

- Support for policies that enlarge the farmer's opportunity to manage his own affairs and give him a greater voice in shaping his own future;

- Effective plant and animal disease control and the control of pests, such as the kharpa beetle, fire ants and the screw worm, to protect our food supplies and farm production;

- Support for agricultural education and experimentation through the land grant college system, while extending the helping hand of the Extension Service to more Americans;

- A sound Federal Crop Insurance program;

- Effective enforcement and ample funding of the Packers and Stockyards Act and other regulatory programs administered by the U.S. Department of Agriculture;

- Vigorous expansion of soil and water conservation programs, including resolution of the constitutional impediment raised by the Administration against the successful Small Watershed program; and

- Improvement and standardization of procedures for the collection, evaluation and dissemination of agricultural statistical data.

I am particularly concerned about the problems of our smaller towns and cities. I believe that it is in great measurer their atmosphere of community spirit, neighborly concern and religious faith that has undergirded and formed many of the most valued ideas and ideals of what we proudly know as the "American way of life." These small communities have long been neglected in the great currents of our society.

And there is a case of even greater neglect. This is the neglect that permitted acute poverty to extend itself through rural areas. As the *Des Moines Register* so aptly observed three days ago, these poor people remain untouched by the Federal anti-poverty programs.

Our rural areas are being depleted of people, due in major degree to the agriculture revolution but due also to inadequate and unwise farm policies. As our farm population has fallen from 18% of our total national population two decades ago to about five percent today, most of these people have moved into our great cities. Thus, we have been generating an urban crush, intensifying problems in the cities to which migrating rural people must go. By de-populating the countryside we have over-populated our cities, and in the process we have created deepening problems in the areas and towns they left behind.

I feel deeply that the time has come for major improvements in the opportunities and quality of rural life. I feel this primarily because it is right for our rural people, especially those trapped in poverty, but also because we can hardly hope to triumph over our city troubles if the heavy migration from rural poverty areas into the cities is not stemmed.

Therefore, I vigorously favor the development of new programs of assistance to rural communities. For the small towns imaginative and comprehensive land use plans can open the way to the location of new industries. Improved transportation facilities, better schools, and more extensive public utilities in rural areas will help toward the same goal. The Federal government can directly assist by emphasis on the dispersal of government contracts to our smaller towns and disadvantaged rural areas wherever possible.

I have stressed before the desirability of tax incentivies—whether direct credits, accelerated depreciation, or a combination of the two—for businesses which locate branch offices or new plants in poverty areas, in rural America as well as in the core cities.

With more than half of our citizens below the poverty level living in rural America—with farm unemployment twice that of the city—with more than half of the nation's inadequate housing in rural areas—such harsh realities cannot be longer ignored.

Here in rural need and blighted opportunity is perhaps one most vivid evidence of the interrelationship of our total society. I propose that we do not treat our farm problems, as I said earlier, as something apart. The hard truth is that many of our city problems are rooted in rural decay. The tragedy is, rural distress has intensified urban distress.

So we must assist rural communities to develop an environment—of community services, recreational facilities, education opportunities, better medical care, and job opportunities—that will alleviate poverty, that will hold out hope for a brighter future, and that will ease the pressures upon these citizens to join the march to the cities.

These areas and these people require better of America than they have been able to acquire. I intend to help them get it.

Looking farther into the future, I stress an interest I have had throughout my public service—the area of new uses for our farm products. I am convinced that if the scientific genius and technological ingenuity of our country are brought adequately to bear in the conversion of farm products into new services to mankind, there can be spectacular advances for our entire society and the world, as well as increased consumption of immense importance to our farmers and ranchers. The capability of transforming agricultural products into startling new substances already exists. I propose that my new Administration vigorously encourage this effort, for here are exciting new prospects for our farm community and the American people.

The programs broadly presented in these remarks are not offered as panaceas, but I submit that in the attitudes expressed here, in the pledges made here, in the programs suggested here, there will be new hope and new opportunity and a new future for the farm people of the United States.

It is with this approach that I believe we can begin the task of service in the 70's toward developing a stronger nation, a better Countryside U.S.A. and more rewarding farming and ranching in America.

Des Moines, Iowa
September 14, 1968

AN OPEN DOOR FOR AMERICAN LABOR

Tonight, I would like to discuss with you the future of the workingman in America.

Take a look at the average factory pay check today and compare it with the pay check of three years ago. The numbers are higher — $11 a week higher. But when you cash that check and take the money to the supermarket, what happens?

This is what happens: the average weekly pay buys less than it did three years ago. Higher taxes and a spiraling cost of living have wiped out the increases.

In terms of real income the average workingman has two dollars less in his envelope now than he did in the first year of this administration. All those hard-won increases at the collective bargaining table have gone for naught.

That's not prosperity — that's treadmill economics. That is where the cost of living undermines the living wage.

Of course, the retired worker is even worse off. He bought his insurance with real dollars; he paid for his Social Security with real dollars; he deposited real dollars in a savings bank.

And what has happened to those real dollars? In eight years they have become 85 cents: the man with the prudence to plan ahead has been sold out.

It wasn't his union who sold him out, and it wasn't his employer; the family on a fixed income today was sold out by an administration that did not have the courage to stop inflation.

If the policies of the past are continued, if the old leadership stays in, what can the workingman expect?

Even the old leadership is alarmed about the highest rate of increase in the cost of living in almost two decades. Now, belatedly, my opponent is thinking of doing something about it.

No, he's not thinking of cutting unnecessary spending programs. He's not thinking of cutting government waste, or reducing your tax burden.

He's not thinking of treating the *causes* of the high cost of living today. The old leadership is thinking of treating the *symptoms* of inflation by bringing to bear the most harmful tool in the economist's kit: Wage and Price Controls.

As recently as one week ago, Hubert Humphrey called for a conference to define what he called "responsible wage and price behavior" and propose "a realistic figure for the year's average rate of wage increase." If labor does not accept the dictates of such a conference — and here I quote directly from the Humphrey task force report on inflation — "a statutory approach will become unavoidable."

In plain language that means the government will say, "Take what we give you — or else." And Hubert Humphrey accepted that report and made it his own policy.

If wage controls go in, the bargaining table will become a bureaucrat's desk — and there'll be no bargaining at all.

It can happen, unless you do something about it this November.

New leadership is determined to protect your earnings, and to increase your ability to earn more real dollars than you are earning today.

Wage security is just one of the issues on the mind of the American worker.

Another is job security.

The election of 1968 has brought a new concern about labor's oldest worry out into the open. A great many union members are troubled about what they suspect is competition for their jobs. They wonder about the impact of competition from people who were disadvantaged before, and who now want — and should have — their share of American opportunity.

Let's get to the heart of the matter: it seems that many wage earners feel that the civil rights movement has come into conflict with the labor movement. And it appears that the basis of this conflict is not racism, but rather the competition of economic interests.

As more disadvantaged Americans are being trained for jobs, the question on many a workingman's mind is this: "Is that my job he's being trained to take over?"

It's a direct question and a real fear. Whether reasoned or valid, we all know that this fear exists, and we must deal with it head-on. It cannot be met effectively by blasts at bigotry or exhortations of equality, because far more often than not, that concern is not rooted in prejudice at all. It is rooted in self-preservation, self-defense — human instincts not easily set aside.

The worker wondering whether his livelihood is threatened is entitled to an answer, not a tirade.

Here is my answer:

Certainly we intend to provide incentives to private industry to help train the unemployed and re-train those displaced by technology.

Certainly we intend to provide educational development and vocational training to the urban poor and the rural poor. They must have an equal chance at the starting line, which is the threshold of genuine economic opportunity.

But we will do this in a way that will help, and not harm, the man with a job today. Our next Administration will offer the workingman more job protection, not less; more security, not less; more opportunity, not less.

In the next four years we must help create *fifteen million* new jobs. And I mean jobs with futures, jobs that give a man's work meaning, not government make-work jobs. More than eight million of those jobs will be needed for those displaced by automation; nearly seven million more will be needed to provide opportunity for those who do not have it now and for the young people entering the work force.

Economic growth is the answer to job security. Economic growth is the best assurance for a workingman that his job will be secure, his real earnings on the rise, his route to advancement open.

Who can best provide that business growth without inflation? The old leadership, with its treadmill economics, has failed; if it adds wage and price controls it will only fail again. The American workingman need not turn to this extreme for his answer. The new leadership we offer will provide

123

the best job protection; an expanded economy will give the present work force a chance to move up, all Americans a chance to move in and up — and nobody need move over.

As we remove that fear of job competition, we will see those who are fearful today not only permitting, but demanding, the training of the disadvantaged.

That's because the unemployed man today is the workingman's burden. Nobody has a greater motive to get the out-of-work to work than today's worker.

When we take a man off the welfare roll and put him on a payroll, we lighten the tax load of the workingman. When the next man is pulling his weight, the strain is less on all of us.

Let's remember that there appear to be at least two forces at work in the mind of the man concerned about the security of his job and his job rights. One is to protect what he has, which is human enough; and the other is to resent the fellow who he believes is taking a free ride on the taxes that he, the worker, pays.

As we increase the number of jobs in the next Administration and end the fear of job displacement, we will turn that natural resentment into a constructive channel. Those truly in need of welfare will receive welfare; the man in need of a job will get off welfare and get on a job.

One area that offers labor and management a chance to broaden the base of taxpayers and meet their own needs is in developing more imaginative training programs. For example, the Transport Workers Union is arranging with the New York City Transit Authority ways to plan ahead to meet the requirements for 1200 to 1500 new, skilled transit workers each year. The program would begin in the first year of high school, as future workers would be paid to train at the transit facilities one day a week during the school season, and all summer long for four years. Upon graduation they would work up to top-rated jobs in two or three years in what is practically a guaranteed lifetime job. A number of these youngsters will come from ghetto communities; many of the jobs they fill will be new jobs. Labor and management, in this case, are cooperating to meet future needs.

124

Under this Administration something has gone terribly wrong with relations between government and public employees in far too many of our states and cities. We must all recognize that there is no right of public employees to strike in a manner that will endanger the public health or safety. Indeed union members have a responsibility to resist efforts to strike against the public interest.

How do we avert these strikes? How do we plan ahead to avoid crisis before it is upon us?

Early in the next Administration, the new Secretary of Labor — someone in the tradition of the late James Mitchell — will assemble a conference of labor leadership, individuals in all these fields, and public officials on every level of government. Their objective will be to to draw up and seek legislative approvals for an Economic Bill of Rights for Public Employees.

Any man who chooses his career working for the public must do so under the clear understanding that public service must not and will not be disrupted.

But the public that rightly demands this has the responsibility to provide acceptable alternatives for these 12 million public employees. Tenure and seniority are a part of it; continuity of employment is another incentive; vastly improved grievance procedures are still another; and improved impasse procedures are vital.

The public interest, of course, is affected by strikes outside the public sector. In this past year alone there have been more strikes than during any year in the past decade. In many cases the public suffered most.

Here is how I feel about the proper role of government in the bargaining process. I believe the Federal government ought not to intervene with the give-and-take of collective bargaining unless there are compelling reasons.

But when those compelling reasons exist, and the government is forced to intervene to safeguard the national health and safety, that intervention must be as a neutral, favoring neither management nor labor.

To be effective in actually resolving disputes, government must have the confidence of both sides; it cannot be under the control of one or the other;

125

it cannot be a captive of either. The President of the United States is the willing captive of the public interest; once he begins to lean one way or the other, he loses his value to both sides and abdicates his responsibility.

For example, in the steel strike of 1959, I recommended a settlement that did not fully satisfy the steel industry nor David McDonald, then the President of the Steelworkers. But it was the best settlement for the nation, and both sides felt treated with complete impartiality.

I do not agree with those who say that government should sit at every bargaining table; that would destroy collective bargaining and undermine free enterprise. In the next Administration hard bargaining will be the order of the day; the Federal government will step in only when the failure of that process endangers the health or safety of our nation, or when other legislation such as the Railway Labor Act requires it.

What can labor expect from a Nixon Administration?

- First, income security: the confidence that the dollar earned and saved today will be worth a dollar tomorrow.

- Second, job security: the greatest protection of all is in an expanding economy — in the next four years fifteen million new jobs to replace those lost to automation and to provide opportunity for all.

- Third, impartial, even-handed fairness and justice to labor and management.

- Fourth, an open door for labor's spokesmen: The Department of Labor will be strengthened, with national labor programs administered in the Department, where they belong. This is where the voice of every workingman will be heard and his rights will be protected.

- Fifth, leadership by example: I believe better occupational safety laws are needed on both Federal and state levels. A good place to begin would be with proper and uniform safety standards on all Federal construction.

- Sixth, an understanding that the workingman in America is not set apart from other citizens in the all-American demand for an end to crime and violence in this nation and for peace without surrender abroad.

126

- Finally, an identification with the great social goals of the labor movement: In its analysis of the 1968 party platforms, the AFL-CIO wrote:

  "The difference between the platforms is less one of ends than of means." I agree. And I believe a great many Americans, weary of failure, are turning to new means to achieve those ends.

There are new needs to be met, new goals to be set. I believe labor will insist on new techniques to make social security truly secure; new incentives to improve the quality of medical care available to the next generation of Americans; new bridges to human dignity that will break the cycle of dependency and despondency.

In the quest for these new goals I believe labor's leadership and labor's rank and file will achieve the best kind of solidarity — the solidarity that aligns itself with all the forward-looking forces in American society seeking new means to accomplish "more" for every American.

In the American system labor is not a class apart, and organized labor is not a separate party; labor is a movement, a progressive force, and now more than ever we need that movement and that progress.

In America's solidarity of purpose, in the new alignment of forces that has come into being, in the exciting new coalition of ideas where labor's voice is heard and heeded, lies hope for a new and creative American unity.

CBS Radio Network
Monday, October 21, 1968

CRUSADE AGAINST CRIME

THE CRUSADE AGAINST CRIME

During the decade of the 1960's, the peace forces of our society surrendered critical ground to the criminal forces. The first right of every American, the right to be free from domestic violence, has become the forgotten civil right of the American people.

As a result, serious crime has been increasing at a rate 7 times as rapidly as the population. In recent years that rate has begun to accelerate. Since Dwight Eisenhower left the Presidency, the annual number of felonies committed in the United States has doubled. At the current rate of increase in crime, the number of rapes and robberies and assaults will double again by the end of 1972.

It is not a Great Society when millions of women refuse to walk in their neighborhood or visit their parks after dusk—out of fear. It is not a Great Society when millions of men buy locks for their doors and watch-dogs for their homes and rifles and pistols for themselves—out of fear.

The American people are bolting their doors and arming themselves because they are rapidly losing confidence in the capacity and determination of government to defend them and their families and their property from crime and criminals. If government does not wish America to become an armed camp of two hundred million people, with vigilante justice as one of its hallmarks, then Government must begin now to reassume the responsibility for domestic peace and security. It is too late for more commissions to study violence; it is time for government to stop it.

We cannot accept a wave of crime as the wave of the future.

The people of this country want an end to government that acts out of spirit of neutrality or beneficence of indulgence toward criminals. They want government that will set itself up as an irreconcilable enemy of crime, a government that will wield its full powers to guarantee that for the criminals that torment the innocent, society's retribution will be ample and swift and sure.

The ideal in a free society is that the chief deterrent to crime lies in the respect for law, in the respect for legitimate authority, in the respect for the rights of others that is the standard moral code of every citizen.

But when the homes and schools and churches of a free society fail to inculcate those standards, or when the moral and opinion leaders of a nation fail in their role as commissioned watchmen of those standards, as they have failed in America in recent years, then the people must fall back for their safety upon police and prosecutors and courts.

This is the last line of defense of a free people. It is these defenses that government patrols; it is these defenses that have crumbled before the rising tide of crime; it is these defenses that government must re-establish and rebuild.

One paramount need is for the men of government at the national level to exert their moral authority to the limit, to marshal the armies of public opinion behind what can be nothing less than a militant crusade against crime. Another is for some recent notions in the administration of the law to be abandoned—and for some principles of justice to be re-established.

Poverty, despair, anger, past wrongs can no longer be allowed to excuse or justify violence or crime or lawlessness.

We must cease as well the granting of special immunities and moral sanctions to those who deliberately violate the public laws—even when those violations are done in the name of peace or civil rights or anti-poverty or academic freedom.

We must return to a single standard of justice for all Americans, and justice must be made blind again to race and color and creed and position along an economic or social line. Long ago in this country we buried the notion that the rich were above the law. Let us now lay to rest the equally deleterious doctrine that those who speak for popular or favored "causes" are entitled to favored considerations before the bar of justice.

We must re-establish again the principle that men are accountable for what they do, that criminals are responsible for their crimes—that while the boy's environment can help to explain the man's crime, it does not excuse that crime.

It does not justify our turning the adult criminal loose to prey again upon society. For too long we have been indulging the criminal poor—at the expense of the innocent poor.

132

But let us be clear about several points. A militant national crusade to protect society from criminals does not preclude a continuing national crusade to eliminate the social conditions from which so many of today's criminals have emerged and tomorrow's criminals are certain to emerge. The two go hand in hand.

Nor is our call for "law" meant to be any code word for the repression of the black American. In the report of the President's Commission on Civil Disorders, it was noted that crimes of violence occur in the slums of some cities 35 times as frequently as they occur in the areas of affluence. It is the poor, black and white alike, that bear the brunt of crime and violence.

We need a new recognition in this country—that a mugging in the ghetto is as serious a crime as a mugging on Main Street. There can be no color line between black murder and white murder, between black safety and white safety. We need not only equal enforcement of the law—but also equal protection of the law.

This country has been on a generation-long experiment of leniency toward all criminals; the result is a society that is increasingly unsafe for all the law-abiding. This experiment has gestated an increasingly bold and successful criminal community and an increasingly fearful and bullied majority of this country.

At every level of law enforcement and criminal justice there are needed men with an awareness of the severity of the crime crisis, men with a new attitude toward crime and criminals. Nowhere is this more necessary than in the judiciary, from the lowest court to the Supreme Court. At the judicial level it is time that the rights of the victimized millions in this country receive at least the same measure of concern and attention and action as have the rights of the criminally few.

From a new attitude about crime, from a new awareness of the severity of the crisis, from a new national priority for crime control, from new leadership of the American people, all else can follow—prison reform at the Federal and State level, judicial reform, better paid, better trained and more police for our undermanned peace forces across this country, increased funds for crime research at the national level.

133

It is difficult to underestimate the impact that a few men of action can have upon the crime crisis in America.

Today—organized crime earns hundreds of millions of dollars a year in the sale of illicit narcotics that both destroy the lives of thousands of children and feed the habit of addicts who commit half the street crime in some of our great cities. These incorporated corrupters of American life cheat union men out of their wages, cheat businessmen of their profits, corrupt government, milk the poor of billions of dollars each year in the numbers racket and additional tens of millions by charging extortionate rates of interest on loans.

Yet, as the profits of organized crime grow prodigiously into untold billions of dollars—the Attorney General of the United States expresses his public distaste for penetrating the secrecy of this organized conspiracy. He has publicly refused to use the strictly limited and carefully safeguarded wiretapping, authorized by Congress and approved by the courts, which is considered by many criminal justice officials as law enforcement's most effective tool against organized crime.

A new Attorney General, with a new attitude and a new awareness and a new determination, could make a world of difference in the quality of American life by making decisive inroads on the security of organized crime.

Only fifty years ago, Americans dreamed of making the world safe for democracy; today, our present leadership cannot even make America safe for Americans.

That is the sad state to which we have fallen. And that will be the duty of this party—at every level of government—to re-establish domestic peace— to restore freedom from fear to the American people.

Submitted to Republican National Convention
Committee on Resolutions
July 31, 1968

TOWARD FREEDOM FROM FEAR

In the last seven years while the population of this country was rising some ten per cent, crime in the United States rose a staggering 88 per cent. If the present rate of new crime continues, the number of rapes and robberies and assaults and thefts in the United States today will double — by the end of 1972.

That is a prospect America cannot accept. If we allow it to happen, then the city jungle will cease to be a metaphor. It will become a barbaric reality, and the brutal society that now flourishes in the core cities of America will annex the affluent suburbs. This nation will then *be* what it is fast becoming — an armed camp of two hundred million Americans living in fear.

But, to stop the rising crime rate and to reduce the incidence of crime in America, we must first speak with a new candor about its causes and cures.

Poverty Not the Cause

We cannot explain away crime in this country by charging it off to poverty — and we would not rid ourselves of the crime problem even if we succeeded overnight in lifting everyone above the poverty level. The role of poverty as a cause of the crime upsurge in America has been grossly exaggerated — and the incumbent Administration bears major responsibility for perpetuation of the myth.

On October 16, 1964, the President said that, "The war on poverty which I started — is a war against crime and a war against disorder." If the President genuinely accepted that proposition, the near 50 per cent increase in crime rate since 1964 would be adequate proof of the utter failure of the government's war on poverty.

But the war on poverty is not a war on crime; and it is no substitute for a war on crime. It is certainly true that rising prosperity will gradually reduce the number of those below the poverty level, and eliminate many of the conditions in which crime is likely to flourish.

But poverty cannot begin to explain the explosion of crime in America. In recent years, this nation has grown wealthier and its riches have been

135

more widely distributed than in any other country in the world. And yet crime has been going up about three times as rapidly as the GNP.

And poverty tells us nothing about the enormous increases in juvenile crime and drug abuse by teenagers in the affluent suburbs of America.

Too Often, Crime Does Pay

The success of criminals in this country plays a far greater role in the rising crime rate than any consideration of poverty. Today, an estimated one-in-eight crimes results in conviction and punishment.

If the conviction rate were doubled in this country, it would do more to eliminate crime in the future than a quadrupling of the funds for any governmental war on poverty.

In short, crime creates crime — because crime rewards the criminal. And we will reduce crime as we reduce the profits of criminals.

There is another attitude that must be discarded if we are to wage an effective national war against this enemy within. That attitude is the socially suicidal tendency — on the part of many public men — to excuse crime and sympathize with criminals because of past grievances the criminal may have against society. By now Americans, I believe, have learned the hard way that a society that is lenient and permissive for criminals is a society that is neither safe nor secure for innocent men and women.

Justice for the Guilty, Too

One of the operative principles of a free society is that men are accountable for what they do. No criminal can justify his crimes on the basis of some real or imagined grievance against his society. And our sympathy for the plight or the past of a criminal cannot justify turning him loose to prey again upon innocent people.

In the preamble of the Constitution of the United States, this country set it as a goal to "establish justice" in these states. Just as justice dictates that innocent men go free, it also means that guilty men pay the penalty for their crimes. It is that second part of justice to which the nation must begin to address itself in earnest.

In the course of presenting these proposals for dealing with the crime problem in America, I have not dealt at all with the urban disorders that have become commonplace in our great cities. Riots are a special problem, a problem apart from the crisis of daily crime in America.

In terms of dollars and cents the toll of the riots is next to nothing compared to the toll of street crime or even the take of organized crime.

But, riots offer their own challenge to the future existence of our society, and that challenge is different than the menace represented in the 88 per cent increase in crime in seven years. Consequently, I have dealt with the riots as a separate problem in other statements.

No Sense of Urgency

The primary responsibility for dealing with that 88 per cent figure continues to rest — as it should — with the local and state government. We want no centralized Federal police force in this country. But crime has become a first priority domestic crisis, a distinct threat to the social order, and it should be a matter of the highest Federal urgency. That urgency has not been reflected in this Administration's actions or recommendations.

Crime today is increasing almost nine times as rapidly as the population.

The Administration in Washington seems to have neither an understanding of the crisis which confronts us nor a recognition of its severity. As a result, neither the leadership nor the necessary tools have been provided to date to enable society's peace forces to regain the upper hand over the criminal forces in this country.

The statistics and evidence are there for all to see.

The last five years have been the halcyon days of organized crime. Gross earnings from illicit gambling, prostitution, narcotics and loan-sharking, have grown prodigiously. One reliable authority places the figure in the neighborhood of $50 billion annually.

As for street crime, for every two major crimes committed in the United States when President Johnson took office in 1963 — there are three committed today — and if the present trend continues, there will be six committed by the end of 1972.

These are the dimensions and the elements, the hard facts and the stark realities of the crime crisis to which this Administration's response has been lame and ineffectual.

Organized Crime

Organized crime is the tapeworm of the American society. In recent years it has prospered as never before and broadened its influence in government and legitimate business and unions. The absence of an adequate response at the national level — to this national threat — is a glaring failure of the present Administration.

One of the most effective groups of men within government combating this kind of criminal activity over the years has been the Organized Crime Section of the Department of Justice. Yet, when President Johnson took office, the number of man days spent in field investigating by members of the OCS, the number of man days spent testifying before grand juries, and the number of man days spent in court all suddenly decreased between 50 and 75 per cent.

This wholesale de-escalation of the Justice Department's war against organized crime has not to this day been adequately explained.

Equally puzzling is the Administration's adamant opposition to the use — against organized crime — of the same wiretap and electronic surveillance the government employs to safeguard the national security. Not only does the Administration oppose the use of these weapons against crime, it has asked Congress to forbid that use by law. Such legislation would be a tragic mistake.

"Give Us the Tools . . ."

Organized crime is a secret society. By denying to State and Federal law enforcement agencies the tools to penetrate that secrecy, the President and the Attorney General are unwittingly guaranteeing the leaders of organized crime a privileged sanctuary from which to proceed with the systematic corruption of American life.

New York County District Attorney Frank Hogan, who has probably convicted more racketeers than any other man in America, has said that wiretapping is:

> "the single most valuable weapon in law enforcement's fight against organized crime . . . Without it, my own office could not have convicted Charles "Lucky" Luciano, Jimmy Hines, Louis "Lepke" Buchalter, Jacob "Gurrah" Shapiro, Joseph "Socks" Lanza, George Scalise, Frank Erickson, John "Dio" Dioguardi, and Frank Carbo."

An overwhelming majority of the President's own blue ribbon crime commission recommended enabling legislation for the use of wiretap. The Judicial Conference, consisting of ranking Federal judges from across the nation, and headed by Chief Justice Earl Warren, has approved such legislation. And the Supreme Court has left the door open to a carefully drawn wiretap measure with proper safeguards.

Safeguards Against Abuse

The Senate is currently considering such a proposal — drawn to conform meticulously to the Supreme Court decisions. That proposal would authorize the use of electronic surveillance on a court order, in the nature of a search warrant, showing probable cause. The court order would be limited to major crime cases, and specified cases involving the national security.

It would be limited as to time, persons and place. Any extraneous evidence gathered by the eavesdrop device would be inadmissible in court and would have to be held in confidence under pain of both civil and criminal penalties. Special precautions would be taken to safeguard those communications regarded by the law as privileged, such as those between husband and wife, doctor and patient, lawyer and client, and priest and penitent. In addition, the bill would outlaw all electronic surveillance by private citizens.

Yet, despite these carefully drawn precautions, the President defends his opposition to wiretapping in major crime cases with the astonishing assertion that "the principle that a man's home is his castle is under new attack."

"Nonsense in its purest form" was the retort by the *Washington Star* which continued:

139

"This is a comment which shakes our faith in (1) whether the President knows what he is talking about in his anti-crime speeches, or (2) whether he will ever support the measures —wiretaps and the like — that are essential investigative tools if we are ever going to wipe out crime — especially organized crime."

Five Immediate Steps

There are other steps which Congress can take independently to strengthen the peace forces in our society against the forces of organized crime. Some of these recommendations have been endorsed by the President's Commission on Crime.

(1) *Infiltration of honest business:* Congress should enact legislation making it a Federal crime to invest in legitimate business either money which has been gathered from illegal racket activities or money that has not been reported for income tax purposes. Such measures would focus the tax enforcement machinery on the problem of organized crime.

(2) *Anti-smuggling:* Congress should authorize substantial increase in the number of Customs Bureau officials. In the last decade while the number of customs officials has risen 4 per cent, the number of people entering the country has risen 50 per cent and the number of aircraft 100 per cent. These would be an effective deterrent to the import of narcotics, a multi-million dollar annual item in the income statement of organized crime.

(3) *Permanent watchdog:* Congress should establish a permanent Joint Congressional Committee on Organized Crime.

(4) *More lawmen:* Congress should authorize whatever Federal personnel are necessary to carry out the new responsibilities under these pieces of recommended legislation.

(5) *Immunity power:* Congress should enact the Republican-proposed organized crime immunity statute. Once granted immunity from prosecution based on his testimony, a witness would be required to testify before a grand jury or at trial, or face jail for criminal contempt. This would be another and an effective legal tool with which to cut through the curtain of secrecy that envelops organized crime. Witness immunity would make it possible to get to the higher echelons of the crime syndicate.

140

These are a few of the steps that can and should be taken if we are to make realistic rather than rhetorical progress in uprooting the infrastructure of organized crime. Yet, both the President and his Attorney General, Mr. Clark, who have the principal responsibility for leading the war on organized crime are either indifferent to or in active opposition to a majority of these measures.

That attitude has made of the President's proposal to the Congress the kind of compromise legislation that organized crime can live with. It has called into question the seriousness of the President's designation of Mr. Clark to be his "Mr. Big" in the war against national crime.

Alerting the People

There is also a need at the national level to awaken and educate the American people to the extent of the threat within that comes from organized crime. The average American — as well as the Attorney General of the United States — seems tragically unaware of the magnitude and immense impact of organized crime upon his society.

This menace which Mr. Clark astonishingly termed a "tiny part" of the crime picture in the United States was more accurately described by his predecessor, Mr. Katzenbach, as constituting "nothing less than a guerilla war against society."

How is the average American affected?

The businessman pays higher insurance rates because of the arson committed under the instructions of organized crime; he loses millions in bad debts annually because of fraudulent bankruptcies. Union workers are cheated out of their just wages when the proxies of organized crime take over and corrupt their unions, arrange sweetheart contracts, exploit mammoth pension funds and intimidate the membership. Organized crime cheats the consumer by its corruption of the free enterprise system. With its gigantic earning power it is able to take over individual businesses, influence prices, and act as unfair competition for honest business and honest labor.

According to Congressman Richard Poff of Virginia, one of the most knowledgeable men in the Congress on the subject, organized crime controls a "reservoir of wealth unmatched by any financial institution in the country."

Crime's War on the Poverty-Stricken

At the same time that the President has asked for a $2 billion appropriation to fund the War on Poverty for one year, organized crime earns an estimated $3.5 billion annually from the numbers racket — a racket that exploits, not the affluent, but the urban poor. Organized crime is taking three dollars in gambling revenues from the urban poor for every two that is put into the poverty program by the nation's taxpayers.

Last year, while the Small Business Administration made some $50 million in loans, the take from loan-sharking amounted to many times that sum. The narcotics traffic in this country, much of it in the urban centers of poverty, netted an estimated $350 million for organized crime last year — the precise sum spent for the Head Start Program.

Organized crime is also directly and deeply involved in street crime. One estimate is that some 50 per cent of the street crime in some of our major cities is the work of addicts attempting to support their habit — and traffic in illegal narcotics is a major enterprise of organized crime.

Street Crime

But organized crime, though a multi-billion dollar enterprise and a major contributing factor to street crime, cannot alone explain the 88 per cent increase in muggings, robberies, rapes and assaults over the past seven years. Another contributing cause of this staggering increase is that street crime is a more lucrative and less risky occupation than it has ever been in the past. Only one of eight major crimes committed now results in arrest, prosecution, conviction and punishment — and a twelve per cent chance of punishment is not adequate to deter a man bent on a career in crime. Among the contributing factors to the small figure are the decisions of a majority of one of the United States Supreme Court.

The Miranda and Escobedo decisions of the High Court have had the effect of seriously hamstringing the peace forces in our society and strengthening the criminal forces.

From the point of view of the peace forces, the cumulative impact on these decisions has been to very nearly rule out the "confession" as an effective and major tool in prosecution and law enforcement.

Justice White, in his dissent in the 5-4 Miranda decision, identified judicial prejudice against the use of confession as the bedrock upon which the majority decision was erected.

"The obvious underpinning of the Court's decision is a deep-seated distrust of all confession . . .the result adds up to a judicial judgment that evidence from the accused should not be used against him in any way, whether compelled or not. This is the not so subtle overtone of the opinion — that it is inherently wrong for the police to gather evidence from the accused himself."

From the point of view of the criminal forces, the cumulative impact of these decisions has been to set free patently guilty individuals on the basis of legal technicalities.

The tragic lesson of guilty men walking free from hundreds of court-rooms across this country has not been lost on the criminal community.

Striking the Balance

The balance must be shifted back toward the peace forces in our society and a requisite step is to redress the imbalance created by these specific court decisions. I would thus urge Congress to enact proposed legislation that — dealing with both Miranda and Escobedo — would leave it to the judge and the jury to determine both the voluntariness and the validity of any confession. If judges and juries can determine guilt or innocence, they can certainly determine whether a confession is voluntary and valid. The rule of reason and justice should replace the Dickensian legalisms that have been obtained as a result of recent Supreme Court decisions.

(In Title III of the omnibus crime bill now pending in the Senate, there is a proposal to correct the imbalance resulting from these decisions; that proposal deserves passage despite the vigorous opposition of the Attorney General.)

The barbed wire of legalisms that a majority of one of the Supreme Court has erected to protect a suspect from invasion of his rights has effectively shielded hundreds of criminals from punishment as provided in the prior laws.

143

If it should become impossible to draw such legislation to the satisfaction of the High Court, then consideration should be given to amending the Constitution. Involved here is the first civil right of every American, the right to be protected in his home, business and person from domestic violence, and it is being traduced with accelerating frequency in every community in America.

Leaning too far Backward

Wade and *Gilbert* are two other decisions of the Supreme Court, the extension of which have added to the problems of effective law enforcement. *Wade* and *Gilbert*, for the first time, ruled that in a line-up confrontation between witness and accused, the absence of a lawyer for the accused could, of itself, render the identification inadmissible in court.

My own view coincides with that of the dissentng minority, who expressed incredulity at the notion that a lawyer's presence at a line-up can somehow be helpful to the quality of the witness' identification. But *Wade* and *Gilbert* were carried to an almost ridiculous, if logical, extreme in *U.S.* versus *Beasley*.

In the latter case, even an accidental, on-the-street confrontation between, in this case, victim and accused, made identification of the accused inadmissible — because of the absence of a lawyer.

(In the Beasley case, police observed three men beating and robbing an elderly man on the streets of Washington, D.C. When they approached, the assailants fled leaving their victim behind. Police gave chase and apprehended one man, and returned with him to the scene to aid the victim and radio for help. There was thus an inevitable confrontation between the suspect and the victim, and the former was positively identified by the latter as one of his assailants. The identification made on the spot was ruled as inadmissible evidence because the alleged assailant did not have an attorney present when he confronted the victim on the street, immediately following the crime.)

It is decisions such as this, suppressing evidence prior to trial, that underscore the merit of the proposal of Congressman Railsback of Illinois, now before Congress.

Currently, a defendant can appeal his conviction to a higher court, if the case can be made that illegal evidence has been used against him. The prosecution, however, except in limited cases, has no similar right to appeal a decision to prohibit the introduction of certain evidence at a trial.

Congressman Railsback's proposal would remedy this situation; it would give government the same right to appeal these rulings now guaranteed the accused. The President's Crime Commission has endorsed this proposal; it would make for more effective prosecution; it would reduce the number of guilty men walking out of courtrooms on technicalities; it deserves passage in this session.

These decisions by a majority of one of the Supreme Court have had a far-reaching impact in this country. They have been the subject of controversy; they were the focus of vigorous dissent on the part of the minority. And I think they point up a genuine need — a need for future Presidents to include in their appointments to the United States Supreme Court men who are thoroughly experienced and versed in the criminal laws of the land.

Strengthening the Peace Forces

A second major deficiency of the "peace forces" in this country is in the number and quality of the men who man the first line of defense—the police.

Today, two-thirds of the community police forces in the country are undermanned. This year there will be 50,000 vacancies for police officers in the United States. To improve the caliber and increase the number of men who volunteer to fill those vacancies, the Federal and State as well as the municipal governments have a role to play.

The primary reason why there are not more and better police officers in our great cities today is quite simply that the rewards — economic and personal — of being a police officer have diminished sharply in the last two decades.

For many years, these men have been in effect increasingly subsidizing the communities which they serve — by accepting a wage rate that gradually fell behind other professions. From 1939 to 1966 while the real income of manufacturing employees in New York increased on the average of 100 per cent, that of a New York City patrolman increased by 20 per cent.

You cannot attract first-class men to do the difficult and complex and dangerous job of police work — if you simply give them a gun and $100 a week — which is the median beginning salary for patrolmen in our greater cities.

The responsibility for rectifying this situation rests largely with the municipalities and the people who live in them. They must be willing to pay the salaries to attract the kind of men they want standing between their property and family and the rising crime rate.

The Blue "Presence"

There is a considerable body of evidence to show that a dramatic rise in the number of patrolmen is followed by an equally dramatic drop in the rate of crime. The New York Subway system is a case in point — where the presence of a patrolman on every train at night brought a reduction of 60 per cent in the epidemic of juvenile terrorism in the first three months they were there. The lesson could be applied to dozens of other cities and communities across the country.

(Along these same lines, a judicious realocation of existing police manpower can often have the same impact on crime as a numerical increase in the force. Systems Analysis can be use to reassign patrolmen from beats and areas where they are not needed to trouble spots. This is one way modern science has been and should be put at the service of justice.)

It would be difficult to exaggerate the urgency of the need for greater police presence — or the danger to the social order if we do not get it. To those who speak and write about that startling 88 per cent increase in crime, the figure is an ominous portent to our society.

Hardest Hit: the Poor

But it is among the urban poor, the silent victims of most of the reported crime and almost all of the unreported crime that these statistics have already been translated into a brutal society. According to the President's own Commission on Civil Disorders, there are cities in this country where the crimes of violence run 35 times as high in the areas of poverty as they do in the areas of affluence. Last fall, a Harlem Pastor spoke out in anguish.

146

"Crime is at its worst; the citizens fear to venture out after dark. Church members are afraid to go out to their meetings at night. The law seems to be in the hands of the muggers and robbers. There's panic among the people."

It would be a dangerous delusion to think that we can either "establish justice" in this country or re-establish peace in the central city, until those who are not the victims of this crime crisis are as indignant as those who are.

We are trifling with social dynamite if we believe that the young people who emerge from these brutal societies in the central cities will come out as satisfied and productive citizens. It is too often the case that "those to whom evil is done do evil in return."

State Help

The State can assist the local community in improving the quality of its law enforcement agencies in a variety of ways. One of the most effective would be to use incentives to accelerate the trend toward larger and more efficient police units.

Today, there are more than 420,000 people involved in police work employed by 40,000 separate agencies. Many of these 40,000 agencies are tiny and inefficient municipal departments wholly inadequate to the tasks assigned them. Consolidation of many of these departments and their merger into city-wide or metropolitan-wide forces would give the peace forces a jurisdictional range and a level of states, we would strengthen law enforcement at a level at which it could deal more effectively with a criminal community that possesses a mobility and strength undreamed of a few years ago.

The shift in emphasis from direct grants to local departments to block grants to the states was written into the Law Enforcement Assistance and Criminal Justice Act of 1967 on the floor of the House largely through the efforts of the Republican leadership there.

In the Upper House, Senator Roman Hruska of Nebraska, one of the most knowledgeable and effective sponsors of anti-crime legislation on the Hill, along with the Minority Leader Senator Dirksen, has worked to have his block grant approach written into the final version of the bill — as it should be.

Setting an Example

There is another area where the Federal Government can not only play a leading role — but where it has the opportunity to make a dramatic demonstration of its concern with the problem of crime, its commitment to new solutions and the efficacy of its proposals. That is in Washington, D.C. — the nation's capital where the authority of the Federal Government is great and its prerogatives many.

Today, Washington, D.C., should be a model city as far as law enforcement is concerned — a national laboratory in which the strength is more commensurate with the criminal forces — which ignore state-lines, let alone the lines that divide tiny municipalities.

Federal Help

The Federal Government can play a leading role as well in furthering this objective of consolidating and reducing the number while improving the quality of law enforcement agencies in this country.

To do so, however, it will have to shift its emphasis from direct grants to local governments, to block grants to the states. The former approach puts the Federal Government squarely into what must and should remain a local function — law enforcement. Direct grants for local police departments could bring domination and control and the door could be opened to the possibility of a Federal police force — a prospect we should avoid. Secondly, the block grant approach to the states will enable them to determine the priorities in the allocation of resources; and that, too, is as it should be. Third, this approach would strengthen the statewide police forces which are, by and large, efficient and professional organizations.

It would also enable the state to strengthen its own investigative and crime laboratory facilities, its intelligence, and records centers — which could be put at the disposal of local police. By providing the assistance to the latest in crime prevention and detection can be tested and the results reported to a waiting nation. The record, however, is otherwise.

If across America the peace forces in city after city and state after state have been gradually giving up ground to the criminal forces — in Washing-

148

ton, D.C., the forces of peace are in disorganized retreat. Since 1960 crime in the nation's capital has increased by 100 per cent.

Again, however, the Administration has been slow to recognize the developing threat. It was only after severe criticism and intense public pressure that the D.C. crime bill was finally signed into law by the President in 1967.

The Prison Problem

No national program for turning back the rising tide of crime can succeed if we continue to ignore a primary headwater — the prisons of America. No institution within our society has a record which presents such a conclusive case of failure as does our prison system.

A recent FBI study of some 18,000 convicts released in 1963 revealed that fully 55 per cent had been re-arrested for new offenses by June 30 of 1966. Of those persons arrested on a new charge within 30 months, 67 per cent had been given a mandatory release by a penal institution.

In short — whether one believes that the purpose of a prison is to punish the criminal or to deter him from future crime or to rehabilitate him and guide him away from a career in crime — by either standard our prison system is a failure.

The American prison system needs to undergo a major overhaul — to be changed from a primary cause of the crime problem in this country into a partial cure. Stated simply and directly, the criminal rate in the United States would be a good deal lower if convicted felons were properly trained and equipped for reassimilation by the outside world.

Both Federal and State Governments share equally in the responsibility for changing our prisons into something other than an ever-normal pool of replacements for the criminal community.

Since, however, the Federal prison system houses only 10 per cent of the penitentiary population of about 200,000 its role will primarily be one of example, of assistance to the states, and of clearing legislative roadblocks to effective prison reform.

149

Recognizing a Mistake

During the depression years of the 1930's, with millions of Americans jobless, many pieces of Federal legislation were enacted calling for discrimination against person-made goods. It was assumed that conscripted labor inside a prison could produce goods at a far cheaper rate and thus enjoy an unfair competitive advantage over both free labor and free enterprise.

This legislation was always questionable, and one certain effect has been to deny to thousands of convicted men the type of work experience that might have given them the essential opportunity to find a job when they left prison. It is time that these existing legal barriers against providing convicts with the type of training and work that will give them a viable employment when they leave — should be removed. According to the President's own Crime Commission, prison labor is no threat to free labor today.

Secondly, of the 120,000 people employed in correction today, five of six are employed in custodial or administrative work, leaving only some 24,000 in treatment activities to handle a combined jail and prison population of 400,000 and a total of some 1.3 million who pass through our system each year. That 24,000 figure includes all the psychiatrists, teachers, psychologists and social workers — and if we are serious about changing the results of prison life — then we have to be serious about increasing that number.

More Prison Reforms

The necessity of other major reforms is equally obvious. A study of the prison population reveals that 50 per cent of it has only a grammar school education or less. Except for New York and California, prison education is provided by inmates — a majority of whom lack college degrees and many of whom are themselves without a high school diploma.

The number of parole officers dealing with that great segment of convict population that has been returned to society is also inadequate to its job. We are thousands of men away from achieving what is considered the desirable ratio of one parole officer to every 37 parolees.

150

To effect these reforms, to provide the personnel in terms of teachers, parole officers, psychiatrists, social workers, to change the American prison system from a pool of replacements for the criminal community into a system of effective correction and rehabilitation will take money. It will require millions of dollars — whether those dollars are taken out at the State or Federal level.

It will take not only more dedicated people, but new ideas and new resources and new tools if we are going to rebuild these broken careers and re-equip these men and women for useful lives.

It will require further the cooperation of both State and Federal Government, for the unreconstructed criminal who walks out of a Missouri or Illinois prison, becomes a threat to the community he visits, wherever he goes in the United States.

These are not all of the steps that should be taken. But here, in these proposals, I believe a beginning can be made toward removing from this nation the stigma of a lawless society.

Right to a Speedy Trial

There are other areas as well where major reform is needed. The judiciary is one of them. In community after community in this country there are great backlogs of criminal cases. Not only does this delay in prosecuting serve as an injustice to the innocent, it does a grave injustice to society by delaying too long the imposition of penalties which are major deterrents to crime.

There is a need for vastly increased resources in crime research. Today, one-half of one per cent of the law enforcement budgets of the State and Federal government — a paltry $20 million — is being spent on crime research.

The potential for law enforcement research is enormous.

Space age tools are available to deal with modern crime. Today, we are still working with the forensic toxicology and forensic medicine of thirty years ago. There are promising areas such as olfactronics waiting to be explored, and tools such as the "voice print" waiting to be exploited.

151

End of a Lawless Society

As this brief statement indicates, there is no shortage of ideas or programs or tools or potential laws to deal with crime in this country. The only shortage is a shortage of leadership that will place this problem in the first priority of American business.

If the American people are willing to commit themselves to pay the necessary price to restore peace to the society, it can be done. If they are willing to commit themselves to the proposition that any man who disobeys the law pays the penalty the law exacts, then we can begin to turn this crime wave back.

We can put an end to an urban situation where the infirm, the old and the women refuse to visit their parks or enjoy the entertainment and good life a city can offer because they are afraid. We can reduce crime by making it a more hazardous and less rewarding occupation.

In connection with the President's Crime Commission Report, a poll was taken of average Americans. It found that of those polled 43 per cent were afraid to be on the streets at night; 35 per cent would not speak to strangers, and 21 per cent used cars and taxis at night to avoid mass transit.

Those are not the statistics of a Great Society; they are the statistics of a lawless society — they are statistics we must and will change.

New York, New York
Wednesday, May 8, 1968

ORDER AND JUSTICE UNDER LAW

Suppose for a moment, my fellow Americans, that you read in your morning newspaper of a great national disaster. It killed 12,000 people. It hospitalized 200,000 more. It produced financial losses of a billion dollars. You, of course, would be shocked. You would demand that every measure necessary be taken to prevent such a thing from occurring again.

And, yet, we undergo just such a disaster every year in America. Each year the losses of life and property are even greater. Violent crime is responsible.

Suppose—again—that you saw cities plagued by fire; entire neighborhoods destroyed, buildings gutted, thousands hospitalized or homeless, businesses wiped out.

You might thing that we had been attacked by a foreign power. Again, you would demand prompt action.

Yet this destruction is the work of other Americans, transformed into a mob.

Let us view one more scene. Another mob surges through the street, shouting political slogans, battling the police, hurling epithets. It barricades itself in public buildings. It vows to paralyze a city, or to bring down an ancient institution of learning—unless its demands are met.

You might think that this was happening under some alien tyranny, where the people had no representation, where there was no ballot, and where insurrection was the alternative to abject submission.

No—again—this is happening in America. It is happening despite the fact that the democratic system in America does allow for change. It allows citizens to bring about change by means of the ballot. But orderly change does not satisfy the violent faction.

How has all this come to pass in America? How have we permitted it to happen? Americans are demanding an answer from those who have a solemn obligation, from those who are obliged by their oath of office, to be the protectors of our liberties.

Some have said that we are a sick society. We're sick, all right, but not in the way they mean. We are *sick* of what has been allowed to go on in this nation for too long.

Skyrocketing Crime Rate

Under the stewardship of the present Administration, crime and violence have skyrocketed in America. Under its stewardship, crime and violence have increased 10 times faster than population.

All you have to do is look at the most recent FBI report. On all the graphs the lines have turned sharply up. Between 1960 and 1967, daytime burglaries against homes rose 187 per cent. Violations of the narcotics laws rose 165 per cent. Murder rose 34 per cent. Assault was up 67 per cent. Comparing the first half of 1968 with the same period of last year, the FBI found an increase of 21 per cent in the seven major crime categories.

Now, by way of excuse, the present Administration places the blame on poverty. But poverty is only one contributing factor. During the Depression the crime rate was at an all-time low in America. Today we are richer than ever before and our wealth is more widely distributed than in any other country. And we have more crime and violence than ever before. There is crime in the suburb as well as in the slum. If poverty were eliminated tomorrow, the violent and the criminal and the depraved would not disappear.

"Safe" Lawbreaking

The truth is that we will reduce crime and violence when we enforce our laws—when we make it less profitable, and a lot more risky, to break our laws.

One lesson has not been lost on the criminal community. Today only one in every eight crimes results in conviction and punishment.

Today, an arrest is made in only one in every five reported burglaries. Today, an arrest is made in less than a third of reported robberies.

Today, it is comparatively safe to break the law. Today, all across the land, guilty men walk free from hundreds of court rooms.

Something has gone terribly wrong in America.

Now, what is the responsibility of the Administration of which Hubert Humphrey is a part? Well, it's time for an accounting. Its responsibility is large. It has failed. It has failed in energy, failed in will, failed in purpose.

The Attorney General, Mr. Ramsey Clark, has the primary responsibility in this area. But listen to him. "The level of crime," he said last year, "has risen a little bit, but there is no wave of crime in this country."

And this is not an isolated statement. It seems to reflect the Administration's overall attitude.

At the present time we are experiencing a prodigious growth in organized crime. The earnings of illicit gambling, prostitution, narcotics and loan-sharking now amount to 50 billion dollars a year in America. And yet the Attorney General has dismissed this as a "tiny part" of the crime picture. He simply has no sense of urgency.

Legalized Wire-tapping

Take the matter of wire-tapping.

The Congress has passed carefully considered and carefully drawn legislation, authorizing wire-tapping with full constitutional safeguards, for the investigation of specific crimes.

The three previous U.S. Attorney Generals not only outlined the need but also sponsored legislation to authorize wire-tapping.

And, *still*, the present Attorney General opposes it.

And what is the attitude of Hubert Humphrey?

Well, his own casual approach to the problem was demonstrated by his recent White Paper on crime. If you were going to issue such a paper, wouldn't you look into the subject pretty thoroughly? Well, apparently, he didn't do his homework. Amazingly, eight of his major proposals are already on the books in the Safe Streets Act. Hadn't he read it?

155

And his proposal to develop sentencing guidelines had already been covered by the new Federal Judicial Center.

How can we expect him to know what still has to be done, when he doesn't know what already has been done?

Does Crime Pay?

Is it any wonder that criminals in America are not losing much sleep over the efforts of the Department of Justice? Is it any wonder that the old saying, "Crime does not pay," is being laughed at by criminals?

The present Administration has failed to enforce the Narcotics Addict Rehabilitation Act of 1966. Even though there are over 60,000 narcotics addicts in this country, the Administration has committed only 305 of them in two years.

Now, would you say that they had much of a sence of urgency about the narcotics problem?

The whole federal effort is handcuffed by red tape. The paper piles up— the criminals go free. If the criminals were this badly organized, they would all be in jail.

Let us recognize that we're in a war, and let us mobilize all of our forces to win that war. Let us resolve that the wave of crime and violence will not be the wave of the future in America.

Protecting *All* Citizens

And now, while we're talking about the rising tide in crime and violence, I'd like to make one thing very clear.

Somehow the idea has gotten around that stressing the need for order, and for progress under the law rather than outside of it, is being secretly anti-Negro. Nothing could be less true. Those who live in our urban ghettos are victims of lawlessness—victims out of all proportion to their numbers.

The poor—those who can least afford it—are the victims of the loan shark and the prey of the narcotics peddler. When the arsonist strikes, their homes burn. Their businesses sometimes never recover. More than any other group in our society, they want and they need the protection of enlightened and progressive law enforcement.

The criminal does not discriminate. He strikes without regard to race or creed. And so when we call for Law and Order, we are calling for the protection of *all* of our citizens.

And somehow another false idea has gotten around—that to criticize some of the decisions of the Supreme Court is to attack the court itself as an institution. This is not true. Some of the sharpest criticism of court decisions has come, in fact, from members of the court themselves.

In their own dissenting opinions, these justices have argued that several recent decisions of the court have tipped the balance against the peace forces in this country, and strengthened the criminal forces. And I agree with those dissenting opinions.

Just consider the three most important and controversial decisions. After convictions for murder, rape and kidnapping, they were reversed by the Supreme Court, and each of the three men involved was convicted of a new major crime.

Those who obey the law surely have a right to as much protection as those who break it.

Some have described criticism of the court's decisions as irrelevant, frivolous. I would like to ask you to make up your own mind about this.

Take the case of the United States vs. Beaseley, for example. Here, police observed three men beating and robbing an elderly man on the streets of Washington, D.C. When they approached, the three assailants fled. The police gave chase, caught one man, returned to the scene to aid the victim and radioed for help. The victim arose from the sidewalk and spontaneously identified the man as one of his assailants. But the identification made on the spot was ruled inadmissable as evidence, because of a Supreme Court ruling—the objection being that the assailant did not have an attorney present when he confronted the victim on the street in the custody of the police, moments after the crime.

I say it is the Court's duty to protect legitimate rights, but not to raise unreasonable obstacles to the enforcement of the law.

National Leadership

In my detailed program for *Freedom From Fear,* issued during the primary campaigns last spring, I discussed many facets of what must be done in this critical area of national policy. It is true that law enforcement is primarily a local responsibility—but the public climate with regard to law is a function of national leadership. And so, in this supplemental discussion, I would like to cite just a few things our incoming administration will do to win the war against crime and disorder in America.

First, we will take the following positive, immediate steps by executive order and other appropriate action.

We will establish a cabinet-level council, the National Law Enforcement Council, to coordinate federal policy on the control and prevention of crime.

We will establish a National Academy of Law Enforcement which would make available to local law enforcement agencies training in the most sophisticated, modern methods as well as information about the social sciences and about community relations for adaptation to local conditions and local situations.

We will promote a series of nation-wide town-hall conferences on crime prevention and control.

We will establish a National Coordinating Center to marshal the efforts of independent groups and institutions.

Council on Law Enforcement

At the present time, as you all know, there are Presidential, cabinet level councils developing and coordinating policy with regard to national security, to economics, and space. But we have no such high-level coordination on our number one national problem today—the control of crime and violence in America. This is why I shall establish such a Council on Law Enforcement, similar to the National Security Council and the Council of Economic Advisors.

In establishing a National Academy of Law Enforcement, we will aim to upgrade and professionalize those who are waging the war against crime.

This would enable our law enforcement agencies to be fully equipped intellectually for the complex tasks they face in our modern world. They would not in any sense be a federal police force. We want no federal police force. But they would have the best training we can provide. And as our local and state law enforcement agencies become more fully professional, they will receive to a fuller degree the respect they deserve. Problems of recruitment will be lessened. Careers in law enforcement will be enhanced. These men will be proud of their profession and the people will be proud of their policemen. In 1968 America cannot settle for less.

Civic Involvement

By philosophy and by ingrained habit the present Administration has neglected to provide the potential of independent sources of energy and creativity in America—civic groups, churches, educational institutions, the mass media, business and industry. Their resources and their skills can make a major contribution to the recovery of order in this country.

Think for a moment of narcotics addiction. Think what progress could be made if the resources of these groups could be brought to bear in a massive educational effort, directed especially at the young and the innocent.

All across the country people are waiting—waiting not for dictation but for guidance. What our independent groups basically need is information—information about what is needed, about what can be done, about what has worked in some other community.

Through the nation-wide town meetings which I will propose, and through the National Coordinating Center which I will establish, we will begin at long last to bring all the energies of our people to bear. The Coordinating Center will be a clearing-house of information, an avenue to effective citizen participation. It will bring together civic groups and law enforcement officials. It will make available the best ideas and help to locate funds. It will be one important way in which government can help to release the creative energies of the American people on this great problem.

Prevention Instead of Permissiveness

Other measures, equally necessary, will require a sustained effort over

159

a long period of time. In this sustained effort we must enlist the entire community, not just the federal government. We do not need mammoth federal grant after mammoth federal grant—what we need is a comprehensive American commitment.

Such a commitment could achieve magnificent results in what is the most basic approach to the problem of crime: prevention.

Our prisons cry out for reform. This is one reason why 60 per cent of all adults discharged from our prisons are back within five years. We must stop this revolving door. Through economic incentives we must develop job training inside the prisons. And we will encourage enlightened methods of rehabilitation, such as half-way houses and work-release time.

And there are many other ways an active and concerned administration will wage the war against crime. Prompt justice is a more effective deterrent than justice delayed; we should accept the recommendations of the American Bar Association for overcoming the delays in our judicial process.

We must block the importation of narcotics into this country. It's a Federal responsibility to do so.

And above all, we must adjust our approach to the needs of the people, remembering that the needs of one community may not be the needs of another.

Social Conditions

Now, finally, I would like to make one important point very clear: We all know that social conditions contribute to disorder and crime. They contribute not only among the poor, but among the alienated as well—among all who feel that they have been cut off from full participation in our American society. For too long we have had government by Big Brother, rather than through the full participation of the people. For too many, in the suburbs as well as in the slums, the American dream has not really been fulfilled. And therefore we must move, as we will move, to bring these people—all of our people within our system—as full participants not only to reduce disorder, but because this is the right thing to do.

160

I would like to make one more point. I think it is the most important point of all.

I know that we need better leadership; I know that we need better law enforcement and more and better trained policemen, better courts, better methods. I commend the Congress for the action it has taken on gun control. But in the end there is a limit to what these things can accomplish.

They are, after all, the tools of order. They are not the sources of order. The law on the books cannot replace the law in the heart.

The American Dream

The sources of moral and civic order are in the family, the church, the school and the community. Have these—let us ask ourselves—have these been doing the best they can to preserve the old and valued standards in this nation? I don't think so.

If violence is met with indifference or appeasement, if the individual is no longer responsible for his actions, if a fog of permissiveness blurs our moral vision, if there has been an erosion of respect and decency, if there is too little concern about the social causes of disorder—then fundamental sources of order bear some of the responsibility.

And so I say—

In every family let us renew our commitment to the traditional American standards.

On every campus, let our college faculties and administrators and students say that the spirit of learning—not the spirit of vandalism—shall prevail.

And let our churches remember their ancient truths about the human heart, and their time-tested standards of moral conduct.

For only if we do these things will we have order and justice in America.

Mutual Broadcasting System
September 29, 1968

UNMET NEEDS AND AMERICA'S OPPORTUNITIES

TODAY'S YOUTH: THE GREAT GENERATION

You can learn a great deal, campaigning for President, if you'll just stop to look and listen.

This is especially true when it comes to understanding what is on the minds of young people.

I have had the chance to sit down and have deep discussions with student leaders; to study suggestions by young people in thoughtful letters and memos; and I have been on the receiving end of some pointed messages on signs carried by young people at our rallies.

One of those signs especially caught my eye. It was at a rally in front of a high school at Burbank, California. It read: "Talk With Us, Not At Us."

There are two major parts to this Presidential Campaign. One deals specifically with the issues of today, highlights the many failures of the policies of the past eight years and offers the voters a clear-cut choice.

The other part of the campaign—the one you hear less about—is just as important; it is the effort to unite, to redirect, and ultimately to lead the United States. Philosophy of government and the sweep of history are at stake in this longer-range campaign: it is concerned with tomorrow, and for that reason it should be especially relevant to our young people today.

This part of the campaign began some months ago with my discussion of the reasons for alienation, the sense of not belonging, as I called for an expanded democracy; it was developed further in a radio talk about my activist concept of the office of the Presidency, as a place for moral leadership. At colonial Williamsburg, I spoke of the yearning of the American spirit to recapture personal freedom. And recently I spoke of more specific ways that freedom could be gained through an enlistment of the powers of the voluntary sector.

Tonight let me discuss with you how our present leadership has failed Young America, and how new leadership can bridge and help to close the gap between the generations.

Too many of us get our impression of American youth from the yippies and the hecklers and the hotheads. These young radicals are no more than a tiny percentage of American youth today. Yes, they must be dealt with and not frozen out; but the vast majority of Americans in their teens and early twenties are accessible to understanding.

However, a great many of these young people are restive and disappointed. Many feel alienated. Not a few refuse to identify themselves with a society they believe is immoral and unjust.

We can begin by admitting that too many of our finest young people feel overpowered, over-patronized, and over-protected.

Overpowered in this way: they feel little or no participation in the decisions that affect their lives. Too often, they feel, government tells them what to do, the schools tell them how to do it, and their parents tell them what not to do. No wonder so many feel powerless and frustrated.

Over-patronized, I say, in this way: far too few of us really listen to what young people are saying. We defend their right to speak up and to dissent, we smile self-righteously at our own tolerance, and then we pay no attention to their message.

Overprotected, they also feel, in this way: the old leadership has offered no challenge, no cause to inspire young people to take as their own.

Understandably, an older generation tries to shield youth from repeating its own mistakes; we don't want youth to suffer the hardship we had to suffer. Sometimes we overreact by sheltering and coddling; some young people come away feeling that the world owes them a living.

What we really owe everyone is a hearing. So let's see how we can come to grips with the first problem—of overpowering our youth.

In high school and college students elect leaders of student organizations. Too often, these student leaders have no real weight with school administrators; students aren't fooled by mere trappings of democracy that have no substance.

We have to level with students. They are entitled to a voice in school affairs, not control of school affairs; they have a right to take part, not a right to take over.

More school administrators have to wake up to the healthy new needs of

166

student participation, and incorporate that activity into the learning process. Unless effective student leadership can be exercised by elected student officials, the leadership will be seized by a noisy and unrepresentative minority.

State government also has a role in giving all young people—students and young workers alike—more of a voice in their own affairs. The states decide on voting age; I believe that all the states should carefully consider giving 18-year-olds the right to vote.

The reason the voting age should be lowered is not that 18-year-olds are old enough to fight—it is because they are smart enough to vote. They are more socially conscious, more politically aware, and much better educated than their parents were at age 18. Youth today is just not as young as it used to be.

This watershed political year of 1968 has shown us that young people need not be of voting age to have a real impact. In a sense, a young person can vote now with his enthusiasm and his political work. In my own campaign, the support of youth has added a tone and a life of immense value.

The Federal government, too, has an opportunity to serve youth; the greatest uncertainty of every young person is the possibility of being drafted. After Vietnam, I believe we should move toward improving the pay and other benefits of the armed forces and making military service entirely voluntary. I will discuss this in detail on radio tomorrow night.

There is a second wedge being driven between the generations, widening the gap: that is overpatronizing.

Some of this is unintentional. Many members of the middle young, aged 12 to 18, resent being called "teenagers" by older people. They react the same way as someone in his thirties or forties when he is called "middle aged."

By overpatronizing, I don't mean the boys-will-be-boys condescension of the past, bad as that was. I mean the cold, smug, dangerous patronizing of today. On one extreme, it dismisses dissent by its refusal to pay attention; on the other extreme, it caves into disruption with a smothering permissiveness.

Youth today has a right to demand that an older generation live up to two responsibilities: to guide and to listen.

We fail our youth when we let a university be shut down; we fail our youth when we permit a peaceful dissenter to be shut up; we fail our youth when we permit wonderment and impulsiveness to be shut out.

There are students today who think the way to make a mark in life is to scrawl a slogan on a wall; we have a responsibility to guide their passion into positive channels.

We must listen to the voices of dissent, sometimes strident, sometimes cool, because the protestor may have something to say worth listening to.

We must firmly guide the anarchists away from disruption. Not because we get any satisfaction out of repression, but because free inquiry can only exist in the framework of order.

But if we dismiss dissent as coming from "rebels without a cause", we will soon find ourselves becoming leaders without an effect.

We must replace patronizing with respect. There will be more respect for law when young people know that justice is not limited to those who are respectable. We will see youth respect its elders when we show some respect for the opinions of our youngsters.

A third problem is caused by overprotection. This is a kind of put-down by pacification.

The most important message I receive from young people today is this: "Don't try to hand us our lives on a silver platter. Don't prepackage our futures. Don't try to play God by making us over in your own image."

Young people today, more than ever before, need a challenge. If an established order cannot provide a worthy challenge, the established order itself becomes the challenge. That is what the old leadership has permitted to happen today. That is what we must change.

The old leadership has provided many of our young people with a fine array of issues to be against; an unending war and the draft; over-centralization of government and impairment of personal freedom; a value system that seems to count the individual merely as a cog in a machine.

Our future leadership must provide our young people with a cause to be for; a commitment to the right to be unique; a dedication to social responsibility on a person-to-person basis.

168

We are not talking here about a way to work off youthful enthusiasm; we are talking about a way to work in a sense of idealism and meaning that will grow throughout a person's life.

Let me be specific.

There are 7 million college students today. The universities they attend are often close to, and sometimes contribute to, urban problems. We have seen how government can make use of academic facilities as "think tanks" to move in on difficult projects. Every university must become a "think tank" for its local community.

In that way students will add realism to their education, as they bring needed services to their communities. A sociology student should have the chance to relate his work to the real problems within walking distance; a science student should be able to take advantage of extracurricular work with an anti-pollution unit; a mathematician into traffic control computers.

Some of this is well under way in pioneering colleges across the country; but now it should become a way of college life. I would hope to see colleges give recognition to students who devote time helping to solve urban problems.

This summer in New York 6,000 students participated in Mayor John Lindsay's Urban Corps, a summer intern program through which the city government and students work together to solve the problems created by poverty.

In Philadelphia about 800 University of Pennsylvania students are working in the ghettos through a variety of voluntary agencies.

Governor Dan Evans' program in the State of Washington, called "Action for Washington," has attracted many young people who are working with the problems of the cities and tutoring slum children. Students across the country —in Los Angeles, Vassar, at Michigan State University and many other places—are involved in similar programs.

Five hundred George Washington University undergraduates are tutoring prisoners, psychiatric patients, and slum children in the city of Washington, D.C. They are helping with recreational programs for retarded children and assisting teachers in music, art, and dancing classes. American University has a similar program in the same city.

More young people are applying for the Vista program every day.

Here are ways of preventing a generation gap of tomorrow.

All across the nation, the Federal government, working with the states, could encourage and help to finance training seminars for college students— and high school seniors as well—to teach them how to teach young children to better their reading and writing skills, as they work under local school teachers to open doors to learning for the disadvantaged.

The young people dealing with children in this way will experience all the frustrations and anxieties of every elder dealing with a member of a younger generation. When a youth encounters a child who doesn't trust anybody over 10-years-old, he will find it both infuriating and uplifting; this kind of service will then contribute toward an understanding of the sources of tension between himself and his older generation.

I have met with members of our student coalition, who are at work now to chart this type of activity in the next Adminstration. The idea of bringing the resources of youthful energy to bear on urban problems is beginning to take root; what is needed now is a national commitment to provide incentive and financing to the great challenge facing this generation of Americans.

Let me sketch the kind of program that the Federal government can and should undertake in its commitment to Young America:

I propose to establish a Youth Service Agency as an independent agency within the Federal government. It would have the mission of bringing together the separate and often duplicating functions dealing with the problems of youth that are now scattered all across the Federal system.

I am well aware that setting up a new agency is all too often an excuse for empire building within the Federal bureaucracy.

In the case of the Youth Service Agency, however, the result will be to focus what is now diffused; to change what is now a lick and a promise by many agencies to genuine performance by one. The goal is not to separate youth; the goal is to bring young people into the decision-making process.

This will be an agency pledged to marshaling the energies of youth to do much for themselves and for others; the byword will be challenge, not handout.

The new Youth Service Agency would encompass these functions:

1. An Open Channel Section, to establish effective two-way communication with organized youth groups, such as student associations, the 4-H Clubs, Jaycees, Boy and Girl Scouts, Future Farmers, YMCA and YMHA groups, the Young Republicans and Young Democrats, ghetto youth (through the Urban Service Corps and similar organizations), and alienated and rebellious groups and individuals as well.

2. A Sports and Fitness Section. The United States is one of the very few major nations without an emphasis on youth and sports. I am speaking here about general physical fitness programs for all young people, not only the gifted few. More than half our young people are rejected by the armed services for physical and mental reasons; right now, a half dozen Federal agencies are conducting research on physical fitness. This could be better handled in one place.

3. A World Youth Activity Section. The youth leaders of foreign nations today will be the national leaders tomorrow; Communist nations wisely cultivate this area and we do not. At World Youth Festivals and sports events the U.S. should be well represented. Support should be openly solicited from private groups, coordinated by this agency; our goals should be full disclosure and full participation. I would include in this agency's charter student exchange programs and other international youth programs now scattered throughout the government.

4. The young people's ombudsman. There should be a single section, staffed by young people well versed in government operations, where youth can turn for cooperation all through the Federal government. The departments of Defense, of HEW, of Agriculture, for example, have enormous influence on the future of young people in America; here too an ombudsman would provide a perceptive entry point for the views of youth and act as a champion and an advocate of complaints and new ideas.

This by no means fully covers the next Administration's commitment to youth: other fields such as education have been and will be discussed in later broadcasts.

But these ideas give some indication of the importance my Administration

171

will be determined to attach to the legitimate demands of young people of America.

In the long perspective of history, one of the most crucial failures of the past Administration has been the breakdown in communications with the younger generation.

By its neglect, by its insensitivity, by its arrogance, our present leadership has caused an unprecedented chasm to develop in our society.

This is not merely a generation gap; not a slight lake of comprehension between the hip and the square; this is a yawning gulf of irritated boredom between the two halves of our body politic.

It is not for us to be patient with young people, waiting for them to grow out of their exuberance and settle down; it is for us to ally ourselves with their impatience, helping them to build the kind of world they want to live in.

We do not pretend to have all the answers, but we are listening to young people, gathering all the questions.

We will develop new ways to challenge the freshly forming minds of children; we will develop new ways to challenge the questioning minds of the "Middle Young" in their teens, and we will develop new ways to challenge the creative energies of the young adults in their early twenties.

These new ways will not be dictated by older Americans; they will be worked out with the young Americans.

I believe in youth; that is another way of saying I believe in America's future. The next Administration will be a young Administration, youthful in staff and young in spirit.

I have seen what young men and women can do in this campaign, when they are given roles of great responsiblity they come through. The problems don't wear them down; they wear down the problems.

That is the spirit we need for tomorrow.

To all my fellow Americans I say: there is a new road ahead, a road wide enough for Americans of every age and color and creed to stride ahead together.

And to the young people of America, I say: that new and relevant road is your road. You will be part of the new leadership. The challenge of change is your challenge, because this land is your land.

What you do for your fellow man is the measure of what you do for yourselves. And as you accept that responsibility, the days of your years will not be labeled the "lost" Generation or the "beat" Generation of the "now" Generation.

If you choose to make it so, yours will be the Great Generation.

The times call out for the Great Generation, generous of heart, questing of mind, committed of spirit, to lift this world into the next millennium.

NBC Radio Network
Wednesday, October 16, 1968

THE ELDERLY: FOR THE ENDURING GENERATION

Tonight I want to talk especially to those 20 million Americans who are over 65 years of age — the generation of my parents, my teachers, and others who guided me through the formative years of my life.

The first thing I am going to do is to *nail,* once and for all, one of those false charges that the political opposition has made in an effort to confuse the older generation. I refer to the charge that I am against the provisions of Social Security and Medicare.

Let me make this very clear: I am not only for the benefits of Social Security and Medicare — I want to improve and extend them so that they will cover more people and be more effective for each person who needs them.

Now, why am I so concerned about communicating my support for these programs so clearly? Obviously, one reason is that I want my record to be clearly and honestly presented and understood in this campaign. But there is another very important reason that reaches well beyond Election Day.

I believe and know that a man cannot be a successful President today unless he has the full support and confidence of older Americans. This country cannot be made whole and healthy again unless we take full advantage of your devotion and your talents.

I say this not only because you are numerically significant — though it is true that a full one-tenth of our population is over 65 years of age. But more important than numbers are the qualities which you, as older citizens, can bring to your country's service.

Think for a moment of what your generation has done! Many of you were born in another century. You have brought yourselves, your families, and your country through the most turbulent and challenging period in the history of man. You have fought two world wars and survived the great depression. You have seen mankind enter the Atomic Age.

You have come through all of this with flags flying. Again and again the familiar ways of life have been uprooted. But you have not been alienated or radicalized. You have not "dropped out." You have endured and adjusted. And you have prevailed.

The qualities which you forged under these pressures and challenges are qualities which America needs more than ever right now: qualities such as perspective and judgment, wisdom and patience, a sense of history and a sense of direction. You can do a great deal to help America renew its faith in the future, for you have seen what this country has accomplished in the past. And you can help restore respect for those enduring values which have brought us through past trials.

For all of these reasons, I say with special emphasis to all older Americans tonight: you must not believe that your service to your country has been completed. For there can never be any retirement from the responsibilities of citizenship.

Now let's look at another side of this matter. We cannot reasonably ask any group of Americans to play a more meaningful role in our national life if we deny them the dignity, the security, and the respect they deserve. For too many older Americans, that too often has been the case. Too many politicians have misled the elderly with lavish promises or patronized them with caretaker attitudes. Too few have addressed themselves to the real problems of the aging.

I want to take up a few of those problems right now. And I want to begin by discussing the rising cost of living — for no group in our society is hurt more by rising costs than those over 65.

For years you have been putting money into savings accounts and pension plans and Social Security. Now that you want to draw it out you find that it is worth only a part of its original value. The rest of its worth has been stolen away — and the thief is rising prices. If you put away $100 25 years ago, for example, today it is worth only $50.

Since President Eisenhower left office, prices have gone up 17 percent; they have gone up 10 percent in just the last three years. And the problem is getting worse instead of better.

No wonder so many older Americans are in a financial pinch.

The only way to stop these rising costs is to end the irresponsible and inflationary spending policies of the present Administration. There is no way to get around that basic point. That is why I am so disturbed by the reckless

175

and rather desperate spending promises of my opponent — particularly his statement that he would increase Social Security across the board by 50 percent. He knows very well that this promise cannot be carried out in the near future. It would cost at least $15 billion a year more than present expenditures and would add significantly to inflationary pressures and soaring prices. Thus it would hurt most those older citizens it is supposed to help.

All of this Mr. Humphrey does not tell us. He dangles what appears to be a generous promise before the aging. But it is a deceptive promise; and that makes it particularly dangerous and cruel.

On the other hand, speaking realistically, how can we deal effectively with the financial problems of older Americans? First, of course, we can bring prices into line by bringing responsible fiscal management to Washington.

In addition I have proposed and I urge an automatic cost of living increase in Social Security and Railroad Retirement benefits; so that when prices go up benefits go up automatically. Some of us have been pushing this for quite a while but the present Administration has actually opposed it and kept it from becoming law.

I have urged other workable improvements in Social Security. For example: an increase in widow's benefits; new permission for those who work past age 65 to build their benefits to higher levels; gradual extension of Social Security to cover all older citizens; and a relaxation of the existing limits on how much Social Security recipients can earn.

In these and other ways we can help to improve the financial picture among older Americans. It is a picture which badly needs improving. It is simply unacceptable in America that a large segment of older Americans have incomes below the poverty line. It is unacceptable that the aged should be the one group in the country where poverty is increasing today.

All of this is evidence that a new and appalling kind of "generation gap" may be growing in America, a gap which separates the affluent young from the dependent old.

This is a danger we simply cannot abide — yet little has been done to turn back that threat during the tenure of the present Administration. I can promise you that the Nixon Administration will change this picture, that we will give priority attention to the problems of poverty among the aging, and that we will do everything we can to generate solutions which are thoughtful, workable, and effective.

Another critical aspect of this whole question is medical care. It is an unhappy fact that Americans over 65 get less adequate medical care than younger Americans, even though they are sick more often. And illness is still a major economic burden for older people, as many of you know only too well. "Wasn't Medicare supposed to take care of all this?" many are asking. "What's gone wrong?" they inquire.

The answer is that Medicare simply has not worked as effectively as it ought to be working. Often it does not *get* to the people who need it most; delays in payment often seem endless; the program is badly tangled in red tape. That is why I propose to make Medicare work better by simplifying the program and by improving its efficiency. In addition I have proposed a 100 per cent income tax deducton for drug and medical expenses which older people still have to pay for out of their own pockets.

It is not enough simply to help older Americans pay for medical care if they can't get adequate treatment.

Did you know that there were ten times as many hospital visits in the United States last year as there were just ten years ago? Needless to say, the supply of doctors and nurses and orderlies, rooms and buildings and equipment just hasn't kept up with that soaring demand. And the sad result too often is a decline in the quality of medical care.

Today we are short some 50,000 doctors, 85,000 nurses, and 200,000 other hospital and nursing home technical employees. The number of hospitals and nursing homes is sadly inadequate, and so is the way many of them are equipped.

As President, I would take immediate steps to meet these shortages, to improve the quality and quantity of medical education, to encourage the development and application of new medical and paramedical techniques. When the health of our people is in question, second best isn't good enough.

Financial and medical problems are not the only difficulties which older people face. I believe that we have paid too little attention to other non-material problems of the elderly — problems such as loneliness, idleness, and a feeling of estrangement.

When leisure time becomes a curse for the aging instead of a blessing, and when the phrase "retirement will kill him" is heard every day, then I say it is time for a basic change in attitude and in approach.

I believe that a special White House Conference on the Problems of Older Americans can help us develop the specifics of such an approach. I support such a conference as a way of bringing together the most creative new thinking from specialists in gerontology, geriatrics, and all the related fields of study. It can be a tremendously informative and useful experience — as was the last such conference held under the leadership of President Eisenhower. In addition I will appoint a special White House assistant on the aging to keep me informed of new ideas and in touch with the many councils and organizations devoted to the cause of the elderly.

This approach will help find new ways of encouraging older citizens to remain active in income-producing occupations or in the voluntary activities of your communities. I believe that job placement services, education and training programs, and various government service corps can do a much better job than they have been doing of involving older people. And those are just a few of the possibilities.

An increased sense of utility and participation can make a vital difference in the lives of older Americans. As Oliver Wendell Holmes said at the age of 90: "The work is never done while the power to work remains. For to live is to function — that is all there is to living."

And the activity of older Americans can be of utmost importance to the country. President Eisenhower put it this way: "Our nation must learn to take advantage of the full potential of our older citizens, their skills, their wisdom, and their experience. We need these traits fully as much as we need the energy and boldness of youth."

Perhaps it is because I have looked *up* to the older generation for so long that I simply cannot accept the idea that the government must now become a custodian or a caretaker for them — or that older citizens should be treated as mere wards of the state. I prefer to see the government — through strengthened Social Security and strengthened Medicare and through other strong programs — entering into a creative partnership with the aging, helping and encouraging them so that they can make the maximum social contribution of which they are capable.

If you, as older Americans, will do that, then all of your countrymen will be the beneficiaries. And you, in turn, will retain the independence, the dignity, and the sense of usefulness that your generation deserves.

For my part I will make this pledge. I will never promise what I cannot deliver. I will level with you, and I will be direct with you. And I will do everything in my power to achieve the goals we have discussed.

Our nation faces many troubles today. But we have known troubles before, and we have survived them all. Often we have emerged stronger for having fought the battle. As I speak to you tonight, I am confident that with your participation and your hard work — in the party of your choice, in the problems of your community, in the programs of your church — the America of which you are so proud will find her way again.

I know that is your prayer. I hope you know that it is mine.

CBS Radio Network
Tuesday, October 22, 1968

EDUCATION FOR EXCELLENCE,
FREEDOM AND DIVERSITY

From among his many achievements Thomas Jefferson toward the close of his life personally selected two he wanted most to be remembered by. He did not select his service as George Washington's Secretary of State — not the monumental fact that he had doubled our nation's area with the Louisiana Purchase — not even that he had served as the third President of the United States.

No, he wanted to be remembered as the author of the Declaration of Independence and as founder of the University of Virginia.

Jefferson knew that the destiny of America was inseparable from education — that in the fulfillment of the promise of this new nation education would be the key.

We have tried hard to hold to Jefferson's ideal. We have seen our schools and colleges flourish and grow, ever enriching our heritage.

Now almost two centuries after Jefferson we also know a sterner truth. The philosopher and educator, Alfred North Whitehead, warned: "In the conditions of modern life the rule is absolute: the race which does not value trained intelligence is doomed." So education, long the key to opportunty and fulfillment, is today also the key to survival.

So I pledge my Administration to be second to none in its concern for education. I pledge it because we will be second to none in our concern for America.

As we move together into the 1970's, we will have to be bold. We must ask again the fundamental questions, for we are entering a new age — a time of tension and danger, but a time of exciting opportunity as well. Like Thomas Jefferson we in our time must have the courage to be founders, to devise new answers. And so let us ask ourselves:

- How we can devise more equitable methods of school support to overcome imbalances among school districts, particularly in urban areas.

- How our basic subjects, the intellectual tools of our civilization, can be better taught.

- How we can encourage the growth of variety and flexibility, even as our society grows more complex, for diversity is inseparable from freedom itself.

- How our schools can be brought closer to the people of our communities and how much they can better serve the community at every level.

- How vocational education can be rejuvenated by making it relevant to the jobs not only of today, but of five and ten years from now.

- How we can make the training of our teachers commensurate with the demands of the space age, and how we can provide more incentive and greater professional recognition for our teachers.

- What role the miracles of technology can play in the schools of tomorrow.

- And how we can best preserve the traditions of our civilization, and whether, too often, we have not allowed inspiration and excitement to disappear from the classroom.

These are some of the urgent questions we all must answer — first as citizens, then as leaders of government. For at every level of government — local, state, and Federal — elected and appointed officials have the duty to listen before they have the right to lead. They do not own the public schools. These schools belong to the people who paid to build them and who pay to support them. And I believe that government has not been listening well enough lately.

We all know, too, that those listen best who are closest to the people, part of the community the school serves. They cannot be deceived in the long run, for they know better than anyone in Washington what is best for their children.

The needs of school children in a small New England town must not be presumed to be the same as those of children in downtown Detroit; and the needs of both may differ from those of a child in suburban Los Angeles or in rural Tennessee. We want no rigid blueprints or inflexible guidelines.

I saw a recent study of the ten best high schools in America; and while each had an outstanding record in preparing its students for college, each had an approach, a technique, an attitude of its own. These are qualities to be guarded and cherished, or else in time we will become deadened by conformity and will lose the creativity and innovative abilities that are the key to our future progress.

So where education is concerned, I deeply believe it is vitally important that local school boards and local and state government have the primary responsibility and the primary right to dispense funds. I will press, therefore, for a federal program to turn back to state and local control, through the bloc grants such funds as are urgently required to upgrade their educational performance. Bloc grants, administered at the state and local levels, provide greater flexibility than any other form of assistance. What our communities want from Washington is not dictation but constructive counsel and sorely needed assistance.

One of the great issues of the 1970's will be to determine the distinctive role of each level of government in the enterprise of education. I believe that our philosophy of encouraging the maximum local control and local participation will provide the answers the times demand.

I consider education a Federal concern, a state responsibility, and a local function.

The Federal government with its ability to raise funds on a national basis should aim at reducing the discrepancies among the various states in their resources for the support of education. State government must bear the legal responsibility of setting standards for attendance, teacher certification, per pupil expenditure, and the development of long range plans. Local school systems should be responsible for developing specific projects and programs, and they should be permitted maximum flexibility, subject only to the broadest of policy definitions.

I believe that on state and local levels many moves should be made as matters of the highest priority as we move into the 1970's.

First of all, serious imbalances exist in the financial support available to many of our school districts. In many states the system of support for schools needs drastic revision. School districts often have developed haphazardly. Some are residential, others possess industry or commercial enterprises, still others are in poverty areas. Many are in transition from one phase to another. As a result, the tax base differs from district to district, and many schools suffer from undersupport. But it is plainly wrong for the funds available to any school to remain indefinitely below an acceptable minimum. It is imperative that our state governments take the initiative here.

One of the most disturbing features of urban educaton today is the tense atmosphere of alienation and mistrust which prevails in some neighborhoods among students, parents, and teachers. We will overcome this when we are able in a variety of ways to bring the schools closer to the people, to bring them into the community. There is no reason why, within broad limits, curricula cannot be tailored to the needs of different groups. Spanish history and culture, for example, could be given more emphasis in one school, and African studies in another. Members of the community could play an important part in the daily program — for example, as teaching assistants.

Buildings, books, administrative structures — all these are important. But everyone knows that the key to learning is the gifted teacher. We must make a serious and comprehensive effort to rejuvenate the teaching profession at the elementary and secondary levels. Too often the gifted teacher, the man or woman of talent and experience, is numbed by routine and stifled by red tape; too often, the incentive to excellence succumbs to a system which fails to distinguish and reward superior performance. We should explore ways of restructuring the teaching profession, and of creating different categories, with different functions and rewards, corresponding to ability and performance. We must also level with ourselves all across this country about teachers' salaries. We tend to fancy that we have done very well in providing for these men and women whose role in our society is so crucially important. Yet one teacher I know in an eastern school still receives only $5,400 a year even though she has taught elementary pupils for 30 years. I say this is wrong for America and a reflection on our sense of values. For too long we have riveted our attention on the needs of higher education. Important these still are, but we must now turn more attention to the quality, effectiveness, and requirements of classroom teachers from kindergarten through the twelfth grade.

Sub-professional personnel, volunteers from the community or salaried individuals, can relieve the professional staff from many of its non-teaching burdens. Many of our future teachers might well be recruited from this group. A junior or apprentice level might assume some teaching duties, but also assist in the performance of routine house-keeping tasks now occupying the teacher. Intermediate ranks would have increasingly advanced classroom responsibilities. Individuals of outstanding experience and ability, who continued to pursue their professional studies and contribute to their fields, would be recognized as master teachers. They would divide their time between the classroom and exploratory work in improving the curriculum and in seeking new and more effective ways of teaching.

The professional teacher should not advance by seniority alone. Imagination, ability, artistry, and achievement deserve to be recognized as we move into the 1970's. We cannot do without this great potential. We must emancipate and honor the great leaders.

It is also essential that our universities take more seriously their obligations in the area of teacher education. Our goal must be to produce teaching scholars and not educational technicians.

Today we are on the threshold of a vast breakthrough, in part brought about by technological advance. Revolutionary possibilities are opening to us. Both elementary and secondary education will increasingly become the province of the highly trained men and women who will be at once scientists and artists. The training of such teachers will be as serious and exacting an enterprise as the training of a nuclear physicist or a heart surgeon. The education of our teachers deserves equal emphasis with other disciplines within the university structure.

We must also take a searching look at our methods of vocational education. Too often such training is geared to jobs which are obsolescent or in short supply. Too often the student loses interest, for he sees, correctly, that there is little or no connection between what he is learning and the realities of the job market. He might well doubt, for example, that there is much point in learning to operate the lathe or the drill press of five years ago, when, increasingly, this function is performed by automated, computerized equipment.

Here private industry and business can play a genuinely creative role. I would urge the leaders of state governments to call for the formation of task forces composed of knowledgeable citizens in business and industry and from the academy. They would ascertain what the job market is likely to be five or ten years hence. Then with the aid of tax incentives business and industry in each state could cooperate with the schools in preparing our young men and women for the real jobs which will await them. As the student moves through his vocational schooling, he should spend some of his time on the actual job for which he is being trained. This connection between training and opportunity would be vivid and concrete.

In vocational education our goal must be a flexible system of training and part-time work experience. Each year it can enable millions of young people with varying abilities, inclinations, and habits to make an effective transition from full-time schooling to full-time productive employment.

And we must get over the idea that vocational and mechanical training is less important than other kinds of education. A skilled worker in industry, a trained technician or machinist, is every bit as important as an office worker; and America cannot survive without them.

Increasing numbers of jobs in our economy require training and education beyond that available in most secondary schools, yet do not demand a college or professional degree. To meet this expanding demand for skilled technicians and semi-professional workers, and to offer the high school graduate a choice other than ending his formal education or pursuing a four-year program, I will press for the expansion and strengthening of two-year technical institutes and community college programs.

As we move into the 1970's, local and community colleges and so-called educational parks will play a more important role. Pioneer educational parks at the secondary school level are already being developed in several states. They consist of a number of schools built in a single park-like setting. They are able to offer a range of possibilities and a degree of flexibility that only a large facility can provide, and they provide ways of economizing through the sharing of such facilities as computers, data banks, and advanced laboratories.

We all recognize how much there is to be done in education on state and local levels. But the individual has an important part to play, too, perhaps the most important part of all. The community must be involved with its schools. Parents must make it their business to find out what their children are learning and ask themselves whether or not the curriculum in their own local schools can be greatly improved. Do the children seem pleased with school? Are they excited by the things learned that day? If not, the chances are it is not because they are lazy and apathetic by nature.

So take an interest in the classroom. After all, it is your school. Are the children learning things that not only interest them, but also are relevant to our history and our civilization? If not, no wonder they learn grudgingly. It is up to you to make it clear to your school board that a good book costs no more than a dull one. It is up to our local communities in all their diversity and with their differing needs and interests to see that education is a living and relevant thing, and that it uses the past in ways that enrich the present.

I would add that the communities of America need to stand behind their teachers in the classrooms insofar as discipline is concerned. For too long an undue permissiveness has been either indulged or imposed. It is time to restore teacher authority where it has been allowed to erode, and parents and community leaders must work cooperatively with teachers to that end. This view is not a punitive one toward the students; rather, it is recognition that good education requires an environment of reason and order. I know of one child who failed admission to the college he had his heart set on, simply because of a math deficiency caused by having seven math teachers in one year. One after another they resigned because they were powerless to enforce discipline in the classroom.

But if education is and should remain primarily the responsibility of the state and local community, the federal government still has a vital role.

Let me highlight a few of the more important needs my Administration will fill. We will seek to:

- Create a National Institute for the Educational Future to serve as a clearing house for ideas in elementary and secondary education and explore the revolutionary possibilities that modern science and technology are making available to education.

- Maintain our national commitment to pre-school education, expanding as necessary such programs as Head Start and Follow Through.

- Create a National Teachers Corps which would bring carefully selected colleges and high school students into action as tutors in core-city schools.

- Encourage diversity by urging states to present plans for federal assistance to be distributed by the states to non-public school children and including non-public school representatives in the planning process.

- Help to encourage the growth of our private colleges and universities by allowing tax advantages for donations up to a specified level.

- Propose the formation of community resource units composed of individuals, organizations, and groups within the community who will make their experience available for the encouragement of education.

- Devise new ways by which, through long-term loans, the federal government can further assist students to gain a higher education, and devise ways by which private capital can expand its participation in the support of students who need assistance.

The National Institute for the Educational Future will be a consortium of educators, scientists, social scientists, and technicians. It will also include classroom teachers with practical experience on elementary and secondary levels. It will have a dual function. First, it will serve as a clearing house of ideas, attacking the problems of communication and coordination. Our far-flung communities have too little communication with one another. Information about programs being instituted throughout the country must be centrally available so the experience of one community can guide another. The Institute will make evaluations and offer advice regarding programs which have succeeded or which have failed.

The Institute will have another important function as well. It will take us into the space age in education. We are on the threshold of great changes, many brought about by the possibilities inherent in new technology; and though in the past, advances in technology have tended to mean standardization and the submersion of the individual, the most recent developments and

187

others in the offing promise the opposite. Our schools a generation from now may be very different from those of today. The use of electronics, of television, of computerized knowledge banks promises to allow far greater scope for programs tailored to the individual. Busy work and dead time may be all but eliminated. Through greater efficiency and effectiveness, the rate of learning may increase geometrically. It is possible that students will spend far less time in the classroom and will also spend less time in school. Through what is called programmed learning, they may be able to learn many things more effectively at home. Learning will be brought closer to daily life, rejoined to the community and to the family. We must be ready to use all possibilities our new technology makes available, and this the National Institute for the Educational Future will help us to do.

While planning for future possibilities, we must not neglect the things only recently found effective. We know now that a child can be so far behind by the time he reaches first grade that he has little or no chance of catching up. The battle for the development of the mind of a child can be lost even before he enters kindergarten. A child who has never learned how to learn, who has never mastered the basic reading skills, the basic mathematical premises, the basic ways of looking at the world which are the heart of all formal education is sure to fall further and further behind. The urban crisis in America will never be resolved until the quality of education for all children attains a level commensurate with the demands of life in our complex urban society.

Effective programs already in operation, such as Head Start and Follow Through, will be expanded as the need grows. When research indicates the desirability of new programs in this area, they will receive support from my Administration. All of us need to understand that perhaps our greatest deficiency today is in the teaching of reading. Moreover, despite the current emphasis on pre-school training, some one-third of our schools do not have kindergartens. I keenly feel these shortcomings and hope to play an important part in their correction.

I would emphasize here, before proceeding on with the Federal effort as a whole, that a critical need exists for consolidation and improved coordination throughout the structure. There are some 60 different Federal programs now that impinge upon education. Our educational system, the states, and the tax-paying public are entitled to a major realignment of this over-proliferated effort.

The problems of the disadvantaged child are too often more than educational. His performance may lag because he has health or diet deficiencies, or because of emotional problems brought about by unstable conditions at home. Early education, therefore, should focus on the whole child. It should involve a flexible cooperation and consultation among teachers, health officers, and social workers, with the school providing common facilities and a central coordinating function.

One of the persistent shortcomings of our society is that it provides too few opportunities for the idealism of our young people to express itself. Yet this is a great resource, one which should be turned to constructive rather than disruptive purposes. This is one reason why we should have a Student Teacher Corps of high school and college students: carefully selected, paid volunteers, who would tutor core-city children. They would aid in extended training programs in core-city schools — programs available after school hours and during the summer months. We want no more talk of "long, hot summers." We must plan for summers of productive learning, summers of hope rather than of idleness and destruction. Nor do we want to "make jobs" — we want to build citizens.

One of the most profound challenges of our time is the preservation of diversity, the preservation of freedom itself, in the face of increasing complexity and interdependence. And yet increasing complexity need not mean standardization, if only we make the decision that it must not. The private schools and colleges of America have always been a source of diversity, of possibility, of experimentation. They have long provided the cutting edge of progress, pushing ahead with new ideas and new techniques.

The private schools and colleges have also provided the diversity which is one of America's great strengths. We must also remember that private schools of various kinds are able to draw upon financial resources not available to public institutions — and which would not otherwise be available to education. Yet our private institutions are now experiencing severe financial pressure as the costs of public education increase. In my view it would be a tragedy of the first magnitude if tax-supported state schools were to drive private institutions out of existence.

Without weakening our commitment to public education, my Administration will protect and encourage the private option. The private option should not be available only to the wealthy: that is not the American way. And America is richer for the diversity of those groups which prefer a distinctive schooling.

Therefore, we will urge state-prepared plans for state-administered Federal assistance to non-public school children and will advocate special tax advantages for donations to private colleges and universities.

For more than a generation we have seen the increasing concentration of power in government. I think the decade of the 1970's will see a reversal of this trend. We are entering a period in which the citizen wants more control over his destiny, more participation in his community, and more responsibility for the quality of his life. In no area is this more relevant than in education. With this in mind I will propose the formation of community resources groups, composed of individuals and organizations who want to help the educational program in the schools of their community.

A local lawyer, a man familiar in the community, might talk to a class of teenagers about the laws which affect their personal lives. He could inspire not only respect for the laws, but also an interest in the process by which laws are made. He could lead the students to thoughts about the sources of law.

A local athlete discussing with a high school class the ceremonial games in the land might make the difference between a dull lesson and a real insight into other cultures and other times.

People from all backgrounds — housewives, businessmen, factory workers, professional people, political leaders — could embody for the students new ways of thinking about the world.

A local businessman and a local labor union leader would be an ideal team to bring home to the children a link between what goes on in the world and what goes on in the classroom.

And finally, my Administration will commit itself to the proposition that no young American who is qualified to go to college will be prevented from doing so because he cannot afford it. I will support existing programs which aid needy students, and will call for their expansion when it is indicated. I also believe, however, that the individual who receives higher education has the primary responsibility of paying for it. I will recommend continuance of Federal grants and loans to students who require such assistance. I will also explore ways in which the private sector of the economy can increasingly become a working partner in enabling more students to go on to higher education. One proposal, which will be carefully considered, would permit private capital to provide loans to students, the interest on such loans to be paid by the Federal government. The student would repay the loan when he became a producing, earning citizen.

I know myself what outside aid can mean to a young man about to embark on his career. I know, because without financial aid I would never have had the opportunity to go on to law school, and so my commitment to such programs is more than just a political commitment to education in this country. It is an expression of my own gratitude to those who, without realizing it at the time, helped a boy discover a new world. I intend to make the new Administration one which will not allow men's worlds to remain closed to those who need only money.

These, then, are some of the educational challenges of the 1970's.

But they are more than that. They are challenges issued by a time of revolutionary change to the very essence of America and to the meaning of the American experience.

To be an American means that you can grow up in a remote town or in the midst of poverty and still go to college and make whatever you can of your own gifts and your own dreams.

When I look at American education, I do not see schools, but children, and young men and women — young Americans who deserve the chance to make a life for themselves and ensure the progress of their country.

If we fail in this, no success we have is worth the keeping. But I say to you tonight that we will not fail.

CBS Radio Network
Sunday, October 20, 1968

PROBLEMS OF THE CITIES

If our cities are to be liveable for the next generation, we can delay no longer in launching new approaches to the problems that beset them, and to the tensions that tear them apart.

The present Administration promised a rebirth of America's cities. But despite the billions spent, its promises have not been kept—and many were unkeepable.

We have not seen the rebirth of a single major city. But we have seen proof of the failure of the old ways. These old ways are still the conditioned reflex of those whose policy approaches are rooted in the 1930's—the old ways of massive spending piled on massive spending, and of looking to Washington to solve the problems of every locality. In the ruins of Detroit and Watts and Newark lie the ruins of a philosophy of government that has outlived its origin and no longer speaks to its time.

A city is many things—homes, offices, schools, factories. But basically, the *people* are the city. The problems of America's cities are the problems of its people; the hope of America's cities lies in the spirit of its people.

This has been the missing dimension of the old way—the old way of government charities that feed the stomach and starve the soul; of government programs that keep a dismal cycle of despair and dependency going from generation to generation.

If our cities are to be saved, the people in them have to be saved—and in the long run, the people will save the cities.

Because of massive and mounting Federal deficits, we face today a fiscal crisis; and the plain fact is that the Federal government today does not have the money to do the job in the cities by itself. But this is not cause for despair and not cause for abandoning the task—because most of these tasks can be done *better* through government encouragement of private energies.

When we think of the urban crisis, we think first of the problems of race and poverty—which too often go hand in hand.

To the problems of poverty, many reply—provide government jobs, government housing, government welfare. Government has a role—a vital role. But what Government can do best is to provide the incentives to get *private* resources and energies where the need is. What we need today is not more millions on welfare roles but more millions on payrolls.

Thus, for example, in the area of jobs I have proposed such measures as tax credits for businesses to hire and train the unemployed; a national computer job bank, to bring job-seeking men and man-seeking jobs together; and special tax incentives to businesses that locate branch offices or new plants in poverty areas.

In the ghetto, providing jobs is an essential first step—but this by itself is not enough. Jobs have to be made available within a framework that establishes the pride, the dignity and the independence of the black American as well as the white. We have to lift the ceiling from black aspirations—and essential to this is the encouraging of more black ownership, more black control over the destinies of black people.

If black and white are to be brought together in peace, the light of hope has to be brought to the ghetto. If we are to bring this light of hope to the ghetto, we have to show by example that the American opportunity is neither a black nor a white opportunity, but an equal opportunity—and to make this opportunity real, we have to begin in the ghetto itself, where the people are and where the need is.

To assist in this, we need new incentives to get capital flowing into the ghetto. We need both technical and financial assistance for the starting of new black businesses and the expansion of existing ones. We need new institutions that can be the channels of enterprise.

What we have to do is to get private enterprise into the ghetto, and get the people of the ghetto into private enterprise—not only as workers, but as managers and owners.

To meet the crisis in housing, again we should turn to where the resources are. Private enterprise built the cities of America, and given the necessary incentives, private enterprise can rebuild them. At the same time we must press forward with imaginative new plans for more widespread home ownership—to put this within the reach of all.

There can be no lasting progress in the cities without a massive upgrading of our educational effort; unless our schools keep abreast of change, our people won't. This includes, quite specifically, such programs as Head Start and Follow Through. It includes compensatory and remedial education for those who need it in order to compete on an equal basis. It includes vocational education, keyed to the needs of today's job market—and tomorrow's. Our investment in education is an investment in America's future; none that we make will pay better dividends.

The problems of our cities are, of course, much broader and much more complex than those of jobs or schools, poverty or race. They are problems of human concentration, with all the abrasive frictions that occur when many people of diverse backgrounds occupy a small place. Increasingly, they are problems of the physical environment we all share—congested streets, fouled air and polluted water. And they are problems of the future. When we look toward the year 2000, we see that population of our cities will have doubled; this means we will need as much *new* city by then as we have *old* city today.

That new city will be built, as the old city has been built in America, by Americans acting individually and by Americans acting together. But Government has a role to play in the building of the new city.

That role is primarily to encourage the energies of individuals and the resources of America's private institutions, business and labor, to become involved in the solution of America's social problems—housing, education and jobs. It is to provide leadership—marshalling the ideas, the intelligence, the vision and the will that can get the job done. It is to use tax incentives and credit incentives to bring to bear upon America's unsolved problems the power of individual initiative and of private enterprise. We can build the housing we need for the urban poor, we can clean up the air above our cities and the water around them—if we get into action the engine of private enterprise that already has performed so many miracles to produce America.

With strong local leadership, with earnest and continuing federal cooperation, with a recognition that we have only begun to tap the enormous energies of private enterprise in meeting public problems, we can have a rebirth and renewal of America's cities. We can restore them as safe and pleasant places to live and as what they should be—places that lift the spirit and cap the glory of our civilization.

Submitted to Republican National Convention
Committee on Resolutions
August 1, 1968

THE RESEARCH GAP:
CRISIS IN AMERICAN SCIENCE AND TECHNOLOGY

Most of our attention in October 1968 is focused on the crucial problems of our country that cry out for solution: war, crime, disorder, injustice and a runaway cost-of-living.

But there is another, quieter crisis at hand. It may seem less urgent and it gets fewer headlines, but it poses unparalleled dangers and opportunities.

I refer to the crisis in American science and technology.

The American scientific and technological community plays a key role in maintaining our well-being and our national security. Science and technology compose a new Atlas that upholds our economic growth, our military defense, our educational system, and our bright hopes for the future of man. The role of science and technology is so large, so complex, and so pervasive, that we sometimes merely take it for granted. At other times, we fear it unreasonably, resent its power, ignore its role and deny its great promise for the future.

Science has served mankind faithfully and well. It has dramatically extended the average lifetime, shortened geographical distances, increased industrial productivity, reduced poverty, and in the long trial of war, contributed significantly to the cause of freedom. Since World War II, it has helped build deterrent forces that have prevented another major conflict among the great powers.

New Dawn for Freedom

If science and technology were to founder or stagnate, many of our hopes would collapse. To the extent that we neglect this source of our greatness, and to the extent that we fail to preserve the conditions of openness and order that made our progress possible, we are living off the land of civilization without refertilizing it. We must not let such a negative drift gain momentum.

Instead, we must bring about a new dawn of scientific freedom and

196

progress. As the world's investment in science expands, the impact of technological progress will be more profound. Scientific knowledge doubled between 1750 and 1900; again between 1900 and 1950; yet again between 1950 and 1960. By 1970 it is expected to double again. In twenty years the world may be as enormously different from today as 1968 is different from 1900.

How much this change will benefit mankind will be determined largely by the location of world leadership in science and technology. If the free world maintains scientific superiority, the growth of science will support the growth of economic and political freedom.

We have this advantage: free societies provide a more attractive setting for intellectual activity than do totalitarian societies. Since World War II almost all the movement in the scientific community has been from East to West. A totalitarian lead in research and development is likely only if the U. S. follows short-sighted policies.

Research Gap

Today, the United States is shortchanging its scientific community. We are risking the opening of a research gap between our effort and that of the Soviet Union.

Faced with dynamic possibilities for science, the current Administration is hobbled by the static philosophy that technological potentialities are limited—that we have reached a technological "plateau."

This attitude is particularly perilous in the realm of defense. The belief that a static balance of power can be maintained, based on a common "plateau" of technological achievement, ignores the dynamic and volatile progress of science today, which is incomparably more rapid and variable than ever before.

In few areas of development is activity so intense and productive as in Soviet military research and development. Although lagging for years, the Soviet Union in 1967 was for the first time estimated to be spending more on defense research and development than the U.S. Thanks to rapid scientific and technological advances, Moscow now commands a full panoply of offensive and defensive strategic weapons, including an orbital nuclear delivery capablilty; ever-improving tactical military equipment, communications facilities, surface navel and merchant vessels; and a large number of nuclear powered, swift and quiet submarines. Together, these advances could — if we stand still — ultimately make the Soviet Union militarily dominant.

The real danger, however, does not stem from existing weapons, but from possible breakthroughs by the huge Soviet research and development establishment. The United States can afford to be selective in our own weapons only if we are resolute in maintaining a comprehensive lead in research and development. Recent events have already put our lead in jeopardy.

Cutback in Development and Education

Soviet scientists have taken a bold new stride in their drive toward a landing on the moon while American scientists have been confronted with short-sighted cutback not only in the space program, but also in over-all American research and development efforts. James Webb, Director of the National Aeronautics and Space Administration, resigned with the prediction that the Soviet Union might soon surpass the United States in space; one week later came the new Soviet moon probe, which Mr. Webb said "shows a capability that could change the basic structure and balance of power in the world."

These events culminate an ominous period in U.S. research and development. While the Soviet Union continues to graduate twice as many scientists annually as the United States, the American scientific community is demoralized by the present Administration's wavering attitude toward research and development.

During the Eisenhower Administration, funds for research and development grew by an average of about 15 per cent annually. By the end of the present Administration, while world scientific knowledge continues to grow at a rate of over ten per cent annually, inflation, spurious economy moves

198

and basic policy miscalculations are effectively reducing U.S. research funds every year.

The sudden decline in the Federal commitment over the last four years coincided with a 20 per cent increase in the number of U.S. scientists. These new men of science, often trained through the Eisenhower Administration's National Defense Education Act, thus faced a contraction of opportunity in the research and development field. Some of them are now turning to other fields.

Scientific activity cannot be turned on and off like a faucet. The withdrawal of support disperses highly trained research teams, closes vital facilities, loses spinoff benefits, and disrupts development momentum. The current Administration has even struck at the lifeline of our future progress —science education. NASA, for example, has cut its graduate student grants from 1300 to 50. The Defense Department cut aid to colleges by $30 million; the National Science Foundation budget was decreased by one-fifth; and the National Institute of Health funds were reduced by an estimated 25 per cent. Especially hard-hit in the reductions is aid for post-doctoral students, who serve as graduate student instructors. The decline of science education is the most damaging indictment of present Administration policy; it threatens to cripple the national effort in science for years to come.

Apart from scientific manpower, fund reductions are idling masses of equipment purchased at great cost in previous years. In the name of economy, the current Administration cut into muscle.

The United States must end this depreciation of research and development in its order of national priorities.

New Emphasis on Peaceful Uses

The importance of new emphasis on research and development in defense needs no further elaboration. The needs and possibilities in the civilian realm, however, are less well recognized. Our future economic growth and competitive trade position depend on maintaining our technological lead. New breakthroughs are likely to improve human life in a multitude of ways—from increasing life expectancy to rebuilding our cities.

If our research priorities are to reflect the national interest in these areas, the Federal Government must offer vigorous leadership. Beyond the need for reasonable and responsible increases in subsidies for basic research, there are several specific goals that are of such commanding importance that the government should commit itself now to their achievement.

For example, we must develop new methods of treating the mentally ill. At present, we spend some $15 billion annually on mental health. One half of the hospital beds in the country are occupied by mentally ill patients. About 10 per cent of the American people spend some time in a mental hospital; the patient load in the country's mental hospitals continues to rise. Research on the molecular and chemical structure of the brain is producing important data relating to certain psychological maladies, including schizophrenia. Further efforts may well lead to medications that allow drastic reductions in the need to hospitalize the mentally ill. This would end untold suffering and save the country billions annually. The benefits are worth a major Federal commitment. At present, the effort is being cut back.

A second imperative worthy of Federal support is development of a source of cheap energy. Dr. Alvin M. Weinberg, Director of Oak Ridge National Laboratory, has said: "The basic raw materials for civilized life are energy, water, food and certain minerals. Energy is the most basic of these. If inexhaustible and really cheap energy were available, we could use it to pump fresh water from long distances or even to extract fresh water from the sea; we could use this water to produce agricultural products; we could electrolyze water . . . get hydrogen . . . and manufacture nitrogenous fertilizer; we could reduce metals from their ores, and even convert coal into liquid fuel. But energy is the primary requirement.

With the goal of fulfilling that requirement, I believe that we should step up the Atomic Energy Commission's breeder reactor project, which could provide virtually inexhaustible energy at an extremely low cost. At present, this project is going forward very slowly though its promise for mankind is as great as any other likely development.

Another area in which there is great potential is the laser—a new device that may be able to accomplish such diverse ends as building tunnels, vaporizing coal, intercepting missiles, communicating in space, and curing retina defects in the eye. Pollution research promises new ways to prevent the poisoning of the air we breathe and the water we drink. The possibilities in the realm of transportation excede most of the dreams of science fiction. New computer technology promises great increases in industrial productivity and great relief from drudgery.

Government and Industry Cooperation

Our firm national purpose should be to stimulate these developments by broad support of science and intelligent cooperation between government and private enterprise.

Today, although Government is to some extent in control of large areas of the nation's research and development effort, it is not really in control of itself in this field. There is little cross-fertilization among agencies and departments of the Federal Government responsible for research and development. Ideas and programs that might have applications in other departments are frequently unknown. The President's science advisors and the National Science Foundation limit themselves chiefly to broad questions of national science policy.

It would be an urgent goal of my Administration to devise effective means by which it could cooperate with industry and the academic community in an effort to make maximum use of scientific advances to help solve major national problems. This effort also would seek to assist state and local governments.

Our goal is to make the United States *first* again in the crucial area of research and development.

Individual Initiative

A new national commitment is a necessary investment in the future. However, this aim must not be exploited as a mandate for the growth of Federal power. There should be no Federal scientific czar. I would propose to use the new miracles of science not to expand the powers of government, but to enhance the vitality of private enterprise and to increase the mastery

201

of the individual over his own fate. Government must support and stimulate technology, but except in the realm of defense and to a large extent in the exploration of space, government must not dominate the effort.

In most areas of science, Washington should serve as a catalyst, sponsoring research and scholarship. Even in areas where Washington must necessarily take the lead, government must stand ready to relinquish to private enterprise projects in which the national security or the national interest do not require public control. One example which could be imitated in other fields is the space communications satellite (COMSAT), a partnership between business and government for the benefit of all.

In other areas such as housing, transportation and medical technology —where the international implications are not so great—private enterprise could take full responsibility. It should always be remembered that most of our greatest inventions were the products not of large-scale planning and control but represented the efforts of individuals working alone or in small groups on the frontiers of science. We must never surrender America's greatest asset—the freedom and initiative of its private citizens and economy. In embracing the promise of technology we must never stifle the spirit of man.

New Horizons

In a way, the feelings of bitterness and frustration in our time stem from a sense of claustrophobia; problems close in on us and we become preoccupied with dangers and difficulties. But by the exploration of the infinite and the infinitesimal, we can gain new perspectives, which offer visions of new solutions. We can cure disease, create cheaper energy, eliminate the pressures of scarcity. We can reinvigorate our society by opening new dimensions of hope, new vistas of change.

We must transcend the cramped horizons of the last few years and embrace the opportunity for genuine progress.

New York, New York
October 5, 1968

THE ALL-VOLUNTEER
ARMED FORCE

I speak tonight about a matter important to us all, but especially to young Americans and their parents.

I refer to compulsory military service—or, as most of us know it, "the draft."

We have lived with the draft now for almost thirty years. It was started during the dark uncertainty before the Second World War, as a temporary, emergency measure. But since then we have kept it—through our ordeals in Korea and Vietnam, and even in the years of uneasy peace between.

We have lived with the draft so long, in fact, that too many of us now accept it as normal and necessary.

I say it's time we took a new look at the draft—at the question of permanent conscription in a free society.

If we find we *can* reasonably meet our peacetime manpower needs by other means—then we should prepare for the day when the draft can be phased out of American life.

I have looked into this question very carefully. And this is my belief: once our involvement in the Vietnam war is behind us, we move toward an all-volunteer armed force.

This means, that just as soon as our reduced manpower requirements in Vietnam will permit us to do so, we should stop the draft and put our Selective Service structure on stand-by.

For the many years since World War II, I believed that, even in peacetime, only through the draft could we get enough servicemen to defend our nation and meet our heavy commitments abroad. Over these years it seemed we faced a Hobson's choice: either constrict the freedom of some, or endanger the freedom of all.

But conditions have changed, and our needs have changed. So, too, I believe, our defense manpower policies should change.

203

Tonight, I would like to share with you some of the reasons why I think this is so.

First, let me talk about what we cannot do.

First of all, we must recognize that conditions in the world today require us to keep a powerful military force. Being prepared for war is our surest guarantor of peace. While our adversaries continue to build up their strength, we cannot reduce ours; while they continue to brandish the sword, we cannot lay aside our shield.

So any major change in the way we obtain military manpower must not keep us from maintaining a clearly superior military strength.

In the short run we need also to recognize the limits imposed by the war in Vietnam. However we might wish to, we can't stop the draft while we are in a major war.

What we can do—and what we should do now—is to commit ourselves as a nation to the goal of building an all-volunteer armed force.

The arguments about the draft center first on whether it's right, and second, on whether it's necessary.

Three decades ago, Senator Robert Taft declared that the draft "is absolutely opposed to the principles of individual liberty which have always been considered a part of American democracy."

I feel this way: a system of compulsory service that arbitrarily selects some and not others simply cannot be squared with our whole concept of liberty, justice and equality under the law. Its only justification is compelling necessity.

The longer it goes on, the more troublesome are the questions it raises. Why should your son be forced to sacrifice two of the most important years of his life, so that a neighbor's son can go right along pursuing his interests in freedom and safety? Why should one young American be forced to take up military service while another is left free to make his own choice?

We all have seen, time and time again, how hit-or-miss the workings of the draft are. You know young people, as I do, whose lives have been disrupted first by uncertainty, next by conscription. We all have seen the unfairness of the present system.

Some say we should tinker with the present system, patching up an inequity here and there. I favor this too, but only for the short term.

But in the long run, the only way to stop the inequities is to stop using the system.

It does not work fairly—and, given the facts of American life, it just can't.

The inequity stems from one simple fact—that some of our young people are forced to spend two years of their lives in our nation's defense, while others are not. It's not so much the way they're selected that's wrong, as it is the *fact* of selection.

Even now, only about 40 percent of our eligible young people ever serve. As our population grows, and the manpower pool expands, that percentage will shrink even further. Ten years ago about a million men became of draft age each year. Now there are almost two million.

There has also been a change in the armed forces we need. The kinds of war we have to be prepared for now include not only conventional war and nuclear war, but also guerrilla war of the kind we are now experiencing in Vietnam.

In nuclear war huge ground armies operating in massive formations would be terribly vulnerable. That way of fighting, where nuclear weapons are in use, is a thing of the past.

An all-out *non*-nuclear war, on the other hand—that is, what we knew before as large-scale conventional war—is hard to see happening again. Of course, a sudden Soviet ground attack from Eastern Europe could mix Soviet forces with the populations in the West and thereby prevent swift resort to nuclear weapons. But even in this situation a massing of huge ground units would be impossible because of their nuclear vulnerability. So again, even this kind of struggle would break up into smaller unit actions.

In a guerrilla war of the Vietnam type, we face something else entirely. Here we need a highly professional, highly motivated force of men trained in the techniques of counterinsurgency. Vietnam has shown us that success in such wars may depend on whether our soldiers are linguists and civil affairs specialists, as well as warriors. Also, the complex weapons of modern war demand a higher level of technical and professional skill.

Of course, we will still need conventional forces large by standards of only a few decades ago to guard our vital interests around the world. But I don't believe we will need them in such quantity that we cannot meet our manpower needs through voluntary enlistments.

Conscription was an efficient mechanism for raising the massive land armies of past wars. Also, it is easier—and cheaper—simply to order men into uniform rather than recruiting them. But I believe our likely military needs in the future will place a special premium on the services of career soldiers.

How, then, do we recruit these servicemen? What incentives do we offer to attract an adequate number of volunteers?

One kind of inducement is better housing, and better living conditions generally. Both to recruit and to retain the highly skilled specialists the services need, military life has to be more competitive with the attractions of the civilian world.

The principal incentives are the most obvious: higher pay and increased benefits.

The military services are the only employers today who don't have to compete in the job market. Supplied by the draft with the manpower they want when they want it, they've been able to ignore the laws of supply and demand. But I say there's no reason why our military should be exempt from peacetime competition for manpower, any more than our local police and fire departments are exempt.

A private in the American army is paid less than a $100 a month. This is a third of the minimum wage in the civilian economy. Now to this we should add food, uniforms and housing which are furnished free. Taken all together, a single young man can probably get by on this. But it's hardly competitive with what most people can earn in civilian life.

Even with allowances, many married servicemen in enlisted ranks have actually been forced to depend on relief payments to support their families.

These pay scales point up another inequity of the draft system. Our servicemen are singled out for a huge hidden tax—the difference between their military pay and what they could otherwise earn. The draftee has been forced by his country not only to defend his neighbors but to subsidize them as well.

The total cost of the pay increases needed to recruit an all-volunteer army cannot be figured out to the dollar, but authoritative studies have suggested that it could be done for 5 to 7 billions of dollars more a year. While this cost would indeed be heavy, it would be increasingly offset by reductions in the many costs which the heavy rate of turnover now causes. Ninety-three percent of the Army's draftees now leave the service as soon as their time is up—taking with them skills that it costs some $6,000 per man to develop. The *net* additional annual cost of shifting to an all-volunteer armed force would be bound to be much less.

It will cost a great deal to move to a voluntary system, but unless that cost is proved to be prohibitive, it will be more than worth it.

The alternative is never-ending compulsion in a society consecrated to freedom. I think we can pay a great deal to avoid that.

In any case, in terms of morale, efficiency and effectiveness, a volunteer armed force would assuredly be a better armed force.

Today, seven out of every ten men in the Army have less than two years' military experience. As an Army Chief of Personnel put it: "As soon as we are able to operate as a unit, the trained men leave and we have to start all over again." A volunteer force would have a smaller turnover; it would be leavened by a higher percentage of skilled, motivated men; fewer would be constantly in training; and fewer trained men would be tied down training others.

The result would be, on the average, more professional fighting men, and less invitation to unnecessary casualties in case of war.

207

The same higher pay scales needed to get more volunteers would also strengthen incentives for career service. I am sure the spirit and self-confidence of the men who wear the nation's uniform would be enhanced.

In proposing that we start toward ending the draft when the war is over, I would enter two cautions: first, its structure needs to be kept on stand-by in case some all-out emergency requires its reactivation. But this can be done without leaving 20 million young Americans who will come of draft age during the next decade in constant uncertainty and apprehension.

The second caution I would enter is this: the *draft* can't be ended all at once. It will have to be phased out, so that at every step we can be certain of maintaining our defense strength.

But the important thing is to decide to begin and at the very first opportunity *to* begin.

Now, some are against a volunteer armed force because of its cost, or because they're used to the draft and hesitant to change. But three other arguments are often raised. While they sound plausible, I say they don't stand up under examination.

The first is that a volunteer army would be a black army, so it is a scheme to use Negroes to defend a white America. The second is that a volunteer army would actually be an army of hired mercenaries. The third is, a volunteer army would dangerously increase military influence in our society.

Now, let's take these arguments in order:

First, the "black army" one. I regard this as sheer fantasy. It supposes that raising military pay would in some way slow up or stop the flow of white volunteers, even as it stepped up the flow of black volunteers. Most of our volunteers now are white. Better pay and better conditions would obviously make military service more attractive to black and white alike.

Second, the "mercenary" argument. A mercenary is a soldier of fortune —one who fights for or against anyone for pay. What we're talking about now is American soldiers, serving under the American flag. We are talking about men who proudly wear our country's uniform in defense of its freedom. We're talking about the same kind of citizen armed force America has had ever since it began, excepting only the period when we have relied on the draft.

The third argument is the threat of universal military influence. This, if ever it did come, would come from the top officers ranks, not from the enlisted ranks that draftees now fill—and we already have a career officer corps. It is hard to see how replacing draftees with volunteers would make officers more influential.

Today all across our country we face a crisis of confidence. Nowhere is it more acute than among our young people. They recognize the draft as an infringement on their liberty—which it is. To them, it represents a government insensitive to their rights—a government callous to their status as free men. They ask for justice—and they deserve it.

So I say, it's time we looked to our consciences. Let's show our commitment to freedom by preparing to assure our young people theirs.

CBS Radio Network
Thursday, October 17, 1968

AMERICA'S NATURAL RESOURCES

This is a time when technological advances have given us material benefits beyond the dreams of all other nations and civilizations, and yet we are confronted with an important and perplexing problem.

Obviously we must make more use of our natural resources to maintain our high standard of living.

But the more inroads we make upon our land and water and air, the less we are able to enjoy life in America.

We need lumber to build up our homes; but we also need untouched forests to refresh our spirit.

We need rivers for commerce and trade; but we also need clean rivers to fish in and sit by.

We need land for homes and for great industrial plants; but we also need land free from man's works, land on which a man can take a long walk, alone, away from the pressures of modern life.

We need the dynamic productivity of industry; but we also need fresh air to breathe.

We need the raw natural materials with which to create the products we desire; but we also need large areas of land in which a man can re-create himself, areas of true recreation.

Today 'natural resources' has a double meaning. It means not only those riches with which we have been so abundantly blessed for our economic and technological advantage, but also those same riches as they exist for our psychological and emotional and spiritual advantage.

We must conserve and use our natural resources because of the numerous things we can do with them.

We must also conserve and use them because of what they can do for us.

We need a high standard of living, but we also need a high quality of life.

We need not only more uses for our natural resources, but also better uses.

We need a strategy of quality for the seventies to match the strategy of quantity of the past.

I was born and spent my early years in the western United States. During my life I have travelled across this country many times. I have never ceased to be inspired by the variety and complexity of the American landscape.

But now man and his works are in places which only a few years ago were untouched by civilization. And now as I fly across the great mountains and deserts, high above the green forests and winding rivers, new questions arise:

Can we have the highest standard of living in the world and still have a land worth living in?

Can we have technological progress and also have clean beaches and rivers, great stretches of natural beauty, and places where a man can go to find the silence and privacy he is unable to find in our increasingly urbanized daily life?

Will future generations say of us that we were the richest nation and the ugliest land in all history?

Are we doomed by some inexorable thing called progress to give to our children a land devoid of beauty, empty of scenes of natural grandeur, filled with gadgets and gimmicks, but lost forever to the wonder and inspiration of nature?

These are the important questions. They deal not with one part of American life, but with life in America itself.

We are faced with nothing less than the task of preserving the American environment and at the same time preserving our high American standard of living.

It would be one of history's cruelest ironies if the American people — who have always been willing to fight and die for freedom — should become slaves and victims of their own technological genius.

The battle for the quality of the American environment is a battle against neglect, mismanagement, poor planning and a piecemeal approach to problems of natural resources.

It is a battle which will have to be fought on every level of government, not on a catch-as-catch-can basis, but on a well thought out strategy of quality which enlists the aid of private industry and private citizens.

At the beginning of this century Theodore Roosevelt called upon the American people to preserve the natural heritage. The time has come to renew that call and to bring to programs of conservation the techniques of the seventies.

Modern technology and old-fashioned pride in America can and must combine to win the battle of our environment.

The technological know-how which will help to place man on the moon can be used to help him keep areas of untouched land, clean rivers and streams and pure air on earth.

I say we can have technological advances and natural beauty. I say we can have fresh ideas in industry and fresh air in our cities.

I say we can have the greatest industrial might in the history of man and have places where man's works seem as distant as the stars.

How can we pursue this strategy of quality?

First: we must re-examine all existing federal programs with the aim of coordinating them. Under the Eisenhower administration such acts as the Federal Water Pollution Act channeled federal funds through a single source eliminating duplication and red tape. There is a grave need for such coordination and cooperation on every level of government, and especially between federal and state and local government.

Second: we must make better use of computer technology, especially in such vital areas as mineral resources. Computer technology can swiftly and efficiently help us to determine the nature and probable effect of existing balances of mineral resources in our own country and throughout the world. Such aid can also be used in helping officials to create multiple use of lands and explore the possibilities of ocean resources.

Third: we must create a national minerals and fuels policy if we are to maintain production needed for our economy and security. The strategy of quality looks upon the oil well and the mine as vital parts of the American economy and of American power. There is no contradiction between preserving the natural beauty of America and assisting the mineral industries which are the primary sources of American power.

Economic incentives, including depletion allowance, to encourage the discovery and development of vital minerals and fuels, must be continued.

Fourth: Federal laws applicable to public lands and related resources should be brought up to date. These lands will be managed to ensure their multiple use as economic resources and recreation areas.

Fifth: although most of our nationally owned land is in the West, most of the population is in the East. We must work in cooperation with cities and states all over the country, but especially in the industrialized East — in acquiring and developing green space. The rugged grandeur of mountains a thousand miles away means nothing to a city child who is not able to get to them. Our cities must not be allowed to become concrete prisons. The creation of national parks and outdoor recreation areas near the large cities is as vital a part of the strategy of quality as the preservation of the great forests and rivers of the West.

Sixth: every effort must be made to purify our rivers and streams and air. Last Sunday in a paper dealing with the pollution of our cities, I outlined a program of anti-pollution measures. Although the paper dealt specifically with problems of our cities, the program is applicable in many parts to the entire problem of pollution. Without repeating the entire six-point proposal, I will mention two key points:

- Regional and Federal approaches to the problem must be perfected and expanded, since air and water pollution spills over traditional political boundaries.
- The Federal government should be the example of the highest standards of pollution control, and all Federal facilities should eliminate pollution if we are to expect the rest of the nation to follow suit.

Seventh: water and soil conservation and development programs must be coordinated. At the present time four Cabinet departments are involved in water resources: Health, Education and Welfare; Interior; Defense; and Agriculture. It often happens that different agencies proceed in contradictory progress programs concerning the same problem. We must improve water resource information, including an acceleration of River Basin Commission inventory studies.

Eighth: we must investigate the possibilities of desalination programs. A limited supply of water is already one of the pressing problems in the world and could become a severe problem in America. A breakthrough in desalination methods could make fresh water available to coastal and surrounding areas throughout the world. Automic desalination offers an exciting possibility of greater output at much lower, perhaps even competitive prices. We must stop talking about the future of water preservation and development and start doing the research and studies which will bring the future to us.

Ninth: we must intensify the investigation of ocean resources. The ocean lies as close as the nearest beach, but in its mystery and promise it is as distant as the fabled lands of gold. We must redouble our efforts in developing oceanography and new methods of harvesting resources from the sea. Vast stores of minerals lie beneath the ocean floor waiting for the ingenuity and courage and determination of man to extract them; the Seventies can be not only the decade when Americans reach for the stars, but when we dive for the riches of the sea, not the traditional sunken treasures, but riches such as protein to feed the world.

We must improve our forestry practices, including protection and improvement of watershed lands. National forests are as important for recreational purposes as for preservation of wildlife, watershed control, and timber production. We must extend methods of fire control in forests by fire presuppression and control work. Public and private agencies must work together to reduce the hazards of fire, pestilence, and disease. Here, as in every area of conservation, coordination of effort is of utmost importance.

Eleventh: we must act to preserve and maintain our wildlife. Already 24 birds and 12 mammals native to the United States and Puerto Rico have become extinct. This is only the beginning: 30 to 40 birds and 35 mammals are currently threatened with extinction unless efforts are made to acquire and maintain sufficient habitats. The preservation of fish and wildlife will require research, more land for sanctuaries, restoration of clean waters, conservation of wetlands, better watershed management, and cooperation between federal, state, and private institutions.

Twelfth: we must make our recreational areas the best in the world. A quarter of a billion people, more than the total population of the United States, visit national parks and monuments annually. The average annual growth in visits to outdoor recreation areas has been ten percent a year.

We are now becoming more aware of the problem emphasized and rigorously attacked during the Eisenhower Administration — overcrowding of our national parks. We have succeeded beyond success in attracting people to our parks. If we continue the present rate of increase, soon everyone will face the crisis of overcrowded parks and recreational areas which already exists in many places.

Again a unified cooperative program is immediately needed if we are to save our outdoor recreation programs and develop new ones. A Recreation Coordination Act can provide integrated planning for recreation in all new federal resources programs.

Conservation cannot be successful unless there is an ongoing commitment based on sound conservation principles by the various government and private agencies. A sudden reaction to a problem which, if proper conservation principles had been followed, would not have needed national publicity to bring it before the eyes of the government.

We cannot afford a policy of conservation which jumps from problem to problem eager to seize on the problem most recently publicized.

Our single goal in this field is the enhancement of the life of every American.

Americans, every one of us, must be able to look at all of America and say: This is my country, not only its material power but its natural glory.

Not only the dynamic sound of its industries but the silence of its great forests.

Not only the march of technological progress, but a casual stroll along a beach at night.

Not only the material benefits of today, but the deeper, richer gifts I can leave my children, gifts of natural grandeur and the solitude which is so necessary for the great search to find one's self.

The boy sitting on the steps of a ghetto tenement deserves and needs a place where he can discover that the sky is larger than the little piece he is able to see through the buildings.

This is our country.

The next administration will do everything it can to keep it great and to keep it, for those who come after us, a land of majesty and inspiration, truly the most powerful and most beautiful country in the world.

CBS Radio Network
Friday, October 18, 1968

RESTORING THE U.S. TO THE ROLE OF
A FIRST-RATE MARITIME POWER

Toward a Revitalized Merchant Marine

The maritime industry of the United States has been permitted to decline to a point at which the nation's defense and economic welfare are imperiled.

The policies of the present Administration have put us on a course toward becoming a second-rate seapower.

Seapower is the ability of a nation to project into the oceans, in times of peace, its economic strength; in times of emergency, its defense mobility.

Seapower is composed of all those elements enabling a nation to use the world ocean advantageously for either trade or defense—its navy, its merchant shipping, its shipbuilding, its fishing, its oceanographic research, and its port facilities.

Even a cursory examination of the United States seapower today makes it clear that our present course has been wrong.

Two-thirds of the Navy's tonnage now afloat was designed during World War II to meet the conditions of that time. The replacement needs of the United States Navy are so great that last year the Secretary of the Navy stated that the Navy needs to build a ship each week for the next 10 years just to keep up.

Our fishing fleet is composed of some 13,000 vessels, most of which are too small and too old for efficient operation. Some 60 percent are more than 20 years old.

Our shipyards have suffered under misguided federal policies which have given them no incentive to increase productivity, to adequately update plant facilities or to introduce new technology.

In oceanographic sciences we have only begun to pierce the surface.

Almost every day a ship leaves the Soviet Port of Odessa with cargoes for North Vietnam. An estimated 80 percent of the materials used by the enemy in Vietnam arrives in Soviet merchant ships. More than 97 percent of all supplies used by the Allied troops in South Vietnam also moves by water, most of it aboard old ships flying the U.S. flag but which are no match for the modern Soviet merchantmen.

Two-thirds of our merchant ships are beyond their economically useful age. By contrast, half the Soviet fleet is less than 5 years old.

The Soviets are adding at the rate of 100 ships or about 1 million tons per year to their existing 1,500 ship fleet.

By contrast, the United States now has an active privately-owned merchant marine of fewer than 1,000 American flagships. We are producing less than 15 ships a year, and we have built only some 300 American flag merchantmen since the end of World War II. In less than a decade, erosion will reduce our fleet to one-third of its present inadequate size unless change is forthcoming.

In the early 1970's the Soviet Union not only will surpass us in number of ships but also in the quantity of goods they can transport on these ships.

They would not hesitate to use this growing economic power as part of their global strategy. At this very moment, the Soviets have created a rate war to undercut the British on the route from Australia to the United Kingdom and Europe.

Apart from its absolute size, our merchant fleet is dramatically unbalanced. The most glaring deficiency is in the dry bulk carrying segment, which is woefully inadequate in lift capability in spite of the vast export and import trade of this country in commodities of this type—imports of raw materials on which this nation's productive capacity depends—exports of farm products that feed the hungry of friendly nations.

In the face of these conditions, there is today in the executive branch of our government a shocking de-emphasis of our national maritime efforts. Continuation of such a lack of interest could only result in making the United States a second-class seapower during the 1970's and beyond.

If we permit this decay to continue we will find that we have abdicated our maritime position to none other than the Soviet Union. Even now their modern merchant fleet ranks sixth in the world—just one place behind our own much older fleet.

In 1965, the present Administration promised to recommend a new policy for our merchant marine.

But the Administration has failed to present a cohesive program to restore the United States as a maritime power.

The void between promise and action of the past four years has halted maritime progress. Our fleet carryings have declined to record lows, our balance of payments has suffered, vessel obsolescence has multiplied, and our ability to meet our maritime commitments overseas has decreasd alarmingly.

Nuclear merchant vessel propulsion, which offers an encouraging possibility, is ready to be junked by the present Administration—this in spite of the long lead we developed in this field during the Eisenhower years with the Nuclear Ship Savannah.

Only through new and advanced technology can the American merchant marine minimize its competitive disadvantage with other merchant fleets. The same holds true in other components of seapower: naval, oceanography, fishing and port facilities.

Commerce

Only 5.6 percent of the U.S. trade is carried on U.S. flagships. This is the lowest since 1921.

Soviet flagships already carry more than 50 percent of Soviet cargoes; Sweden, 30 percent of her own commerce; Norway, 43 percent; Great Britain, 37 percent; France, 48 percent; and Greece, 53 percent. Japan is carrying 46 percent right now, but Japanese shipping policy has prescribed that by 1975, the Japanese flag merchant marine should carry 60 percent of Japanese exports, and 70 percent of Japanese imports.

219

These nations have determined that a high degree of reliance on their own shipping resources is important to their own self-interest. We have not.

To state it bluntly, our trade is predominantly in the hands of foreign carriers, some of whom may be our trading competitors. We must have more control over the movement of our own cargoes not only for competitive reasons, but also because of the contributions our ships make to our balance of payments.

The stability of the dollar is vital to the whole free world. Increasing our exports is probably the healthiest method of removing our balance of payments deficit.

Exports of those services as well as goods, therefore, is essential to increase U.S. flag participation in our overseas shipping as part of our export promotion policy.

This cannot be done with our present fleet or under our present maritime policy.

Shipbuilding

Continuing neglect of vessel replacement has led to an antiquated current fleet.

The new Administration's maritime policy will seek a higher level of coordination between naval and merchant shipbuilding.

In that way we can create a climate in which shipbuilding can attract the capital, as well as the stable labor force, needed to make it competitive with foreign yards and to provide an expansion base for national emergencies.

In turn I would expect initiative and cooperation from both industry and labor. Throughout the maritime industry, a new outlook must be encouraged to replace the current divisiveness and short sightedness.

Until such time as American yards can be independently competitive, I recognize that shipbuilding subsidies are necessary to enable shipyards to build ships and deliver them to operators at competitive world prices.

We must set as our goal a sharp increase of the transport of U.S. trade abroad American flagships. The present rate is 5.6 percent; by the mid-seventies, we must see that rate over 30 percent and the growth accelerating.

I support a building program to accomplish that objective.

In keeping with the traditions of private enterprise, our efforts will be directed toward the creating of a favorable shipbuilding environment through a better use of credit facilities and amortization procedures. The use of long-range government cargo commitments should be explored as a means to stimulate unsubsidized financing of ship construction.

Shipbuilding is not all financing and steel. This is an industry where many of our hard-core unemployed, and those whose jobs are displaced by automation, might be channeled and trained. During World War II, the United States established records for turning out nearly 6,000 merchant ships. Many of the people who participated in achieving these records had been classified as "untrained." This should serve as an example to us today.

Operating Subsidy

Since the Merchant Marine Act of 1936 was passed, we have been living with an operating subsidy system. The system has been aimed primarily at removing the wage-cost disadvantage of the American operators who must pay seamen under U.S. working standards and levels of living.

The subsidy system has had its shortcomings. It has been extended exclusively to liner operators in the foreign trade; it has grown more costly; it has not created a modern merchant fleet even among its recipients nor has it had as a basic ingredient enough reward for increasing efficiency.

I propose, therefore, an immediate re-evaluation of this program, in consultation with industry members and labor representatives, with the goal of providing more incentives for productivity.

The unsubsidized sector of our merchant fleet must be given attention, so that it, too, can replace its deteriorating fleet in the immediate future. Included in this category are those who carry farm products to the under-developed nations, and the Great Lakes operators who daily face competition from their government-assisted Canadian counterparts.

Although the Eisenhower Administration provided the United States with a fourth seacoast through the St. Lawrence Seaway, the present Administration has chosen to turn its back on this inland network of water transportation.

Certainly these segments of our merchant marine can be stimulated by tax incentives and cargo assistance. The United States, in turn, can expect them to make a capital commitment in new ships and facilities.

Oceanography

This Administration has paid too little attention to the new opportunities that science and technology can open beneath the surface of the sea.

New leadership will stimulate exploration and scientific study of the ocean depths, bringing to light hidden resources. And, we must never lose sight of the importance of oceanography to our nation's security.

My Administration will make full use of the Marine Resources Engineering and Development Act passed in 1966. That Act established a cabinet-level council and a study commission, which I will ask next year to submit to the new President and to the new Congress recommendations for bringing about a unified effort in the field of marine sciences and engineering.

Food from the Sea

The present Administration also has permitted a deterioration in our seafood industry. Under new leadership we may discover beneath the sea a food supply that will satisfy the growing needs of humanity.

In 1957 the U.S. imported only one-third of all the seafood we consumed. Today that figure has jumped to a startling 71 percent. In 1938 the U.S. ranked second to Japan in the amount of fish it caught. By 1965 the U.S. had slipped to 5th place, passed by Peru, Japan, Communist China and Russia, in that order. During this period, Russia more than tripled her catch, and Japan almost doubled hers, while the U.S. catch remained about the same.

This reflects a failure of our existing federal programs to encourage the fishing industry to modernize fast enough so that it can counter foreign competitors. Meanwhile, Soviet trawler fleets virtually dominate the Grand Banks off our shores. These trawlers have a multiple capacity—fishing and oceanography and electronic snooping.

At the present time, there is not one modern long-range trawler in service in the U.S. fleet. While the fleets of other countries roam the oceans, our fleets too often can only hug the coastlines.

The maritime policy of the new Administration will be to accelerate the technological improvements which we know can be achieved today in our fishing industry to make it competitive world-wide.

Ports

Federal maritime policy must recognize not only how essential the fleet is, but also how essential are the facilities and capabilities to handle the fleet's cargo.

Cooperating with local port authorities, the new Administration will encourage further modernization and development of our existing port facilities to meet the needs of the future.

Summary

All our goals will not be accomplished overnight. Restoring the U.S. to the role of a first-rate maritime power requires the cooperation of management, labor, local port authorities, and government; but the leadership for a national policy can and will come from a new Administration.

To overcome the present maritime crisis, I recognize that we have an opportunity and an obligation to reverse the gross deficiencies that have marked the present Administration's performance in this field.

We shall adopt vigorous research and development programs designed to harness the latest and best technology to the needs of our maritime fleet.

We shall adopt a policy that recognized the role of government in the well-being of an industry so vital to our national defense, and stimulate private enterprise to revitalize the industry.

We shall adopt a policy that will enable American flagships to carry much more American trade at competitive world prices.

The old ways have failed, to the detriment of the seamen, the businessmen, the balance of payments and the national defense.

The time has come for new departures, new solutions and new vitality for American ships and American crews on the high seas of the world.

Seattle, Washington
September 25, 1968

QUEST FOR PEACE

TO KEEP THE PEACE

Anyone who travels extensively abroad comes back with one indelible impression: whether peace and freedom survive in the world depends on what we do here in America—the leadership we give, the decisions we make.

Of all the tasks facing the next Administration, none is greater than this: establishing the basis for a just and a lasting peace.

We have lived for a generation now with the abrasive tensions of the Cold War, with the threat of nuclear weapons, with the explosive instabilities that rose from a rapid dismantling of the old colonial empires. We have fought World War II, Korea, Vietnam; we have poured out $150 billion in foreign aid; we spend nearly 80 billion dollars in a year on arms —and still we live in a world in which tyranny and greed and fanaticism march behind the barrels of guns.

It's time for a new beginning.

It's time for a new commitment to preventive diplomacy, to persistently seeking out ways in which wars can be averted and peace can be strengthened.

It's time for a creative new approach to our structure of alliances, not only adapting that structure to the changed conditions of the world today, but also enlisting our allies more effectively in achieving our common aims.

In policy planning it's time for a determined shift of emphasis from crisis management to crisis prevention. The key to peace lies in anticipating trouble, not merely responding to it. As part of our missile defense, we have a Distant Early Warning System stretched across Canada; we also need a Diplomatic Early Warning System to cope with threats to the peace while they still are manageable short of war.

Within the term of the next President I believe the foundation for a lasting peace can be laid. But we cannot have peace by wishing for it, however fervently we wish. We cannot secure it by proclamations or declarations or pious exhortations.

Peace today requires strength of will, strength of arms, and strength of purpose. It has to be pursued with a combination of relentless passion, calm reason, and cold logic. By itself neither logic nor reason nor passion is enough.

In its preoccupation with the war in Vietnam the present Administration has lost America's leadership in the world. If we are to make progress toward a durable peace, we must recover that leadership.

Increasingly today, we find ourselves confronting a paradox of American power: never has a nation had such power, and never has a nation sought to use its power for better purposes—but seldom has a nation been so mistrusted in its purposes or so frustrated in its efforts.

Our example has lost its fire. Our leadership has lost its drive. The world has lost its respect for our judgment, its faith in our ideals, its confidence in our dollar, its trust in our word.

If we are to regain our lost leadership, there are four things we must do.

We must see the world as it *is*, not as it was or as we wish that it were.

We must face facts with a new realism.

We must speak with a new candor.

We must act with a new urgency.

We live in a new world.

It is a world of new nations and a world of new people. Half the world's nations have been born since World War II, and half the world's people have been born since World War II.

It is a world of new ideas. The old isms—communism, socialism, anti-colonialism—that summoned men to revolution after World War II, have lost their appeal.

But if the new generation is no longer prisoner of the old isms, neither is it sold on the American idea.

When people abroad look at America, they see violence, intolerance, lawlessness; and too often they see us as stodgy champions of the status quo rather than what we are: the boldest architects of change and progress in the world's history.

Keeping the peace is inseparable from defending freedom. If we hope to inspire others to the defense of freedom, we must show a decent respect for the uses of freedom. If we expect others to follow our lead in keeping the peace abroad, we must show ourselves capable of maintaining peace at home. If our ideas are to command respect from a new world in search of a direction, they have to be made relevant to the needs of that world.

The time has come when America must reappraise—in a most searching, measured, and fundamental way—its role and its responsibilities in the world and the resources which we and other nations can bring to the task of keeping peace and defending freedom.

Economically, diplomatically, militarily, the time has come to insist that others must assume the responsibilities which are rightfully theirs. We must do our full share. But the free world can no more afford to base its security and prosperity on a system of permanent welfarism abroad than the progress of our own people can be based on permanent welfarism here at home. Peace is everybody's business, and the pursuit of peace is everybody's responsibility.

To insist that others do more is not a retreat into a new isolationism. Rather, it faces up to one of the blunt facts of life in the world today: that even if the United States had the will, it no longer has the capacity to do all that needs to be done. If the other nations in the free world want to remain free, they can no longer afford the luxury of relying on American power.

When President Eisenhower left office, the United States held a massive advantage in strategic nuclear power—and it was that advantage which enabled President Kennedy to face down the Soviet leaders in the Cuban missile confrontation. But under the short-sighted defense policies of the present Administration, that advantage has been dissipated; a determined Soviet drive for supremacy has very nearly achieved its goal. As a result,

229

even where the thinly stretched forces of the United States can be deployed, they no longer are backed by the decisive nuclear superiority which in past crises made our power fully credible.

In Europe—as I indicated in a major address last weekend—NATO must be strengthened, with our European allies not only asked for a greater contribution but also given a greater voice in the policies of the alliance.

Southeast Asia presents a special case because of its proximity to Communist China, its history of conflict, and the designs of Hanoi—which has troops fighting in Laos and Thailand, as well as in South Vietnam.

But if Asia has special needs, it also presents a special opportunity.

All around the rim of China, nations of non-Communist Asia have been growing phenomenally in wealth and achieving a new stability. It's in non-Communist Asia that the world's most exciting records of economic development are being written. At the same time there is a developing spirit of Asian regionalism, with old rivalries giving way to new ventures in economic and cultural cooperation.

Almost without exception, the leaders of non-Communist Asia recognize the threat from Communist China. They want protection against it.

The American commitment in Vietnam has bought time for this to take place. The time bought at such terrible cost must now be used to ensure that any future aggression is held in check—*without* another unilateral American commitment on the pattern of Vietnam.

I look back over a generation of Americans that has been called on to fight three wars—and I know that for the next generation, we must do better.

In Korea and again in Vietnam the United States furnished most of the money and most of the arms in defense of freedom—and also most of the men. We are a rich nation and a powerful nation, and we have 200 million people. But there are 2 billion people in the free world—and it's time we made sure that in the future we help others fight their wars, if necessary, but that we don't do the fighting for them.

The nations of non-Communist Asia must be brought to accept the need for their own mutual security arrangement, able to deal both with old-style wars and with new—with traditional wars in which armies cross over national boundaries, and with the so-called "wars of national liberation" in which they burrow under them in the guise of revolution.

It is not for the United States to prescribe the pattern for such an arrangement; this must be determined by the Asian nations themselves. But whatever its form, the important thing is that the Asian nations themselves be prepared in the future to make the initial response to any new aggression in their area.

This has a purpose beyond sparing American lives and beyond even ensuring that aggression would be effectively resisted at a time when the American people would be deeply reluctant to become involved in another Asian war.

Its larger purpose is this: if another world war is to be prevented, every step possible must be taken to avert direct confrontation between the nuclear powers. Whenever the United States sends its forces in to block a Communist advance, the danger of a confrontation between nuclear powers arises. This danger can be reduced by the development of regional pacts in which other nations undertake, among themselves, to contain aggression in their own areas. The regional pact thus becomes a buffer separating the distant great power from the immediate threat—and the danger of a local conflict escalating into world war is thereby reduced.

In the case of Asia by joining forces the non-Communist nations would also lessen the temptation to Chinese adventuring, and thus speed the day when Communist China could return to the family of nations.

Vietnam has been a profoundly sobering lesson in the limits of U.S. power. But it is not enough to lament these limits or to criticize the commitment or to wish that history had dealt differently with that tormented corner of the world.

What we must do is to work—with a sense of urgency that has so far been lacking—toward ensuring that we have no more Vietnams.

If this requires concerting the power of the free world, it also requires tapping the best brains of the free world.

231

All around the globe there are far-sighted statesmen, men of extraordinary vision and extraordinary brilliance—in small nations as well as large.

We can't afford go-it-alone diplomacy any more than we can afford go-it-alone defense. When peace requires mobilizing the support of the world's people, we cannot continue to neglect the enormous resources that the ideas and insights of these leaders represent.

As we look to the future, it is clear that the years just ahead must be a time of intensive and sustained negotiation with the Soviet Union. The primary purpose of this is not to secure Soviet friendship, though friendship we seek; the primary purpose is, more modestly and more realistically, to seek out those areas of mutual interest on which accommodation can be reached, while making it abundantly evident that the profit has gone out of aggression.

If the Soviets believe they can extend their influence by arms or the threat of arms, their interest in peaceful agreements will be limited. To the extent they become convinced that they cannot win their way by force, their interest in peaceful agreements will increase. But in any case they do share with us a common interest in preventing the dread specter of nuclear holocaust; as their economy grows richer and more complex, they share a greater interest in stable arrangements for international trade. Faced with frictions and rivalries within the Communist bloc, they may from time to time seek respite from the cold war tensions they themselves have created.

Looking further into the future, we must also anticipate eventual conversations with the leaders of Communist China. In the short run we should not reward China's present tactics with offers of trade or recognition; but taking the long view, we simply cannot afford to leave China forever outside the family of nations, there to nurture its fantasies, cherish its hates, and threaten its neighbors. There is no place on this small planet for a billion of its potentially most able people to live in angry isolation.

The world has a long way to go before the rule of reason prevails in international relations, before those who seek domination renounce their ambitions and agree to respect the rights of their neighbors. But rather than grow discouraged, we should grow firmer in our resolution; precisely because the world does contain persistent threats of war, we should redouble our efforts for peace.

CBS Radio Network
Saturday, October 19, 1968

VIETNAM

With regard to the war in Vietnam, the Republican party faces the question of how a complex, emotionally-charged and highly sensitive issue can be handled during an election year in a responsible way.

The manner in which we conduct ourselves on this issue can bear heavily on the chances for peace.

The Republican party must address this issue in its platform. What I intend to do, and what I believe the party should do, is to separate those questions that *can* responsibly be discussed from those that cannot. The present Administration's emissaries in Paris must be able to speak with the full force and authority of the United States. Nothing should be offered in the political arena that might undercut their hand.

But there is much that can and should be discussed.

The war must be ended.

It must be ended honorably, consistent with America's limited aims and with the long term requirements of peace in Asia.

We must seek a negotiated settlement. This will require patience.

Until it *is* ended—and in order to hasten a negotiated end—it must be waged more effectively. But rather than further escalation on the military front, what it requires now is a dramatic escalation of our efforts on the economic, political, diplomatic and psychological fronts. It requires a new strategy, which recognizes that this is a new and different kind of war. And it requires a fuller enlistment of our Vietnamese allies in their own defense.

I have long been critical of the Administration's conduct of the war. Specifically:

• Our massive military superiority has been wasted, our options frittered away, by applying power so gradually as to be ineffective. The swift, overwhelming blow that would have been decisive two or three years ago is no longer possible today. Instead, we find that we have been locked into a massive, grinding war of attrition.

234

• The Administration has done far too little, too late, to train and equip the South Vietnamese, both for fighting their own war now and for the task of defending their own country after the war is settled.

• The Administration has either not recognized that this is a new and more complex kind of war, or has not seen its significance. The result is that the old-style, conventional military aspects have been overemphasized, and its other dimensions—psychological, political, economic, even diplomatic—have gotten too little attention.

• The Administration has failed in candor at home and in leadership abroad. By not taking the American people into *its* confidence, the Administration has lost *their* confidence. Its diplomacy has failed to enlist other nations to use their influence toward achieving a peaceful settlement.

These are failures of the past. In terms of what the United States should do *now*, we start with the fact of the Paris talks. These impose limits on what a Presidential candidate can responsibly say—not because of what the American people might think, but because of how Hanoi's negotiators might interpret it.

A Presidential candidate is in a different position than is a private citizen, an editor or even a Senator. He may soon bear the responsibility for conducting the negotiations. Anything he might offer as a candidate would become unavailable for bargaining when he became President. Anything he might say, any differences he might express, would be taken by Hanoi as indicating the possible new direction of the next administration.

Our negotiators in Paris represent not only the present administration, but the United States. In the spirit of country above party, as long as they have a chance of success—and as long as the Administration remains committed to an honorable settlement—they should be free from partisan interference, and they should have our full support. The pursuit of peace is too important for politics-as-usual.

If the talks fail, or if they drag on indefinitely, new approaches both to the conduct of the war and to the search for peace will be needed.

235

There is no Republican way or Democratic way to end a war, but there *is* a difference between an administration that inherits the errors of the past, and an administration that can make a fresh beginning free from the legacy of those errors.

There is a difference between an administration burdened by accumulated distrust, and a new administration that can tell the truth to the American people and be believed.

However cruel its military aspects, this new kind of war is not primarily a military struggle in the conventional sense. It is primarily a political struggle, with the enemy conducting military operations to achieve political and psychological objectives. It is a war for people, not for territory. The real measure of progress is not the body-count of enemy killed, but the number of South Vietnamese won to the building and defense of their own country.

This new kind of war requires greater emphasis on small-unit action, on routing out the Viet Cong infrastructure, on police and patrol activities, on intelligence-gathering, on the strengthening of local forces. This kind of war can actually be waged *more* effectively with *fewer* men and at *less* cost.

The fact is that our men have not been out-fought; the Administration has been out-*thought*.

At the same time, we need far greater and more urgent attention to training the South Vietnamese themselves, and equipping them with the best of modern weapons. As they are phased in, American troops can—and should—be phased out. This phasing-out will save American lives and cut American costs. Further, it is essential if South Vietnam is to develop both the military strength and the strength of spirit to survive now and in the future.

It is a cruel irony that the American effort to safeguard the *independence* of South Vietnam has produced an ever-increasing dependency in our ally. If South Vietnam's future is to be secure, this process must now be reversed.

The context in which the final negotiations will occur cannot be predicted, but the far-reaching implications of the war in Vietnam plainly indicate

236

that the conference table must be wide enough, and the issues placed upon it broad enough, to accommodate as many as possible of the powers and interests involved. In particular, there should be the most candid and searching conversations with the Soviet Union.

Vietnam does not exist in isolation. Around the world, we should mobilize our diplomatic forces for peace—through our embassies, through the United Nations and elsewhere. We need such effort not only to speed an end to the war in Vietnam, but also to lay the groundwork for the organization of a lasting and larger peace. Certainly one of the lessons from the agony of Vietnam is that we need a new diplomacy to prevent future Vietnams.

If the war is still going on next January, it can best be ended by a new Administration that has given no hostages to the mistakes of the past; an Administration neither defending old errors nor bound by the old record. A new Republican Administration will be pledged to conduct a thorough reappraisal of every aspect of the prosecution of the war and the search for peace. It will accept nothing on faith, reputation or statistics. In waging the war and making the peace, it will come with a fresh eye and act with a free hand. And it will do what the present Administration has so signally failed to do: it will arm the American people with the truth.

Submitted to Republican National Convention
Committee on Resolutions
August 1, 1968

THE SECURITY GAP

For eight months I have criss-crossed America discussing major national problems. Tonight I report on the greatest Federal effort of all — our nation's defense.

The hard truth is this: the present state of our defenses is too close to peril point, and our future prospects are in some respects downright alarming. We have a gravely serious security gap.

When the Eisenhower Administration took office, one problem we faced was much as it is today. America was hopelessly bogged down in a quicksand war — Korea.

Very quickly, we ended that war. When we left the government, America was still at peace, and not one American boy had been killed or wounded on any battlefield for eight years.

Moreover, our nation was the acknowledged leader of the Free World. Our superiority in weapons was unquestioned. Our planning of diplomatic and military ventures had been conducted in a way to hold the initiative for peace. There was no waiting for crisis to develop. No wandering aimlessly into trouble and frantically devising patchwork solutions.

In those days America's policies recognized that if we were weak on small issues, we would soon be challenged on large issues. The Eisenhower position was that prudent firmness under-girds peace, but timidity, impulsiveness, and indecision lead toward war — further, that a consistent display of strength and determination prevent the miscalculations that stumble nations into dangerous encounters and war.

I retrace this history because it explains why, during the eight Eisenhower years, there was not a Berlin wall, no Bay of Pigs, no Cuban missile crisis, no Americans fighting in Southeast Asia, no Pueblo piracy. It also explains why our globe-encircling alliances stayed strong and firm.

The point is: a nation doesn't *accidentally* keep the peace; it takes strength, careful planning, holding to principle — yes, and determination and courage as well — to keep American boys out of war.

Now let's measure where we are today, eight years later. First, let's check our weapons.

Eight years ago, when the Eisenhower Administration ended, we had a 50 percent advantage over the Soviet Union in the number of land-based intercontinental ballistic missiles — the crucial weapon. Today that advantage, so important during the Cuban crisis, has become only marginal. The trend is that even this slight edge will soon be gone.

Eight years ago our numerical advantage over the Soviets in bombers was 30 percent. Now it's more than the other way around. Today the Soviets are 50 percent ahead of us.

Eight years ago, in nuclear submarines, we had a 500 percent advantage. Already it is down four-fifths and each year shrinks still more.

Eight years ago we had a decisive lead in tactical aircraft. Now the Soviets are ahead not only in numbers but also in quality. We have produced only one new aircraft of this type since 1960 while the Soviets have put out seven. Nearly all our planes today were developed by the Eisenhower Administration 10 or 15 years ago.

Eight years ago we had a large strategic stockpile of defense supplies and weapons. But the present Administration has used it to support the Vietnam war. Now it is seriously depleted. And so also is our ability to meet a future major crisis.

There are other examples, but already you know the disturbing truth. Simply this: in recent years our country has followed policies which now threaten to make America second best both in numbers and quality of major weapons.

That is why I charge the opposition with creating a security gap for America.

What is at stake here is far more than military hardware — ships, missiles, tanks, and guns. Our huge defense apparatus is our guardian of peace.

If we allow our superior strength to become second best — if we let those who threaten world peace outpace us — in time we will generate tensions which could lead to war, first, by our display of physical weakness and flabby will, and second, by tempting an aggressor to take risks that would compel us to respond.

I stress that point, because soon after our Eisenhower team left office, the new Administration reached a grave misjudgment. The idea was, if America kept up her numerical superiority, if we also stayed ahead in new weapons, we would provoke the Communist leaders, and this would dash our hopes for friendly relations and peace.

Apparently these planners had persuaded themselves they could quickly reconcile our differences with the Communist world. The Soviets, they reasoned, had tired of trouble abroad; they had troubles at home; they had lost their expansionist fervor; they had become defensiveminded.

It was concluded that, by marking time in our own defense program, we could induce the Communists to follow our example, slacken their own effort, and then we would have peace in our time.

Such were the dreams that crimped our national defense program. Out of it all evolved a peculiar, unprecedented doctrine called "parity." This meant America would no longer try to be first. We would only stay even.

This concept has done us incalculable damage.

We must move, if we can, from confrontation to negotiation, and as President I would actively pursue that goal. But, just as it takes two to negotiate, so it takes two to avoid confrontations.

In a very real sense we are always in a confrontation with actual and potential adversaries in the world. There is a constant question: is the continuing confrontation to be kept limited and safe or is it to become all-out and dangerous.

The gross national product of the United States is nearly double that of the Soviets, and we have a superior technology. In order to arrive at a meaningful power balance with the Soviets these basic economic and technological strengths would also have to be equalized.

For us deliberately to let a weaker but basically expansionist nation achieve parity with us indicates an erosion of our commitment and will. It encourages the Soviets to press eagerly on — to step up their drive for strategic superiority — and then they would harshly exploit their superior strength against our sagging capabilities. In short, this "parity" concept means superiority for potential enemies. We cannot accept this concept and survive as a free people.

Other notions of this same cult of planners have hurt our country.

The Vietnam war is a tragic example. It has been painstakingly nurtured year after year by a new policy of "gradualism" until it has become the longest and one of the bloodiest, more costly military ventures in our history.

With these mistakes respect abroad for America has plummeted, to the point where a fourth rate military power, North Korea, felt free, impudently, to seize the U.S.S. Pueblo on the high seas. Today, ten months later, the ship is still in their hands. The crew is still held captive. It is an incredible humiliation of the United States.

I cannot presume to explain why such peculiar ideas were found worthy by our government, particularly in view of the emphatic Soviet declarations of their own designs. As long as six years ago the Soviet Minister of Defense, the late Marshall Malinovski, stated: "We do not intend to fall behind in development or be inferior to our public enemies in any way . . . In the competition for quality of armaments in 'the future' . . . (our) superiority will evermore increase."

So the Soviets have vigorously advanced their military effort as we put ours in second gear. They have raised the quantity and quality of their ballistic missiles. They have greatly increased their submarine-launching ballistic missile capability. They have developed a land-mobile version of an inter-continental missile.

For the first time the Soviets have moved large modern naval forces into the Mediterranean.

They have deployed an anti-missile defense system. They have tested and developed an orbital bombardment system.

Their rapid advances in tactical aircraft have brought Communist bloc countries to near equality with the United States and the free world. In submarines they have made major quality improvements and have a vast numerical advantage. They are still building and stockpiling immensely powerful nuclear weapons, even as they test entirely new families of smaller tactical and naval nuclear weapons.

Recently we learned they are perfecting ballistic-missile multiple warheads far more powerful than our own. This is a grave menace to the United States, as well as a body blow to our continuing efforts toward effective arms control.

And, as all Americans bitterly know, the Soviets have been and still are the arsenal and the trainers of the North Vietnamese and have escalated this jungle battle into a major war. In addition, they continue to add fuel to the Mideast tinderbox.

Considering these developments, it is evident the last two Administrations failed in their defense responsibilities. Worse, they have so positioned our country that by 1970 or 1971 we could find ourselves with a "Survival Gap" — discovering then that we are irretrievably behind in the most critical areas.

I must add one further criticism.

Earlier I mentioned the careful planning of the Eisenhower period. I was referring particularly to an official body known as the National Security Council. This Council, chaired by the President, was established by law to integrate our diplomatic, military, and economic policies. It was our assurance that America would not aimlessly drift in world affairs, but would control and direct their course.

Throughout the Eisenhower period this Council met week in and week out under President Eisenhower's personal direction. I attended these weekly meetings for eight years, and during the President's absences due to illness, it fell to me to preside. The process was, of course, not flawless, but it was the controlling element in our success in keeping the peace throughout our eight White House years.

Since 1960, this Council has virtually disappeared as an operating function. In its place there have been catch-as-can talk-fests between the President, his staff assistants, and various others. I attribute most of our serious reverses abroad since 1960 to the inability or disinclination of President Eisenhower's successors to make effective use of this important Council.

So the risks facing our country have intensified these past eight years. Wrong policy assumptions — unrealism in numbers and kinds of weapons — laxity in research and development — flaws in the decision making process — a disregard of timing — allowing the Soviets to move rapidly toward parity and in some areas to achieve superiority — a near breakdown of top policy-making procedures — these have been somber developments for our country.

I am intensely dissatisfied with these conditions.

As President I would move promptly to correct these mistakes of judgement and action.

I intend to initiate a major reorganization of the Department of Defense to correct its overcentralization and streamline its top level over-staffing.

I intend to restore ready access of our top military professionals to the President of the United States, as contemplated by the National Security Act.

I intend to root out the "whiz kid" approach which for years in the Defense Department has led our policies and programs down the wrong roads.

I intend to restore our objective of clear-cut military superiority — meaning by this the aggregate that constitutes real superiority rather than competition weapon by weapon.

I intend to revitalize research and development, for our success in deterring war may wholly depend on our success in keeping the United States first in military science and technology.

I intend to restore the National Security Council to its pre-eminent role in national security planning.

And I intend to do away with wishful thinking either as to the capability or the intent of potential enemies.

It is clear from what I have reported tonight that America urgently needs new leadership for tomorrow — a new leadership to restore our world position — a new leadership so our nation can apply its great power and influence to the building of a stable, international order.

I repeat: the peace we won and kept during the Eisenhower Administration was not accidental or lucky. We stayed at peace because of careful planning, diplomatic skill, national strength, and constant vigilance in the day-to-day interaction of statesmen. Thus we prevented the false moves and miscalculations that bring on crises and wars.

This, then, is why I have dealt so extensively tonight with the state of our defenses. In calling for strength — in resisting deterioration of our position relative to the Soviet Union — in stressing vigorous development of new weaponry — our object is not belligerency, not turning ourselves into an international bully, not truculence or arrogance — but the very opposite. Strength we want and strength we need — to win and hold the peace. Our next President must be able to negotiate effectively with the Soviet Union and other nations on such issues as limitation of armaments. We will need to bargain on our side not with concern but with confidence — not from weakness but with the persuasiveness of respectable and evident power.

As President Kennedy said, "Let us never negotiate out of fear. But let us never fear to negotiate." The United States was in that position of assurance through strength when President Kennedy took office. He was still in that position when he suddenly confronted the Cuban missile crisis. For America's sake — for the cause of world peace — our next President must be in the same position.

This is, then, a fateful election year. Let us together refashion the conditions, the atmosphere, the environment that can lead to a durable peace. In that great effort I ask your confidence and your support.

CBS Radio Network
Thursday, October 24, 1968

THE CRADLE OF CIVILIZATION MUST
NOT BE ITS GRAVE

Dr. Wexler, Madam President, all of the distinguished guests at the head table, including Mr. Klutznick, who was the presiding officer the last time I was here nine years ago, and all of those who are attending this great Triennial Convention:

It seems very hard for me to realize it was eleven years ago, 1957, that I addressed you before. As I stand here and as I see so many who were here then and also as I hear the eloquent words, I say "eloquent," because they were much too generous, by my friend Max Fisher, I am most grateful for his introduction and for your very warm reception.

I would like to point out at the outset that I come here knowing that this is a political year. I guess you are aware of that, too. I know, too, that earlier today one of the other contestants for the office I seek was present— not the third one, but the second one, I think.

While I would not want to prejudice your judgment on such an important decision—this is a non-partisan group as Max Fisher has pointed out— I should say that this is a very unusual time in America's history as far as the two candidates for the Presidency are concerned. This is the first time in history when two men who have served as Vice President of the United States have run for the office of President.

When I used to address organizations like this in years like this, I often used to say, after the election in 1960 that I only wish I had been a member of an organization in which the Vice President automatically became President. As a matter of fact, I think I said that in 1957. I can't say that tonight, not that I am prejudiced, of course. I just simply want to say that I have been trying to figure a way that I could get one up on my good friend Mr. Humphrey, and it occurred to me that both of us have served in the United States Senate. We are, therefore, highly aware of the rules of seniority. It is true that both of us have also served as Vice President, but he has been Vice President only four years, I was Vice President eight years. I have seniority. And so I think it is my turn.

Incidentally, when I heard about the mortgage on that building that I dedicated nine years ago, all that I can say is that in return for the very generous comments made by my friend Max Fisher, in the party which I happen to represent which I will not mention because this is a non-partisan organization, I can assure you that in all this great nation there is no man that I know who has been a more effective money-raiser, fund-raiser, than Max Fisher. Let him pay the mortgage. He can do it—after the election, however, I need it first.

Now, if I could talk to you quite seriously about the subjects that I know that are in your hearts tonight and that you would want me to discuss in the great tradition of this organization, I say in the great tradition because while this is a non-partisan organization, you are naturally interested in the great political decisions that will be made by your Government, the Government of the United States, and, consequently, you should know how a potential President of the United States, a candidate for that office, feels on those particular positions which would be of interest to you.

Naturally, I cannot discuss them all and I tried to select those that I think would be of great interest, greatest current interest at this moment for this group. I would like to tell you at the outset the direction of my remarks, the sense of them.

I am not here to make any kind of an attack on the other man who seeks this office. I respect him. We differ. I am here to present my views. I believe that my views will speak for themselves, and then after you have heard us both, of course, you will make up your own minds.

In presenting my views, what I would like to do first is to point out that this organization—and I am going to be quite candid—is known, of course, as a Jewish organization. Whenever this organization takes positions or its members take positions, there is a tendency to say, "That is a Jewish position."

For example, this organization, its members, people like my good friend Max Fisher, Dr. Wexler, others, are tremendously interested in what is going to happen to the State of Israel. There is a tendency in an election campaign when the State of Israel is discussed by a political candidate to say, well that is all politics. They are after the Jewish vote.

Then in the field of civil rights, this organization is tremendously dedicated to that great cause. It has been for 125 years. But the observer who is superficial tends to think this organization is dedicated to the cause of civil rights in terms of civil rights for Jewish people, not for all people. I happen to know differently.

I happen to know that you believe, just as Theodore Roosevelt stated, that if this country is not a good country for all of us, it is not going to be a good country for any of us, and I believe that.

I happen to know, too, that while you have a tremendous interest in the State of Israel, you also have a primary interest in the United States of America. Tonight what I would like to do, I would like to stand aside, if I might, from the B'nai B'rith organization. I would like to speak to you as I know you would want me to speak to you, as an American. I would like to speak to you about the interest that we have in the two great issues of our time: Peace abroad and peace at home.

In talking about those two issues, I naturally will have to be selective. In talking about the issue of peace abroad, I am going to talk about the Mideast. I will tell you why that should be discussed tonight, not because this is the B'nai B'rith, but because in terms of the potential areas of the world that could explode into a nuclear confrontation, the Mideast today presents the greatest danger.

This is not true of Vietnam. Vietnam presents many other dangers, and a current problem very difficult for all of us, as we know. But when we look at the Mideast, all of us realize that there, if the great powers come in confrontation, the possibility of an explosion on a massive basis is there before us, because the interests are so great, much greater, for example, than those involved in what is happening in Vietnam.

For that reason, anyone interested in peace, in world peace, world peace in the sense of the absence of a nuclear confrontation that could destroy civilization as we know it, must look at the Mideast today. It is the primary area at this time that could explode.

I am not predicting that it is going to explode next week, next year, two years, three years from now, but I think it is well for us to look at it in those terms. I think as we look at Mideast policy, it is well for us tonight to consider what has been right about American policy, what has been wrong about American policy, consider it not in partisan terms, but in terms, again, of what are the interests of America in peace.

Now, that brings me to my formal remarks, a major statement that I have prepared on the Mideast situation for this meeting—not, I say again, because this is a Jewish organization, but because at this time in America's history it is essential that we understand the great stakes involved there and the need for new policies to deal with the new problems.

There are four fundamental facts of life that are evident in the Mideast today:

First, the danger of war increases in direct ratio to the confidence of certain Arab leaders that they could win that war.

Second, the Soviet Union has the definite aggressive goal of extending its sphere of influence to include the Middle East, and shall I point out here that when I was here in 1957 I would not have said that? That is something new in the situation.

Third, the United States has a firm and unwavering commitment to the national existence of Israel, repeated by four Presidents, and after Inauguration Day next year, it will be repeated by another President, whichever candidate is elected President of the United States.

Fourth, the foundations for a permanent peace will be laid when hunger and disease and human misery have begun to disappear in the Arab world, and the breeding ground of bitterness and envy is removed.

America must look hard at these facts of life to determine how we can change the collision course of the nations of the Middle East and avert a confrontation of the major powers.

Let's look at these four points that I have raised quite specifically, quite directly, and reach some conclusions.

First, the danger of war increases in direct ratio to the confidence of certain Arab leaders that they could win the war. Here we face a hard fact. Since the six-day war the Soviet Union has systematically rebuilt the armed forces of the U.A.R. and of Syria. Their goal was not to restore a balance of power. Their goal was to further Soviet ambitions. To a disturbing extent they have introduced new and more sophisticated weapons. Their Middle Eastern clients are growing more confident that they could win a war of revenge and drive Israel into the sea. That is what has happened.

Now, what should we do? The free world must act to maintain a balance of power to remove the confidence of would-be aggressors. Certainly a balance of power, as we all know, is only a short-term solution, but when survival is at stake, short-term solutions are necessary.

Israel must possess sufficient military power to deter an attack. As long as the threat of Arab attack remains direct and imminent, sufficient power means the balance must be tipped in Israel's favor.

Let me explain that from a highly technical standpoint. An exact balance of power, which in any case is purely theoretical and not realistic, would run risks that potential aggressors might miscalculate and would offer them too much of a temptation.

For that reason—to provide Israel a valid self-defense—I support a policy that would give Israel a technological military margin to more than offset her hostile neighbors' numerical superiority.

I am not a military expert, and I will rely on the judgment of military experts if I hold the office which I seek. If maintaining that margin of superiority should require that the United States should supply Israel with supersonic Phantom F-4 jets, we should supply those jets so they can maintain that superiority.

Now, let us look at our second hard fact. The Soviet Union has the definite aggressive goal of extending its sphere of influence to include the Middle East. In the Middle East, in the Mediterranean, along the southern flank of NATO, we have been witnessing the advancement of Russian imperialism. This is no Communist innovation, but it the age-old Russian geopolitical goal that the Soviet leaders inherited from the Czars.

Look at the pattern. In June of 1966, as far back as that, the Warsaw Pact nations blatantly declared the incorporation of the Middle East into the Communist sphere to be one of their aims.

During the next year, they provided the weapons and unleashed a propaganda campaign that inflamed tensions and led to the six-day war which they considered only a temporary setback.

Since June of 1967 the Mediterranean complement of Soviet ships has more than quadrupled from 11 to nearly 50 ships, and for the first time in 60 years, the Soviets have moved a fleet into the Persian Gulf which extends into the heart of West Asia.

Since the takeover of Czechoslovakia, the Soviets—and this is a very significant point—have stepped up their anti-Semitic propaganda, concocting a "Zionist plot" in Prague. Why? To win the support in the Middle East.

Now, that is the fact. These are the clear-cut moves of a superpower seeking domination. Confronted with this diplomatic and military policy and expansionism on the part of the Soviets, I believe that the American response has been uncertain and ineffectual. We can hardly ignore the fact that during the past five years of active Soviet penetration, the United States Government has at times seemed to hide its head in the sands of the Middle East. The Administration has failed to come to diplomatic grips with the scope and seriousness of the Soviet threat.

Now, what do we do? Short-range, we must counter the military build-up, as I have indicated. We must take the initiative for near-term settlements. Looking ahead, we must deal directly with the Soviets diplomatically on the subject of the Middle East.

Without belligerence but with complete firmness, we have to make it crystal clear that the stake of the free world in the Middle East is great. We must impress upon the Soviets the full extent of our determination. Then, and only then, will we cause them to re-examine their own policy to avoid a collision course.

Some may call this a hard line. But I insist that when you are confronted with a potential aggressive power, the most important thing to remember is that he must not miscalculate. So let him know in advance that we have a great interest. That is why we must speak firmly.

Now, let's look at the third fact of life in the Middle East. The United States has a firm and unwavering commitment to the national existence of Israel.

I think most of us are aware in this room of some of the reasons for that commitment. America supports Israel because we believe in self-determination of nations. We support Israel because we oppose aggression in every form. We support Israel because it is threatened by Soviet imperialism, and we support Israel because its example offers long-range hope in the Middle East. What they have done there offers hope of what could happen elsewhere.

There is another reason that goes beyond diplomacy. Americans admire a people who can scratch a desert and produce a garden. The Israelis have shown qualities that Americans identify with: guts, patriotism, idealism, a passion for freedom. I have seen it. I know. I believe that.

So we can justify our firm support on the basis of principle, but there is also this human element involved as well. All these reasons taken together add up to why we are not about to abandon Israel. America's word is good. It has cost us enough to prove that. We recognize Israel's predicament. One fact is this: Israel's enemies can afford to fight a war and lose. They can come back to fight again. But Israel cannot afford to lose even once. America knows that and America is determined that Israel is here in the family of nations to stay.

Now we come to the positive side, the fourth fact of life, the foundations for a permanent peace will be laid when hunger and disease and human misery have begun to disappear from the Arab world.

Some Arab leaders equate America's support of Israel as being against them. That is absolutely untrue. The United States should work with every nation in the Middle East willing to live in peace with its neighbors in a far-reaching development program.

The imaginative Eisenhower Plan to bring water—and thus food and employment to the Middle East—is one such proposal. This plan would provide atomic plants for the desalting of seawater, water so desperately needed to irrigate deserts. The first of these plants would produce as much fresh water as the Jordan River system does today. It would open a new life to hundreds of thousands of Arab refugees. We must explore every avenue to turn the arms race into a race for development.

Right now, the United States must take the lead in forming an acceptable settlement in the Middle East.

Listen to the terms: Included in those terms should be solid guarantees that the currently occupied territories will never again be used as a basis of aggression and sanctuary for terrorism.

Access for the ships of all nations through the re-opened Suez Canal and the Straits of Tiran should be guaranteed.

The settlement should include recognition of Israeli sovereignty, its right to exist in peace and an end to the state of belligerency.

It is my view that for Israel to take formal and final possession of the occupied territories would be a grave mistake. At the same time it is not realistic to expect Israel to surrender vital bargaining counters in the absence of a genuine peace and effective guarantees, and that is what this is all about. I recognize, as all of you recognize in this room that to find a just peace in an area of the world that has only known armed truces and three major and bitter wars in a generation is not an easy task. But the United States is not without diplomatic and economic resources, and its private and public men are not without cogent ideas to get directly at the underlying problems of refugees and water.

We should thwart the temptation for aggression by helping Israel maintain a defense, we should engage in some direct hard negotiation, hard and fair, with the Soviet Union, to remove one underlying cause of the tension.

We should assert some leadership in bringing about talks with the moderate Arab leaders and then with the militants, and we should open up vistas of growth and development that can gradually end the bitterness and envy that exist. This is an ambitious task, but the only way to succeed or even partially to succeed is to make the effort.

252

Any future Mideast war could bring together in a sudden collision not only the nations of the Mideast but the great powers of the East and West. We must not allow the cradle of civilization to become its grave. That is what is at stake in the Mideast.

Let me turn from the subject of peace abroad, of which the Mideast is such an important part. It is an example, of course, of the type of diplomacy we need all over the world in these critical flashpoints—Let us turn from the subject of peace abroad to the equally important subject of peace at home.

One thing that we must all recognize in this room is that the United States of America, which is destined, whether we want it or not, to lead the forces of peace and freedom abroad in this last third of the century—we are not going to be respected, we are not going to be able to fulfill the mission of bringing peace abroad unless we can demonstrate that we can keep the peace at home.

So we look at the United States today in this year 1968. We see problems that deeply concern us, concern us as Americans. We see the rise in crime, we see the riots in our cities, we see the problems in the ghettos, the problems in the universities.

We understand as we look at these problems that they are not partisan problems. They are ones that are not going to be solved only by laws or programs. They are ones that are going to take a commitment by a people, a people who will recognize that we need the best efforts of all of the American people if we are to have now an era of reconciliation after an era of revolution.

Here I want to talk bluntly about another subject that will be before you, has been before you, and will be before this nation in the months ahead. Often you hear it said that when an individual comes before an audience and talks about the necessity for order, or law and order, that that is simply a code word for racism.

The answer on the other side, of course, is that rather than talking about order, we should talk about progress. Let me give you my view. We need both because order without progress is tyranny. You cannot have order without progress in a free society. Eventually there will be an explosion.

But there is another side to that coin. Progress without order is anarchy. You cannot have progress with disorder. You look back to the history of this country. We were born in revolution, but what we must recognize is that our Founding Fathers had the genius to set up a system of government which provided a method for peacefully changing what we do not like about our country.

In a country which provides a method for peaceful change, there is no cause in my view that justifies lawlessness or violence. This we must understand in the United States of America. That is the "order" side of the equation.

Let's look at the progress side of the equation. We can talk about the necessities for law and order, we can pass laws, we can have better police and more police, but if the people who live in some of the great cities of our country have no hope, they have nothing to lose, they will explode. So progress is essential.

We must light the lamp of hope in millions of homes tonight in which there is no hope. This is what we must do. Again, this is not Republican talk or Democratic talk. It is what we Americans have always believed. It is the American dream.

For virtually everybody in this room the American dream has come true. We have had an equal chance. We have moved up. But for millions the American dream is a nightmare. There is no chance. You have heard this said before.

The question then is not the objective. The question is the means. Here I believe it is essential that the United States move toward new means and on a new road. I do not mean that Government cannot play a great role, but I do say that when you say that the answer to the problems of our cities is simply to pour billions of dollars more into programs for Government jobs and Government houses and Government welfare, what we are doing is to go down a road which we have been proceeding down and which has not brought us to the destination that we want to go to.

254

What we must recognize is that Government has its role to play, but if you are going to have progress, if you are going to rebuild the cities of America, if you are going to provide the jobs and the training for jobs that you need to be provided for those that do not have that kind of training, the great instrument of progress in America is private enterprise rather than government enterprise.

We must enlist private enterprise in the job of rebuilding America. That is why—and I will not spell them out tonight—I have emphasized and will continue to emphasize the necessity for a new approach: Government playing its great role where private enterprise cannot do it, education and the like—but private enterprise having a tax credit to train the unemployed for real jobs that will be there rather than jobs that will not be there; private enterprise having a tax credit to bring private housing into the cities and into the ghettoes so that people can have the pride of owning their houses with all that that means in pride and dignity and self-respect; private enterprise receiving again tax credit and incentives in other ways not only to train the unemployed for jobs but to give people, black Americans, Mexican Americans, others who have not had that equal chance, give them a chance to become owners and managers, to have a piece of the action, because—let me be quite direct—Government can provide a job for a man, it can provide housing for a man, it can provide clothing for a man and shelter for a man, but Government cannot provide dignity and pride and self-respect. That will only come when people get that ownership, a piece of the action in America.

That is why I think that now we need to enlist the great private community of the United States, this great engine of progress, in the unfinished business of America, rebuilding the cities of America and also in the unfinished business of poverty in rural America.

Then, finally, one other area which is particularly appropriate to mention before this organization. I refer to the fact that apart from what private enterprise may do, do for profit as private enterprise must operate from profit, what we have is an engine for progress in this country, and a third dimension, an extra dimension, which deTocqueville pointed out 100 years ago when he traveled over the young America at that time was unique among the nations of the world, and that is what Americans do in their volunteer capacities. There are thousands of organizations across the country like B'nai B'rith, organizations of people who in terms of heart, in terms of dedication, in terms of devotion, help less fortunate people in a way that money cannot buy.

We need more of that. I simply want to say that as I talk to this organization, I am aware of the fact, and I get back to my original theme, that your interests are far beyond the Jewish community, that your interests extend to good causes in all of the cities in which you live, and I would say that as I look to the future of America that the next President of the United States can call upon the Congress to enact laws and he can call upon the Congress to appropriate money, and he can call upon the Congress to provide tax credits to private industry, but if we are going to have the true reconciliation, if we are going to have the true progress that we need, we need a total commitment from the whole American community.

That is why it is so important that organizations like this one with a heart recognize how much they can contribute to bringing the reconciliation which is so deeply needed in America.

Could I be permitted to put this as I conclude in the semantics of religion? The Christians, most Catholics and most Protestants, in referring to the kind of voluntary activity that I have just described, used the word "charity," a great word.

The Quakers, my Quaker mother, my Quaker grandmother, used the word "concern." I recall my mother and my grandmother saying, "I have a concern for peace. I have a concern for this person or that person. Thee must have a concern for someone who is less fortunate than thee.

When I was ten years ago in St. Louis dedicating a building, a friend of mine, Sam Krupnick—it happened to be a Jewish building—told me that the Hebrew word which was similar to these two words was "seddukah." I said, "What does it mean?"

He thought a moment, and said, "It means 'Do justly.'" Do justly not because the law requires it, not because your religion requires it, but because this is what every man owes to his fellowman.

256

As I stand before this group tonight, I think there is no greater message that could emanate from this triennial convention of B'nai B'rith than across this land of ours for Americans to get the message "Seddukah"—Do justly, because if we feel that in our hearts, then we are going to be able to make progress in these very difficult times in which we live.

Finally, since I began in discussing the problems of peace abroad and have finished by talking about the problems of peace at home, it would seem to me that it would be only appropriate since I understand 45 other nations are represented here today to tell our friends from abroad what I think is America's foreign policy objective, whether it is Vietnam, whether it is in the Mideast, whether it is in Europe or any place in the world.

In the last third of this century, whether peace or freedom does survive will depend upon the leadership of the United States of America. The question arises, What does the United States want? On this score we are different from the powers that preceded us. This is no reflection on them because that was a different time.

We do not seek colonies. We do not seek economic concessions. We seek only the right to live in peace with other nations. We do not try to impose our system upon them. We like our system but we recognize that for some other countries it may not work. We want each of them to select his own system, and we want our ideas to travel on their own power and not on the power of our arms. That is the American ideal.

I think I can best put it in terms of one of the shortest and one of the greatest speeches ever made in the English language. It was 150 years ago at a happier time in Britain's history, right after Nelson's great victory at Trafalgar. A great dinner was held in London's Guild Hall. William Pitt, the Prime Minister, was toasted at that dinner as the savior of Europe. He rose to his feet, he answered the toast. Listen to his words.

"I return you many thanks for the honor you have done me, but Europe will not be saved by any single man. England has saved herself by her exertions and will, I trust, save Europe by her example."

I would say to you tonight, looking at America and its role in the world, the world will not be saved by any single man, but America can save herself by her exertions and will, I trust, save the cause of peace and freedom in the world by her example.

B'nai B'rith Convention
Washington, D.C.
Sunday, September 8, 1968

THE TIME TO SAVE NATO

Ever since our birth as a nation, close ties of history and kinship have bound America to Europe. But since World War II, we have also been bound by new ties of vital national interest. The Atlantic Alliance—formalized in the North Atlantic Treaty Organization—has been the cornerstone of our own network of defensive alliances, and the world's strongest bulwark of peace.

But the structure born of necessity in the bitter aftermath of World War II has fallen on days of neglect. The United States has been pre-occupied in Asia. Many of our European partners have been caught up in their own concerns, or grown dissatisfied with the functioning of the alliance, or changed their estimates of the Soviet challenge.

As a result, as it approaches its 20th anniversary, NATO is in trouble about the Atlantic Alliance, what it represents, and how we can preserve it.

Let me begin by sharing with you a report I received just a few days ago.

Last month I asked former Governor Scranton of Pennsylvania to make a fact-finding tour of Western Europe on my behalf. He visited France, Germany, Italy, Belgium, the Netherlands, and Britain. In each country he talked at length with the leaders of government and with private citizens about many of the problems confronting Europe today. This past week he returned, and on Thursday he gave me his report.

The first of his findings explains many of our other difficulties. America's voice in Europe, once so strong and so respected, is, in his words, "Now muffled in confusion — if it is listened to at all."

Why is this?

There are many reasons, he learned. Vietnam is one. But even more, the Europeans were appalled at what they daily saw happening in America: at the violence, the lawlessness, the prejudice, the hate, the disenchantment of our youth, the decline of our dollar, the loss of credibility by our national leadership. These, he said, leave our friends in Europe bewildered and disappointed. They expect the leader of the free world to do better.

259

They expect us to set standards. When we fail their expectations, we lose their attention and their respect.

The meaning is clear.

If we are to restore the effectiveness of our leadership, we have to restore the credibility of our leadership. If we are to be trusted to maintain peace abroad, we have to show that we can maintain peace at home. If our example is to be followed rather than spurned, it has to be an example of what other nations seek to be, not what they seek to avoid.

That was one lesson.

Another concerns NATO itself.

One high official summed up the mood of many when he told Governor Scranton: "Czechoslovakia breathes new life into the old girl, but I wonder how long it will last."

What the official was referring to is this: NATO's troubles have left it weakened, its future uncertain. France has withdrawn its forces; other members have let theirs lag well below the prescribed levels: coordination has sometimes been lax; faith in the firmness of the American commitment has been eroded. Many have questioned whether the alliance would long survive at all, or whether it would soon be left to die.

But when the Soviets invaded Czechoslovakia, shock waves swept suddenly across Europe.

NATO members felt a new anxiety about their defenses.

The Soviet takeover of Czechoslovakia helped pass the Marshall Plan in 1948; 20 years later, the Soviet invasion of Czechoslovakia has helped— for a time, at least—to revive the spirit of NATO.

The result is that if NATO is to be saved, now is the time to save it.

If the Czech crisis demonstrated the continuing need for NATO, it also pointed up some of the problems that have to be overcome.

For example: despite meetings galore at NATO Headquarters, the only collective response by NATO to the Czech invasion has been to advance a December ministerial meeting to November.

More ominously, the NATO posture is based on a political assessment of Soviet intentions. As it turned out, the judgment that the Soviets did not plan to attack a NATO member proved correct. But on the other hand, virtually no NATO political leader had predicted the invasion of Czechoslovakia. In short, NATO did miscalculate Soviet intentions; it did underestimate the risks the Soviets were willing to take.

If this miscalculation could be made, might the next miscalculation be greater? And is NATO strong enough to allow a margin for miscalculation?

These are questions NATO must address.

They are heightened by another lesson of the Czech episode: there appear to be major elements of instability in the Soviet leadership, with a hard-line faction having increasing influence. These instabilities make it even more difficult to predict how far the Soviets might go in the future. How much would they risk? What would be their assessment of Western intentions?

Among the other questions facing NATO in the wake of the Czech invasion is the changed balance of conventional power in Europe. The Soviets already had dramatically enlarged their naval presence in the Mediterranean; now they have brought half again as many troops into Eastern Europe as they had there before, and placed them farther forward than ever. At the same time, the Czech operation was carried out with a crack efficiency and speed that many thought the Soviets not capable of.

In the face of this, U.S. troops in Germany are poorly equipped; other NATO partners have let their contributions fall below the prescribed force levels. The increased Soviet strength would seem to suggest that as a minimum response, those forces should be brought up to the strength prescribed before Czechoslovakia.

In a larger sense, revitalizing NATO involves much more than troop levels.

It requires a new attitude on the part of the United States.

Increasingly, the Atlantic Alliance has suffered from American neglect. It was symptomatic of this that Europe was not even mentioned in this year's State of the Union Message. There has not been a NATO summit since President Eisenhower went to Paris in 1958. Actions have been taken by the United States which vitally affected the security of our European partners, without even the courtesy of prior consultation. In its preoccupation with bilateral detente with the Soviet Union, the Administration has too often pursued it in ways that seemed to our European allies to jeopardize their interests, without having those interests represented.

It's time we began paying Europe more attention. And if our ideals of Atlantic interdependence are to mean anything in practice, it's time we began lecturing our European partners less and listening to them more. What we need is not more proclamations and declarations, but a greater attention to what our allies think.

One of the chief values in having allies is the access it gives to their ideas. Too often, America's world view has been narrowed to the view from a Washington window. What we need from our NATO partners is not only their strength, but their experience and their judgment.

If the Free World is to meet its challenges, it's going to take the best brainpower that all of us together can contribute.

One of the most encouraging things I have found in my own travels abroad is that all around the world there are outstanding leaders, many of them in small countries, who have a keen perception of the forces moving the world—of both the threats to peace and the paths to peace. Their insights are not limited to their own areas.

In NATO, for example, there is an enormous fund of wisdom not only about Europe, but also about Asia and Africa and the Middle East. Ten years ago, five years ago, many of these Europeans were not accepted in former colonial areas. But this is changing.

NATO thus has a role to play beyond Europe—not with its arms, but with its insight, and by helping build those bridges that are so urgently needed between the rich and the poor nations of the world. On the foundation of cooperation that has been built with NATO, we can build for the tasks beyond.

This is one of the reasons why I hope to establish a greater openness, more communication, within NATO — not only on a protocol basis, and not simply about whether we should establish a base here or conclude an agreement there, but free and far-ranging discussion of all the problems that confront the free world.

I would hope this could include quite specifically, new conversations with President De Gaulle.

Nearly a quarter-century has passed since the end of World War II, and nearly 20 years since the creation of NATO. This has been a period of extraordinary change and development. Only, if it keeps abreast of change can the Alliance retain its vitality.

The world has changed.

As we look at the world, we find for the first time ever a genuinely global community, however wracked it may be with turmoil and quarrels. Asia is no longer an appendage of Europe; neither are the nations of Asia what they once were, as remote from the West as if they had been on a separate planet. Africa, in a ferment of new nationhood; Latin America, still developing economically but rich in culture: the Soviet Union, tough, expansionist, but making giant strides in industry and technology — it's a world of new nations, new people, new ideas, all part of a great, global village.

The Soviet Union has changed.

Many have interpreted that change as allowing the West to relax its guard. But in its relations with the rest of the world, the Soviet Union has had a change of the head, not the heart. The change was gradually brought about as Western strength and Western unity persuaded the men in the Kremlin that expansion by crude force had reached its limits. If the process of change is to continue, the maintenance of Western strength and unity is essential.

Any sign of Western weakness or Western irresolution would only tempt the Soviets to new adventures and strengthen the hand of the hardline faction within the Kremlin. Far from accelerating the hopeful change, it would reverse it.

Despite the recent setbacks, the years just ahead can bring a breakthrough for peace. They must be a time of careful probing, of intensive negotiations, of a determined search for those areas of accommodation between East and West on which a climate of mutual trust can eventually be built. But this can only succeed if Western strength is sufficient to back up our diplomacy. As one of Europe's leading statesmen has phrased it: "Genuine detente presupposes security; it does not replace it."

The world has changed; the Soviet Union has changed; Western Europe, too, has dramatically changed.

Since World War II, Western Europe has seen its empires dismantled and its pre-eminence in power taken by others. Yet at the same time, its economies have been rebuilt, its societies restructured, a new set of political relationships pioneered.

After centuries of intense nationalism, new international organs have sprung into being in Europe on a scale unmatched in the world, and unmatched in history: the Western European Union, the European Coal and Steel Community, the Common Market, the European Free Trade Association, Euratom, the Organization for Economic Cooperation and Development, and many more — not least of them NATO itself.

The result is that Western Europe today is self-assured, strong, and growing stronger. If a greater measure of European union can be achieved, its potentials for development are almost limitless. It has the resources, the skills, and the educated people to make it another superpower.

Some argue that we should not encourage further European unity, precisely because Europe does have so great a power potential. But a strong, independent Europe within the Atlantic Alliance could make for a healthier Atlantic Community at the same time providing a strong negotiation hand with the Soviet Union.

Whatever our own feelings in the matter, however, we should recognize that the shape of Europe's future is essentially the business of the Europeans. If greater European unity is to be achieved, it will have to be through European initiatives and on European terms; it is not our place to meddle, to prescribe, or to sponsor schemes to bring it about.

We can, however, cooperate with initiatives the Europeans take — for example, with the stirrings within NATO of an informal European caucus to deal with the United States on matters of defense.

A revitalized NATO, a strengthened European Community, a new spirit of cooperation between the U.S. and Europe — all these together can contribute to a stronger defense, to the concerting of new initiatives for peace and not least to the coordination of effort needed for crisis prevention.

The surest way to invite a crisis is to be unprepared for it. The present Administration has lived from crisis to crisis, improvising here and temporizing there — a practice that makes for a lively drama, but poor diplomacy. In these times of uneasy peace, we need a shift of emphasis from crisis management to crisis prevention; to anticipating trouble, rather than merely responding to it. And in today's global village, crisis prevention requires allies who consult.

We live in a condition, as it once was described, of "neither war nor peace". But in its halting, often disappointing way, the progress of civilization has been toward a world at peace.

The best example is Western Europe.

For centuries, the continent was wracked by wars, as armies surged back and forth in pursuit of conquest. But finally, out of the terrible catharsis of World War II, the spirit of peace finally rose triumphant. A new era began, there in the very place where Western civilization developed: an era in which, for the first time, war ceased to be an instrument of national ambition.

Whatever the needs of defense, the war of conquest has been abandoned by the nations of Western Europe.

It's easy to forget how recent a change this it, and how monumental a development.

It's this great change that NATO represents, this great ideal that NATO embodies. The task of the years ahead — a task we share with our European partners — is to coordinate our strength in the service of peace, and to make this ideal the governing doctrine of man.

CBS Radio Network
Sunday, October 13, 1968

THE ALLIANCE FOR PROGRESS

Eight years ago—during the last year of the Eisenhower Administration —the Act of Bogota, the forerunner of the present Alliance for Progress, was concluded. The noble concept set forth in this agreement, reached after years of work and consultation, provided the groundwork and the inspiration for a genuine partnership for progress in Latin America.

Now, seven years after President Kennedy called upon the nations of the Western Hemisphere to join in a massive program of economic and social development and democratic progress, the Alliance is foundering.

Economic and social development has not kept pace with demands, and democratic progress has been only halting. The already ominous gulf between North and South America continues to widen at an alarming pace.

Statistics bear out this gloomy picture:

Since World War II, Latin American exports to the United States have been cut in half. In 1967 alone, these exports dropped more than $300 million.

Since 1962, the beginning of the Alliance for Progress, Latin America's share in world trade has dropped from 6.5 to 5.4 percent.

An Inter-American Development Bank report shows that the per capita growth rate is only 1.5 percent per year, far below the 2.5 percent goal established by the Alliance.

Interest payments and other debt servicing has doubled in the seven years of the Alliance and now absorbs almost 75 percent of the money coming into the area.

The sharp drop in exports is causing acute balance of payments problems.

The U.S. food and agriculture organization estimates that food production must increase over the next few years at an annual rate of 7 percent in order to make up for short-falls since 1964. This is considered an impossibility.

Despite the optimistic tone set by the Administration at the April 1967 Punta Del Este meeting of heads of state, the highly touted "action program" has failed to bring action.

Except for cutbacks in military expenditures, none of the goals has been

266

advanced in the first year. Several, in fact, have been hopelessly retarded. For example, a major item on the Punta Del Este agenda was the modernization of agriculture. But, in the months since the meeting, the problem has become even worse. Hunger and malnutrition are more widespread in Latin America today than eight years ago, there are now some 60 million more mouths to feed.

While all of this seems to add up to a doleful prospect, the lack of progress under the Alliance should never lead our nation into a sense of resignation. Such an attitude would jeopardize both the fundamental ideals and the interests of the American people. We cannot and should not ignore the needs and aspirations of our immediate neighbors. The continuing problems present a constant challenge to the imagination and innovative abilities of free people.

What is needed is an action program of realistic dimensions to attack the problems of Latin America's unencumbered ideological dogmas and platitudes. The present Administration has clearly shown its unwillingness and inability to give our neighbors the priority status and effective aid which they deserve. It has utterly failed even in the basic requirement for effective cooperation: an integrated strategy of assistance with clear priorities. Money and energy have been dissipated without a realistic assessment of the most efficient methods for achieving established goals.

Now, before it is too late, and before Latin America is engulfed in disillusionment brought on by grandiose and unrealistic schemes emanating from Washington, we must make sweeping reevaluation of the Alliance. Without jeopardizing the national security of any Latin American nation, we must terminate those over-bureaucratized forms of aid which are of little benefit to the economies of Latin America, and redirect all available resources for an attack on the real problems of hunger and sagging growth rates.

First, we must make more conscious efforts toward "Latinizing" our actions in Latin America. This will not only serve as a positive, self-help motivation for the Latin Americans; but it would also serve to open the way for the United States to play a more constructive role on a partnership basis in the area. On my most recent trip to Latin America in 1967, I noted with great interest the emerging middle class, a crucial factor in this phase of cooperation.

The Latinization moves should be designed as a part in establishing a truly regional approach. While success in regionalism and development in general will depend upon the response of Latin Americans, the initiative in this movement can come from Washington. We should gear our machinery to such an approach, which first of all means the establishment of one rather than several voices and agencies. To date, dispersion of responsibilities and functions has made it virtually impossible for Washington to speak with one voice in the Alliance for Progress.

Second, we must honestly re-evaluate the Agency for International Development Program in terms of its capacity for promoting necessary reforms. In the final analysis, the only means for opening up Latin America will be capital, technical skills and more hard work and intimately connected with these key elements must be a recognition that a significant portion of profits generated by free enterprise will remain in Latin America.

Third, our emphasis should be upon trade instead of aid. Proposals deserving full consideration include; a new inter-American fund to assist in the stabilization of prices of Latin American commodities; special financial assistance to those countries burdened with interest loads on their debts; and a system of tariff preferences for Latin American exports. It is urgent that we help restore forward momentum to the Latin American economies.

Fourth, U.S. policies should always reflect our concern that the Organization of American States become a truly international political body with vigorous political and economic programs.

Fifth, by word and deed, the United States and its hemisphere partners must make clear their support of constructive change in both the private and public sectors. We should reinforce our opposition to mere maintenance of the status quo.

Sixth, the United States would take steps toward a strategic approach in agricultural development, education and technical assistance. All aspects of agricultural development should take priority at this stage, as food production falls hazardously behind population growth. The great irony is that Latin America is not an over-populated continent, but an under-populated one. What the Alliance has not provided are the tools and technology required to till the land. With knowledge, seed, and fertilizer, Latin Americans can feed themselves. Then they can begin the task of exploiting in a serious way the vast untapped resources of the continent.

There are various ways in which we can aid our Latin American neighbors in developing their economies and in meeting the challenge of exploiting the continent's vast pool of untapped resources.

Walter Lippmann has suggested that the key to progress in Latin America is the opening of the Latin American heartland. As I have stated previously, I would favor instituting a crash program to finish the highway net down the center of the continent, with a goal of completion in five years. To accomplish this we must marshal all available resources.

Of course, this will not solve all problems immediately or automatically. It will not do away with the need for other programs. But the opening of the heartland of South America will have an immense effect economically and will open more doors to development for our neighbors.

The opening of the continent would also do more to facilitate the growth of a Latin American common market than any massive government-to-government aid program.

Education must also take a top priority position. While the Alliance proclaimed the goal of eradicating illiteracy in the 1960's, it appears, in fact, that illiteracy will get worse. Expanding the regular educational process is only half the goal. Vocational training is also a requirement, for Latin Americans need to know not only how to manage a government, but how to run a lathe, how to run a tractor and a harvestor.

In assisting Latin America to expand its educational systems of all types, it should be clearly understood that the United States has no interest in establishing the curriculum, but seeks only to assist our neighbors to adapt their systems to their own needs. It is neither possible nor desirable to expect that our own educational techniques and curriculum structures can automatically be transferred to fill the needs of others. But once the Latin American countries sense that the United States is genuinely committed to meaningful and measureable progress on their behalf, a genuine alliance based on true partnership can be more effectively forged.

This confidence cannot come about with switching, veering and uncertainty on the part of Washington. Our neighbors to the south have appreciated neither the hard line nor the soft line; they need a straight line and that line adhered to.

Most important, our policies must be as flexible as changing conditions require. In the search for alternatives to caudillos and communists, we would do well to keep in mind that Castro-communism constitutes a threat, not because it is strong, but because its target is weak. To meet this threat, what Latin America really needs is fewer marching feet and more helping hands.

The last third of the Twentieth Century may well be our final chance to solve these problems by means of peaceful change. As we enter this critical period, our friends in the western hemisphere must be equipped—both materially and spiritually—to grapple realistically with the mounting problems. And it is only with new leadership from the United States, a new leadership capable of marshalling all the resources at our command, that this regeneration can begin.

New York, N.Y.

Monday, October 14, 1968

IN THE ARENA

LESSONS OF CRISIS

(Preface to 1968 edition of *Six Crises*)

This book was written between defeats. The 1960 presidential campaign was history, and I was soon to lose the 1962 campaign for Governor of California.

At that point I retired from politics, moved to New York and entered the private practice of law. For the first time, I was able to provide for the future of my family. And with no political future of my own, I was able to reflect about and comment on the American political scene with complete objectivity.

"No political future" was a fair statement. As a lawyer, I had a good career ahead, but as a political force, as I said at my "last press conference" in 1962, I was through.

I wish I could analyze the workings of American democracy and the mystery of public opinion that took a man from "finished" in 1963 to candidate for the Presidency in 1968. I cannot. Not even a statesman who was also a great historian — Winston Churchill — could adequately explain why, after a decade in political eclipse, he was the one called upon to lead his nation in a time of crisis.

There is no doubt, however, about what was *not* the reason for my candidacy today: it was not by dint of my own calculation or efforts. No man, not if he combined the wisdom of Lincoln with the connivance of Machiavelli, could have maneuvered or manipulated his way back into the arena.

Sometimes a nation is ready and a man is not; sometimes a man is ready and a nation is not; sometimes a nation decides that a man is ready for leadership and his is the right kind of leadership for the time. Only time will tell what course destiny will take in this watershed year of 1968.

Crisis is a recurring theme in American history. In 1776, Tom Paine titled a series of pamphlets *The American Crisis,* and every schoolboy is familiar with its most famous line: "These are the times that try men's souls."

Not every schoolboy is familiar with another line from *The American Crisis:* "Not a place upon earth might be so happy as America."

273

That counterpoint of sacrifice and optimism is built into the discussion of every crisis in this book, and every crisis America faces today.

Six Crises was intended to be, and is, a personal memoir and not a history of the Fifties. I wrote in 1961 about the moments of tension and drama that were closest to me, with no presumption that they were the most important events of the time.

How are these personal crises in one man's life relevant to Americans in 1968? Perhaps in these ways:

The number of crises a man has been through is relatively unimportant; what counts is what he learns from them and how he applies what he has learned in one to the next crisis.

The major crises of John F. Kennedy's administration are a case in point. During the Bay of Pigs disaster, the new President learned about the dependence of expert advice, the need to exercise enough power to guarantee success, and the requirement of leadership to assume responsibility for failure.

At the next major crisis, the Cuban missile confrontation with Khrushchev, the lessons of the Bay of Pigs served him in good stead. The President's ability to understand the proper use of power learned tragically at the start of his term led to what was undoubtedly his finest hour in turning back an unacceptable threat to our security.

The crises of the Eisenhower years, and of the Kennedy administration, were on the whole short-term moments of tension; they were resolved one way or another with national leadership strengthened.

But with the Johnson-Humphrey administration, the nature of crisis has changed. The remarkable characteristic of the crises of today is their continuity — they have moved in, it seems, to stay. Let us examine some of them:

1. The continuing crisis in Vietnam. The decision to rise to this crisis was, in my view, the right decision; the method of meeting it was wrong. We frittered away our power through piecemeal escalation that locked us in a long land war in Asia; we had no global strategy to induce the Soviet Union to stop making it possible for the war to go on. And so that crisis has dragged on for years.

2. The crisis of the American city. A welfare philosophy tuned to the Thirties that overlooks the need for human dignity, combined with the frustration of unfulfilled promises, has led to riots and sustained civil disorder. The two-day crisis of a riot led to the summer-long crisis of 1966 and 1967 and to the year-round crisis of today.

3. The crisis of the American dollar. A policy of heavy government spending has led to runaway inflation, which in turn has led to a worldwide loss of confidence in the American dollar — endangering jobs and hurting most those on fixed incomes. And this crisis is not being resolved, as the cost of living rises at an ever-faster rate.

4. The crisis of crime. As the forces of justice were hampered by court decisions that put the scales of individual liberty and public protection out of balance, crime in America has increased by 55% — and this crisis is getting worse every day.

Add to these the growing crises of housing, of pollution, of inadequate education, and a picture emerges of government by crisis, of "crash programs" that only lead to crashing hopes.

The next President cannot be expected to lead an administration of serenity and calm, of no crises. Too many events press in upon us from abroad to hope for that; the momentum and ferment of change at home clearly means that the "revolution of rising expectations" will cause crises for us at home as well.

But someting can be done to alleviate the *continuity* of crisis, the atmosphere of crisis, that pervades American life today.

We need not wait for explosions in our cities to begin realistic programs that restore self-respect to the poor and open up opportunity for the jobless man who wants to work. We need not wait for infiltration and invasion abroad to practice the kind of preventive diplomacy that averts crisis rather than responds to crisis; we need not wait until inflation backs us to the wall to start to get our economic house in order.

Some crisis is unavoidable, and proves a test for leadership; some crisis is healthy, when it snaps us out of our lethargy; but crisis cannot be allowed to become the American way of life.

A national crisis is a shock to the body politic. Too many shocks, especially long-sustained shocks, drain a nation of its energy; it can cause a national punchiness, and even worse, cause a rebellion against creative change and progress.

There are more than enough "natural shocks that flesh is heir to" — crises that cannot be avoided — for us to add to them by lack of foresight or a willingness to act in time. This may disappoint those who are attracted by the excitement of high drama, but the best way to meet a crisis is to anticipate it and avoid it. Those who ignore impending crisis are condemned to live through it.

(Preface to 1968 edition of *Six Crises*)

I SEE A DAY...

Mr. Chairman, delegates to this convention, my fellow Americans.

Sixteen years ago I stood before this Convention to accept your nomination as the running mate of one of the greatest Americans of our time—or of any time—Dwight D. Eisenhower.

Eight years ago, I had the highest honor of accepting your nomination for President of the United States.

Tonight, I again proudly accept that nomination for President of the United States.

But I have news for you. This time there is a difference.

This time we are going to win.

We're going to win for a number of reasons: first a personal one. General Eisenhower, as you know, lies critically ill in the Walter Reed Hospital tonight. I have talked, however, with Mrs. Eisenhower on the telephone. She tells me that his heart is with us. And she says that there is nothing that he lives more for and there is nothing that would lift him more than for us to win in November and I say let's win this one for Ike!

We are going to win because this great Convention has demonstrated to the nation that the Republican Party has the leadership, the platform and the purpose that America needs.

We are going to win because you have nominated as my running mate a statesman of the first rank who will be a great campaigner and one who is fully qualified to undertake the new responsibilities that I shall give to the next Vice President of the United States.

And he is a man who fully shares my conviction and yours, that after a period of forty years when power has gone from the cities and the states to the government in Washington, D.C., it's time to have power go back from Washington to the states and to the cities of this country all over America.

We are going to win because at a time that America cries out for the unity that this Administration has destroyed, the Republican Party—after a spirited contest for its nomination for President and for Vice President—stands united before the nation tonight.

I congratulate Governor Reagan. I congratulate Governor Rockefeller. I congratulate Governor Romney. I congratulate all those who have made the hard fight that they have for this nomination. And I know that you will all fight even harder for the great victory our party is going to win in November because we're going to be together in that election campaign.

And a party that can unite itself will unite America.

My fellow Americans, most important—we are going to win because our cause is right.

We make history tonight—not for ourselves but for the ages.

The choice we make in 1968 will determine not only the future of America but the future of peace and freedom in the world for the last third of the Twentieth Century.

And the question that we answer tonight: can America meet this great challenge?

For a few moments, lets us look at America, let us listen to America to find the answer to that question.

As we look at America, we see cities enveloped in smoke and flame.

We hear sirens in the night.

We see Americans dying on distant battlefields abroad.

We see Americans hating each other; fighting each other; killing each other at home.

And as we see and hear these things, millions of Americans cry out in anguish.

Did we come all this way for this?

Did American boys die in Normandy, and Korea, and in Valley Forge for this?

Listen to the answer to those questions.

It is another voice. It is the quiet voice in the tumult and the shouting.

It is the voice of the great majority of Americans, the forgotten Americans—the non-shouters; the non-demonstrators.

They are not racists or sick; they are not guilty of the crime that plagues the land.

They are black and they are white—they're native born and foreign born —they're young and they're old.

They work in America's factories.

They run America's businesses.

They serve in government.

They provide most of the soldiers who died to keep us free.

They give drive to the spirit of America.

They give lift to the American Dream.

They give steel to the backbone of America.

They are good people, they are decent people; they work, and they save, and they pay their taxes, and they care.

Like Theodore Roosevelt, they know that this country will not be a good place for any of us to live in unless it is a good place for all of us to live in.

This I say to you tonight is the real voice of America. In this year 1968, this is the message it will broadcast to America and to the world.

Let's never forget that despite her faults, America is a great nation.

And America is great because her people are great.

With Winston Churchill, we say: "We have not journeyed all this way across the centuries, across the oceans, across the mountains, across the prairies because we are made of sugar candy."

America is in trouble today not because her people have failed but because her leaders have failed.

And what America needs are leaders to match the greatness of her people.

And this great group of Americans, the forgotten Americans, and others know that the great question Americans must answer by their votes in November is this: Whether we shall continue for four more years the policies of the last five years.

And this is their answer and this is my answer to that question.

When the strongest nation in the world can be tied down for four years in a war in Vietnam with no end in sight;

When the richest nation in the world can't manage its own economy;

When the nation with the greatest tradition of the rule of law is plagued by unprecedented lawlessness;

When a nation that has been known for a century for equality of opportunity is torn by unprecedented racial violence;

And when the President of the United States cannot travel abroad or to any major city at home without fear of a hostile demonstration—then it's time for new leadership for the United States of America.

My fellow Americans, tonight I accept the challenge and the commitment to provide that new leadership for America.

And I ask you to accept it with me.

And let us accept this challenge not as a grim duty but as an exciting adventure in which we are privileged to help a great nation realize its destiny.

And let us begin by committing ourselves to the truth—to see it like it is, and tell it like it is—to find the truth, to speak the truth, and to live the truth —that's what we will do.

We've had enough of big promises and little action.

The time has come for honest government in the United States of America.

And so tonight I do not promise the millennium in the morning.

I don't promise that we can eradicate poverty, and end discrimination, eliminate all danger of war in the space of four, or even eight years. But, I do promise action—a new policy for peace abroad; a new policy for peace and progress and justice at hime.

Look at our problems abroad. Do you realize that we face the stark truth that we are worse off in every area of the world tonight than we were when President Eisenhower left office eight years ago. That's the record. And there is only one answer to such a record of failure and that is a complete house-cleaning of those responsible for the failures of that record. The answer is a complete re-appraisal of America's policies in every section of the world.

We shall begin with Vietnam.

We all hope in this room that there is a chance that current negotiations may bring an honorable end to that war. And we will say nothing during this campaign that might destory that chance.

But if the war is not ended when the people choose in November, the choice will be clear. Here it is.

For four years this Administration has had at its disposal the greatest military and economic advantage that one nation has ever had over another in any war in history.

For four years, America's fighting men have set a record for courage and sacrifice unsurpassed in our history.

For four years, this Administration has had the support of the Loyal Opposition for the objective of seeking an honorable end to the struggle.

Never has so much military and economic and diplomatic power been used so ineffectively.

And if after all of this time and all of this sacrifice and all of this support there is still no end in sight, then I say the time has come for the American people to turn to new leadership—not tied to the mistakes and the policies of the past. That is what we offer to America.

And I pledge to you tonight that the first priority foreign policy objective of our next Administration will be to bring an honorable end to the war in Vietnam. We shall not stop there—we need a policy to prevent more Vietnams.

All of America's peace-keeping institutions and all of America's foreign commitments must be re-appraised. Over the past twenty-five years, America has provided more than one hundred and fifty billion dollars in foreign aid to nations abroad.

In Korea and now again in Vietnam, the United States furnished most of the money, most of the arms; most of the men to help the people of those countries defend themselves against aggression.

Now we are a rich country. We are a strong nation. We are a populous nation. But there are two hundred million Americans and there are two billion people that live in the Free World.

And I say the time has come for other nations in the Free World to bear their fair share of the burden of defending peace and freedom around this world.

What I call for is not a new isolationism. It is a new internationalism in which America enlists its allies and its friends around the world in those struggles in which their interest is as great as ours.

And now to the leaders of the Communist world, we say: After an era of confrontation, the time has come for an era of negotiation.

Where the world's super powers are concerned, there is no acceptable alternative to peaceful negotiation.

Because this will be a period of negotiation, we shall restore the strength of America so that we shall always negotiate from strength and never from weakness.

And as we seek peace through negotiation, let our goals be made clear:

We do not seek domination over any other country.

We believe deeply in our ideas, but we believe they should travel on their own power and not on the power of our arms.

We shall never be belligerent but we shall be as firm in defending our system as they are in expanding theirs.

We believe this should be an era of peaceful competition, not only in the productivity of our factories but in the quality of our ideas.

We extend the hand of friendship to all people, to the Russian people, to the Chinese people, to all people in the world.

And we shall work toward the goal of an open world—open skies, open cities, open hearts, open minds.

The next eight years, my friends, this period in which we are entering, I think we will have the greatest opportunity for world peace but also face the greatest danger of world war of any time in our history.

I believe we must have peace. I believe that we can have peace, but I do not underestimate the difficulty of this task. Because you see the art of preserving peace is greater than that of waging war and much more demanding. But I am proud to have served in an Administration which ended one war and kept the nation out of other wars for eight years. And it is that kind of experience and it is that kind of leadership that America needs today, and that we will give to America with your help.

And as we commit to new policies for America tonight, let us make one further pledge:

For five years hardly a day has gone by when we haven't read or heard a report of the American flag being spit on; an embassy being stoned; a library being burned; or an ambassador being insulted some place in the world. And each incident reduced respect for the United States until the ultimate insult inevitably occurred.

And I say to you tonight that when respect for the United States of America falls so low that a fourth-rate military power, like Norh Korea, will seize an American naval vessel on the high seas, it is time for new leadership to restore respect for the United States of America.

My friends, America is a great nation.

And it is time we started to act like a great nation around the world. It is ironic to note when we were a small nation—weak militarily and poor economically—America was respected. And the reason was that America stood for something more powerful than military strength or economic wealth.

The American Revolution was a shining example of freedom in action which caught the imagination of the world.

Today, too often, America is an example to be avoided and not followed.

A nation that can't keep the peace at home won't be trusted to keep the peace abroad.

A President who isn't treated with respect at home will not be treated with respect abroad.

A nation which can't manage its own economy can't tell others how to manage theirs.

If we are to restore prestige and respect for America abroad, the place to begin is at home in the United States of America.

My friends, we live in an age of revolution in America and in the world. And to find the answers to our problems, let us turn to a revolution, a revolution that will never grow old. The world's greatest continuing revolution, the American Revolution.

The American Revolution was and is dedicated to progress, but our founders recognized that the first requisite of progress is order.

Now, there is no quarrel between progress and order—because neither can exist without the other.

So let us have order in America—not the order that suppresses dissent and discourages change but the order which guarantees the right to dissent and provides the basis for peaceful change.

And tonight, it is time for some honest talk about the problem of order in the United States.

Let us always respect, as I do, our courts and those who serve on them. But let us also recognize that some of our courts in their decisions have gone too far in weakening the peace forces as against the criminal forces in this country and we must act to restore that balance.

Let those who have the responsibility to enforce our laws and our judges who have the responsibility to interpret them be dedicated to the great principles of civil rights.

But let them also recognize that the first civil right of every American is to be free from domestic violence, and that right must be guaranteed in this country.

And if we are to restore order and respect for law in this country there is one place we are going to begin. We are going to have a new Attorney General of the United States of America.

I pledge to you that our new Attorney General will be directed by the President of the United States to launch a war against organized crime in this country.

I pledge to you that the new Attorney General of the United States will be an active belligerent against the loan sharks and the numbers racketeers that rob the urban poor in our cities.

I pledge to you that the new Attorney General will open a new front against the filth peddlers and the narcotics peddlers who are corrupting the lives of the children of this country.

Because, my friends, let this message come through clear from what I say tonight. Time is running out for the merchants of crime and corruption in American society.

The wave of crime is not going to be the wave of the future in the United States of America.

We shall re-establish freedom from fear in America so that America can take the lead in re-establishing freedom from fear in the world.

And to those who say that law and order is the code word for racism, there and here is a reply:

Our goal is justice for every American.

If we are to have respect for law in America, we must have laws that deserve respect.

Just as we cannot have progress without order, we cannot have order without progress, and so, as we commit to order tonight, let us commit to progress.

And this brings me to the clearest choice among the great issues of this campaign.

For the past five years we have been deluged by government programs for the unemployed; programs for the cities; programs for the poor. And we have reaped from these programs an ugly harvest of frustration, violence and failure across the land.

And now our opponents will be offering more of the same—more billions for government jobs, government housing, government welfare.

I say it is time to quit pouring billions of dollars into programs that have failed in the United States of America.

To put it bluntly, we are on the wrong road—and it's time to take a new road, to progress.

Again, we turn to the American Revolution for our answer.

The war on poverty didn't begin five years ago in this country. It began when this country began. It's been the most successful war on poverty in the history of nations. There is more wealth in America today, more broadly shared, than in any nation in the world.

We are a great nation. And we must never forget how we became great.

America is a great nation today not because of what government did for people—but because of what people did for themselves over a hundred-ninety years in this country.

So it is time to apply the lessons of the American Revolution to our present problem.

Let us increase the wealth of America so that we can provide more generously for the aged; and for the needy; and for all those who cannot help themselves.

But for those who are able to help themselves—what we need are not more millions on welfare rolls—but more millions on payrolls in the United States of America.

Instead of government jobs, and government housing, and government welfare, let government use its tax and credit policies to enlist in this battle the greatest engine of progress ever developed in the history of man—American private enterprise.

Let us enlist in this great cause the millions of Americans in volunteer organizations who will bring a dedication to this task that no amount of money could ever buy.

And let us build bridges, my friends, build bridges to human dignity across that gulf that separates black America from white America.

Black Americans, no more than white Americans, they do not want more government programs which perpetuate dependency.

They don't want to be a colony in a nation.

They want the pride, and the self-respect, and the dignity that can only come if they have an equal chance to own their own homes, to own their own businesses, to be managers and executives as well as workers, to have a piece of the action in the exciting ventures of private enterprise.

I pledge to you tonight that we shall have new programs which will provide that equal chance.

We make great history tonight.

We do not fire a shot heard 'round the world but we shall light the lamp of hope in millions of homes across this land in which there is no hope today.

And that great light shining out from America will again become a beacon of hope for all those in the world who seek freedom and opportunity.

My fellow Americans, I believe that historians will recall that 1968 marked the beginning of the American generation in world history.

Just to be alive in America, just to be alive at this time is an experience unparalleled in history. Here is where the action is. Think.

Thirty-two years from now most Americans living today will celebrate a new year that comes once in a thousand years.

Eight years from now, in the second term of the next President, we will celebrate the 200th anniversary of the American Revolution.

And by our decision in this election, we, all of us here, all of you listening on television and radio, we will determine what kind of nation America will be on its 200th birthday; we will determine what kind of a world America will live in in the year 2000.

This is the kind of a day I see for America on that glorious Fourth—eight years from now.

I see a day when Americans are once again proud of their flag. When once again at home and abroad, it is honored as the world's greatest symbol of liberty and justice.

I see a day when the President of the United States is respected and his office is honored because it is worthy of respect and worthy of honor.

I see a day when every child in this land, regardless of his background, has a chance for the best education our wisdom and schools can provide, and an equal chance to go just as high as his talents will take him.

I see a day when life in rural America attracts people to the country, rather than driving them away.

I see a day when we can look back on massive breakthroughs in solving the problems of slums and pollution and traffic which are choking our cities to death.

I see a day when our senior citizens and millions of others can plan for the future with the assurance that their government is not going to rob them of their savings by destroying the value of their dollars.

I see a day when we will again have freedom from fear in America and freedom from fear in the world.

I see a day when our nation is at peace and the world is at peace and everyone on earth—those who hope, those who aspire, those who crave liberty—will look to America as the shining example of hopes realized and dreams achieved.

My fellow Americans, this is the cause I ask you to vote for. This is the cause I ask you to work for. This is the cause I ask you to commit to—not just for victory in November but beyond that to a new Administration.

Because the time when one man or a few leaders could save America is gone. We need tonight nothing less than the total commitment and the total mobilization of the American people if we are to succeed.

Government can pass laws. But respect for law can come only from people who take the law into their hearts and their minds—and not into their hands.

Government can provide opportunity. But opportunity means nothing unless people are prepared to seize it.

A President can ask for reconciliation in the racial conflict that divides Americans. But reconciliation comes only from the hearts of people.

And tonight, therefore, as we make this commitment, let us look into our hearts and let us look down into the faces of our children.

Is there anything in the world that should stand in their way?

None of the old hatreds mean anything when we look down into the faces of our children.

In their faces is our hope, our love, and our courage.

Tonight, I see the face of a child.

He lives in a great city. He is black. Or he is white. He is Mexican, Italian, Polish. None of that matters. What matters, he's an American child.

That child in that great city is more important than any politician's promise. He is America. He is a poet. He is a scientist, he is a great teacher, he is a proud craftsman. He is everything we ever hoped to be and everything we dare to dream to be.

He sleeps the sleep of childhood and he dreams the dreams of a child.

And yet when he awakens, he awakens to a living nightmare of poverty, neglect and despair.

He fails in school.

He ends up on welfare.

For him the American system is one that feeds his stomach and starves his soul. It breaks his heart. And in the end it may take his life on some distant battlefield.

To millions of children in this rich land, this is their prospect of the future.

But this is only part of what I see in America.

I see another child tonight.

He hears the train go by at night and he dreams of far away places where he'd like to go.

It seems like an impossible dream.

But he is helped on his journey through life.

A father who had to go to work before he finished the sixth grade, sacrificed everything he had so that his sons could go to college.

A gentle, Quaker mother, with a passionate concern for peace, quietly wept when he went to war but she understood why he had to go.

A great teacher, a remarkable football coach, an inspirational minister encouraged him on his way.

A courageous wife and loyal children stood by him in victory and also defeat.

And in his chosen profession of politics, first there were scores, then hundreds, then thousands, and finally millions worked for his success.

And tonight he stands before you—nominated for President of the United States of America.

You can see why I believe so deeply in the American Dream.

For most of us the American Revolution has been won; the American Dream has come true.

And what I ask you to do tonight is to help me make that dream come true for millions to whom it's an impossible dream today.

One hundred and eight years ago, the newly elected President of the

United States, Abraham Lincoln, left Springfield, Illinois, never to return again. He spoke to his friends gathered at the railroad station. Listen to his words:

"Today I leave you. I go to assume a greater task than devolved on General Washington. The great God which helped him must help me. Without that great assistance, I will surely fail. With it, I cannot fail."

Abraham Lincoln lost his life but he did not fail.

The next President of the United States will face challenges which in some ways will be greater than those of Washington or Lincoln. Because for the first time in our nation's history, an American President will face not only the problem of restoring peace abroad but of restoring peace at home.

Without God's help and your help, we will surely fail; but with God's help and your help, we shall surely succeed.

My fellow Americans, the long dark night for America is about to end.

The time has come for us to leave the valley of despair and climb the mountain so that we may see the glory of the dawn—a new day for America, and a new dawn for peace and freedom in the world.

Republican National Convention
Miami Beach, Florida
August 8, 1968

PUBLISHED BY NIXON/AGNEW Campaign Committee
450 PARK AVE., NEW YORK, N.Y. 10022
Maurice H. Stans, Fin. Chmn.   Peter M. Flanigan, Dep. Camp. Mgr.

 362